DEALING WITH COMPLEXITY

An Introduction to the Theory and Application of Systems Science

D1345470

DEALING WITH COMPLEXITY

An Introduction to the Theory and Application of Systems Science

Robert L. Flood

and

Ewart R. Carson

City University
London, England

PLENUM PRESS • NEW YORK AND LONDON

Library of Congress Cataloging in Publication Data

Flood, Robert L.
    Dealing with complexity: an introduction to the theory and application of systems
science / Robert L. Flood and Ewart R. Carson.
        p.   cm.
    Includes bibliographical references and index.
    ISBN 0-306-42715-X
    1. System analysis. 2. Computational complexity. I. Carson, Ewart R. II. Title.
QA402.F55   1988   87-29814
003 – dc19   CIP

First Printing – March 1988
Second Printing – October 1989
Third Printing – September 1990 (with corrections)

© 1988 Plenum Press, New York
A Division of Plenum Publishing Corporation
233 Spring Street, New York, N.Y. 10013

PREFACE

With technological advance, the difficulties faced by decision makers and researchers become even more complex and hence more difficult to understand and manage. Traditional approaches have their limitations, particularly when dealing with issues that span many fields of endeavor. Fortunately there has emerged, particularly over the past four decades, the discipline of systems science, which provides a framework for dealing with such complexity. This book gives an account of the underlying theory of systems science and illustrates its applicability to a range of "real-world" problems.

To gain an understanding of systems science and what motivates the systems scientist requires at least a reasonable degree of literacy and numeracy, a consequence of the interdisciplinary nature of the subject. The numerate content of this book, however, is almost entirely confined to Chapters 8 and 9. As a result, those who class themselves as nonnumerate are not continually confronted by equations that would, in some cases, prevent satisfactory completion of the text. Nevertheless, it has not been possible to exclude totally all aspects of numerate thinking from the remaining chapters. It would be useful, therefore, for those who class themselves as nonnumerate to read initially the section of Chapter 8 entitled "Using Letters Instead of Numbers." This provides sufficient material to enable the nonnumerate reader to deal with the small amount of quantitative material outside Chapters 8 and 9.

Finding a logical sequence in which to read this book is really a matter of personal choice and interest. However, the following observations on Figure

1.1a (p. 3) might help. Here we see three distinguishable levels. Level A consists of chapters that cover systems terms and concepts and a definition of complexity and considers some important philosophical issues. This level thus contains the fundamental material that underpins the remaining two levels. Level B is essentially concerned with modeling of structured situations. This ranges from qualitative to quantitative representations in Chapters 3 and 9, respectively. These chapters are supported by the fundamental issues of measurement (Chapter 4) and quantification (Chapter 8). The ideas of methodology are also introduced at this level. Level C moves away from the structured situations of the natural sciences (to a large extent) to consider the unstructured or "messy systems" of the social situations. In Chapter 5, social systems theory, management, and the organization provide the theme for discussion. The closely related areas of "problems" and problematic issues, which stem from the study of management and organizations, follow in Chapter 6. Along a different track, but still within the social sciences, a systems view of international relations is presented, and the use of systems thinking in theory building is discussed.

The following logical orderings of chapters suggest a number of ways to read the text. An insight into systems and the social sciences can be gained by reading Chapters 1, 2, 5, 6, 7, and 10, with a deeper view being attainable by reading Chapters 1, 2, 3, 4, 5, 6, 7, and 10. An in-depth study of structured situations and their modeling is obtainable by reading Chapters 1, 2, 3, 4, 8, and 9. For a thorough introductory insight into the theory and application of systems science, reading sequentially from Chapter 1 up to and including Chapter 10 is necessary.

In terms of content, Chapters 1 and 2 constitute the introductory phase of *Dealing with Complexity*. Chapter 1 offers a brief historical look at systems science and highlights four interrelated development cycles associated with the evolution of this area of study. The chapter then draws together systems terms and concepts, commonly found in systems publications, and, in as logical a sequence as is possible, provides clear and generally accepted definitions and illustrations of them. Chapter 2 answers the question "What is complexity?" by providing one possible definition, which acts as a transportable conceptual framework for use in the remainder of the book (and beyond).

Chapter 3 constitutes the first phase of the modeling component. The chapter is concerned with qualitative representations, concentrating on diagrammatic approaches. The rules associated with the variety of approaches are clearly defined, and removal of ambiguity is stressed. Following this, the difficult task of setting boundaries around systems of interest is discussed. Some guidelines and rules are presented, and a novel way of conceptualizing a system and its boundary is offered. Subsequently, Chapter 4 considers ways of bridging the gap, by means of measurement, between the real world and the various forms of system representation that may be adopted.

A systems view of management and the organization is considered in Chapter 5. This covers a large volume of theory and application in social systems theory, considering cybernetics in some detail, while not neglecting the experiential viewpoints. Chapter 6 continues along similar lines dealing with methodology in the context of "problems" and/or problematic issues. The concern is essentially with human activity systems (defined in Chapter 1). Again, a variety of viewpoints on this matter are covered, and some ideas on integrating the methodological approaches are considered. Chapter 7, still in the area of the social sciences, is concerned with the ways that systems science has been used in the study of international relations and some major criticisms of the use of the approach in this area. These are answered by highlighting the inappropriate structural paradigm of orthodox international relations and by offering an alternative behavioral approach. The usefulness of systems science in social theory building is discussed.

Up to this point, the reader has essentially been presented with some fundamental concepts of systems science (including terms and concepts, system identification, and measurement) and shown how these have been used in the social sciences. The two main philosophical viewpoints of so-called hard and soft thinking in these sciences have also been drawn out.

The following two chapters concentrate on systemic scientific methods in the natural sciences, looking at quantification and subsequently modeling at both a basic and more advanced level, and considering both theory and application.

Chapter 10 adds the final systems component, which, in conjunction with Chapters 1 and 2, underpins the rest of the text. The controversial ideas that emerge during the course of the book are considered in the light of a conceptual framework developed from Chapters 2 and 4. The issues are presented in such a way as to allow readers full opportunity to consider their own viewpoint on these matters.

One final but crucial point concerning the content has to be made here. Throughout the text the reader must at all times recognize that systems are objects as perceived by people (see Chapter 2). This is obvious when conceptual models and the like are being discussed. However, it is less obvious when the words are formed something like—"There are a number of reasons why we may want to distinguish a system from its surroundings"—(which could be the first sentence of Chapter 3) suggesting something very real "out there." This is not so. The most positive we can be is that a system is a perception of "what might be out there," and so the example of Chapter 3 above (and all other cases) must not be given literally in the manner by which we are accustomed. When referring directly "to what might be out there" we have used the term situation, for want of a better expression, or may have used labels (like dog, cat, etc.), where these are generally well understood terms (consensus agreement), or the word thing, or put the term in question in single quotes. When reviewing the work of other authors, however, we have used their terminology, which usually incorporates the word system when referring to the real world. If at any place we have failed to do this it is a consequence of having lived for many years in the traditional paradigm of Western culture and having to use the language that has evolved therefrom.

There are a number of people who warrant acknowledgment for a variety of reasons, both individually and/or jointly from the authors, and for both personal and/or formal reasons.

No one person deserves our joint appreciation more than Louis Flood. His contribution has come in many forms, including editing, idea generation, and help in the preparation of the line drawings as well as preparing the entire manuscript. Ian Flood prepared all but a few of the line drawings.

Alex Ellison contributed through the many days and evenings she spent with Robert Flood in the preparation of Chapter 7. Keith Ellis contributed to "The Evolution of Management Theory" and "Administrative Management" in Chapter 5, and gave us permission to document one of his consultancies in Chapter 6. Similarly, thanks to Steven Edmunton and Ferranti Computers Ltd. for allowing us to publish material in Chapter 6. Other direct contributions have come from Afshin Sha ɔolmaali and John Hamwee. Rosalind Flood prepared Figures 1.7 and 2.1

A special thank you is extended to M. C. Jackson for his comments on the manuscript. Others who have contributed via discussions and/or reading of the manuscript include our editor at Plenum, Ken Derham, and the following staff of the Department of Systems Science at the City University in London: Fred Charlwood, Ross Janes, Ray Jowitt, Philip M'Pherson, Chris Mitchell, Sionade Robinson, and Peter Willetts; and from the Royal Free Hospital and School of Medicine in London, Derek Cramp and Mark Leaning.

On a personal note, Robert Flood wishes to extend his thanks to Mandy, Ross, and Marjorie Flood.

Finally, an intellectual debt is owed to Philip M'Pherson since our department exists only because of his forward thinking in the 1960s.

Robert L. Flood and Ewart R. Carson
City University, London
December, 1986

CONTENTS

CHAPTER FIVE. SYSTEMS VIEW OF MANAGEMENT AND THE ORGANIZATION 73

CHAPTER SIX.   SYSTEMS VIEW OF PROBLEMS
                AND PROBLEMATIC SITUATIONS **105**

CHAPTER SEVEN.   SYSTEMS THEORY IN
                  INTERNATIONAL RELATIONS **159**

CHAPTER EIGHT. SYSTEMS QUANTIFICATION:
                  FROM STONE AGE TO SPACE AGE . . . 169

SYSTEMS

Origin and Evolution, Terms and Concepts

1.1. INTRODUCTION

When asked to explain "what systems science is all about," a systems expert is confronted with a rather daunting task. Indeed, it was precisely this difficulty that identified the need for a comprehensive well-documented account such as is presented here in *Dealing with Complexity*. As far as we are aware, there is not a single consolidated text on the nature and content of systems science that is both (1) an introduction to the systems concepts that provide the structural components that make up the systems framework of thought, and yet (2) broad enough in its outlook to provide an insight into the breadth of application achievable with such a framework.

This introductory book cannot hope (and does not pretend) to chart the frontiers achieved in systems thought and activities. That special task continues to be performed via writings with a narrower focus of attention. The reader would need to consult the works of Bertalanffy, Boulding, Bunge, Klir, Laszlo, Rapoport, Wiener, and others for the major milestones of systems science. Recently, Checkland has brought to the surface an alternative stream of systems thinking, working in a tradition also explored by writers such as Ackoff and Churchman. New arguments have emerged at the methodological level, while the underlying philosophy is somewhat controversial, questioning more traditional systems philosophies.

In due course, *Dealing with Complexity* will necessarily touch on these points; however, let us now return to the question: "What is systems science all about?" A standard answer is "it is all about dealing with complexity." This clearly identifies the need to fully understand the concept of complexity, but we have deferred this until Chapter 2 (the second part of the introductory phase). Before pursuing that path, it is necessary to understand the fundamentals that underly systems thinking and complexity, and that allow us to be bold enough to state that mankind can at last begin to understand and therefore manage complex situations. This will go some way to answering the question posed above.

Chapter 1 (the first part of the introductory phase) will, therefore, be concerned with a thorough review of systems terms and concepts. Before exploring these issues, however, let us briefly set the scene. Why and where did systems science originate? How has it evolved?

1.2. THE ORIGIN AND EVOLUTION OF SYSTEMS SCIENCE

Any subject area with "science" in its title strongly implies a distinct branch of systematic and well-formulated knowledge and the pursuit of principles for achieving this, suggesting that a science should have a clearly recorded and coherent historical development. However, this is not the case for systems science, which has a somewhat fragmented history. For instance, some fundamental concepts now used in systems science have apparently been present in other disciplines for many centuries, while equally fundamental concepts have emerged as recently as 40 or so years ago.

Cybernetics is a good example of an area of systems thinking that has been in existence for many centuries. The origin of the word is the Greek *kybernetes* (steersman) and *kybernetics* (Plato's art of steermanship). Subsequently, Maxwell in 1864 used the word cybernetics to describe feedback in mechanical governors, and Ampère in 1884 used the word to refer to the art of government in the context of social science (Robb, 1985). The contemporary definition of the word has rightly been attributed to Wiener (1948) and relates to control and communication in the animal and machine.

The principal coming together of systems ideas (those relating to wholes) occurred in the field of biology. The initiator of this consolidation is recognized as being Bertalanffy in the 1940s. Bertalanffy envisaged a framework of concepts and theory that would be equally applicable to many fields of interest. This original work is entitled General Systems Theory (GST) and is still actively pursued today (see for instance, Rapoport, 1986). It is based on the idea that homologies exist between disciplines that have traditionally been considered as being separated by their different subject matters. Mathematics is favored as the medium by which these ideas are expressed. GST is therefore defined as a metatheory.

The Second World War, with its attendant problems of logistics and resource management, acted as a catalyst for the growth of systems science. The nature of the application area lent itself to a holistic and quantitative analysis. Operations research and management science (ORMS) emerged from these studies, and its close association with systems ideas is still evident today (see, for instance, Daellenbach *et al.*, 1983). This catalyst directed systems science further toward "hard" quantitative analysis. The trend has, however, been broken in recent times with, for example, Checkland's work on human activity systems (defined later).

By the early 1950s (as a result of the development of GST and ORMS) the cycles shown in Fig. 1.1 (b) (the development processes of systems thinking, theory, and application) had become at least loosely coupled and over the following decades became fully engaged. Looking at the figure we can see four interlinked cycles, which, we believe, fairly represent the evolutionary

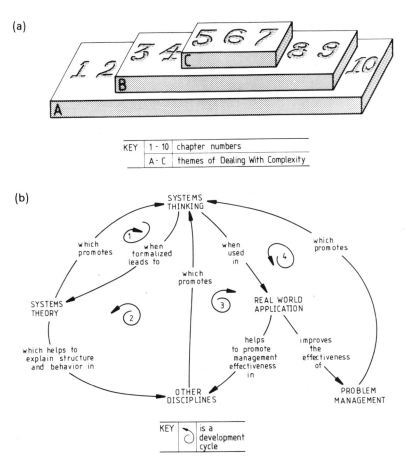

FIGURE 1.1. (a) Three levels or themes of structure of *Dealing with Complexity.* (b) Four development cycles of systems science.

process associated with systems science. We shall use this dynamic configuration as a base on which to mold our continuing discussion.

DEVELOPMENT CYCLE 1. Systems thinking, when formalized, leads to systems theory, which promotes systems thinking.

Systems thinking is a framework of thought that helps us to deal with complex things in a holistic way. The formalization of (giving an explicit, definite, and conventional form to) this thinking is what we have termed systems theory. Conventions are subsequently adopted in the thinking process. However, theory and thinking are never synonymous, as it is the latter that remains looser and provides the lubricant for application.

DEVELOPMENT CYCLE 2. Systems thinking, when formalized, leads to systems theory, which helps to explain structure and behavior in other disciplines, which promotes systems thinking.

During the initiation phase of GST, Development Cycles 1 and 2 were effectively the only ones in action. Thought revolved around the need to develop a metatheory that could be used to explain much of the dynamics associated with situations of separate disciplines in a single operation.

Thus, over the years, many systems writings (mostly of a GST nature) involved the discussion of systems theory in other disciplines. This stimulated criticism from Berlinski (1976) and Lilienfeld (1978) as pointed out by Checkland (1981), who also quotes Naughton's suggestion that there is nothing approaching a coherent body of tested systems knowledge (Naughton, 1979).

These criticisms can be considered in the light of Figure 1.1(b). To a large extent they have been made without fully appreciating the four development cycles associated with systems science. Many of the criticisms are unwittingly directed at Development Cycle 2 only, which is merely one (very necessary) part of the overall development of systems science. It is only when formalization of thinking is significantly developed that it is possible to go on and effectively accrue tested knowledge. It is evident, however, that a portion of systems theory does exist that is unlikely to be directly useful in application and thus will remain more or less isolated from practical experience. Nevertheless, these quasi-isolated components of systems theory provide an important contribution to the overall systems view.

A good example of Cycle 2 is the mutual development of international relations and systems science as presented in Chapter 7. Additionally, management (human), organization theory, and systems science have close links, with systems science offering a novel view as discussed in Chapter 5.

DEVELOPMENT CYCLE 3.   Systems thinking, when used in real-world application, helps to promote management effectiveness in other disciplines, which promotes systems thinking.

Real-world, or practical, application of systems science may be found in many disparate disciplines, and has included modeling approaches with both systemic scientific and utilitarian objectives—for instance, studies of technological advances and man's involvement in them, respectively. Another example is the in-depth study of complexity in structured situations. For instance, in computer science this has proved to be crucial in handling and developing new technology. We offer an example of this cycle via the modeling case studies of Chapter 9 (which are of a medical flavor).

DEVELOPMENT CYCLE 4.   Systems thinking, when used in real-world application, improves the effectiveness of problem management, which promotes systems thinking.

"Real-world problem solving," adopting a hard methodological approach, has been successful in design and decision making. In fact, systems analysis (promoted by the RAND Corporation) and systems engineering, for decision making and real-world problem solving respectively, emerged as the norm in systems applications during the 1960s. However, early attempts to apply this approach in a social problem-solving context in California were rightly criticized by Hoos (1972).

The main difficulties have, however, been remedied to a large extent by more sophisticated systems engineering (M'Pherson, 1980, 1981) and with Checkland's work on soft systems methodology (Checkland, 1972, 1981). Application of systems thinking to problem management has achieved notable success. These contemporary approaches now date the comments of Hoos and others.

Recently, GST has also had its say in, for example, Miller's Living System Model (Miller, 1978), and Klir's General Systems Problem Solver (GSPS) (Klir, 1985a), a fascinating account of how "a finite number of types of general systems . . . [has] . . . a finite set of relevant and desirable methodological distinctions." A comprehensive insight into these and other issues is given in Chapter 6, which looks at the systems approach to problems and problematic situations.

To summarize, in systems science, thinking leads to application, which feeds back to (re)thinking. Figure 1.1(b) then, defines the process by which systems thinking and theory have developed and identifies the role of application, not only in real-world use, but also in the further development of systems science itself. A detailed summary of the many facets of systems science, which are the output of the development processes discussed above, is given in

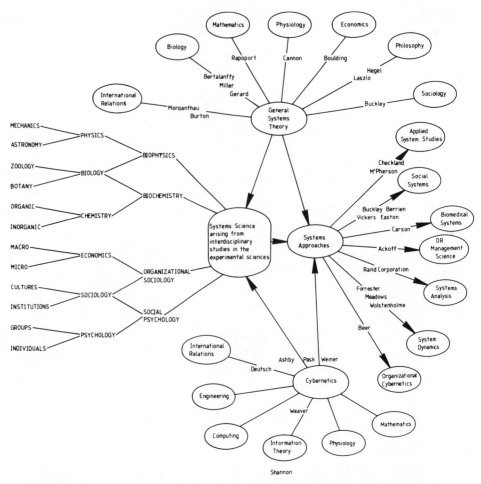

FIGURE 1.2. Systems science, its origin and evolution (Beishon, 1980, with international relations and biomedical systems added. Reproduced by permission of Open University Press).

Figure 1.2. Here we see how systems science has arisen from interdisciplinary studies, and how it can itself be categorized into distinct areas. On the diagram a number of the major contributors in each area of systems studies are given.

1.3. SYSTEMS TERMS AND CONCEPTS

1.3.1. Introduction

In this section a pencil sketch of systems terms and concepts will be developed, indicating the colorful richness of their full form and their multi-dimensional nature. Our task is then to take this picture and animate it, in so

doing reflecting the dynamic nature of situational behavior. Such a picture
7

*Systems: Origin
and Evolution*

doing reflecting the dynamic nature of situational behavior. Such a picture
will necessarily be presented in an abstract way (the notion of a system is
abstract); however, we intend to follow a policy of realism in the sense that
situations of interest here are of the world—that is, they are earthly (of the
earth and man's life on it).

1.3.2. Terms and Concepts

A systems description of a situation is: an assembly of elements related
in an *organized whole*. An **element** may be anything that is discernible by a
noun or a noun phrase that all informed observers would agree exists. An
element must normally be capable of behavior such that it has some significant
property(ies) that may change. A **relationship** can be said to exist between *A*
and *B* if the behavior of either is influenced by the other (Jones, 1982).
Relationships between elements may be flows of materials, information, or
energy.

Any characteristic quality or property ascribed to an element or process
is termed an **attribute** of that element (color, texture, size, strength, shape, and
permeability, for example) or process (intensity, speed, throughput, and rate,
for example). It is the changes in the elemental and processual attributes of
interest that are of prime concern.

The concentration of relationships between elements helps us to distinguish a system (with concentrated feedback relationships) from its **environment**
(input–output relationships with the system). The demarcation between a
system and its environment is made explicit by defining a **boundary** of the
system. This distinction is absolute in the theoretical construct of a **closed
system** where relationships do not exist between elements of a system, and
everything external to that system. Conversely, an **open system** exchanges
material, information, or energy with its environment across a boundary. The
difficult task of boundary identification is tackled in Chapter 3.

Other less influential component parts that indirectly affect a situation
under study, via the ability to significantly change the surroundings, are
represented as members of a wider environment. It is sometimes useful to distinguish a **narrower system of interest** (NSOI) from a **wider system of interest**
(WSOI). This may be necessary where the application domain of a study
relates to the NSOI, although there are also some elements that are closely
associated (having feedback relationships) and clearly do not belong in the
outside environment. These then form a set labeled WSOI. These ideas are
expanded in Chapter 3.

The fundamental ideas of a system are illustrated in Figure 1.3. Here, (a)
shows a set of elements devoid of relationships, which is no more than an
aggregation of parts; while (b) shows a set of elements with only limited
relationships, which does not constitute a system; (c) suggests that identifying
the concentrations of relationships between elements helps to identify a boundary of a system, its inputs and outputs; and (d) shows that a system may
comprise a number of subsystems, and each subsystem can be thought of as

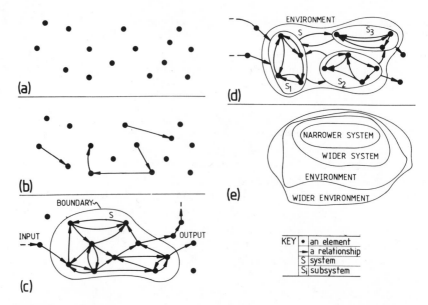

FIGURE 1.3. Defining a system: (a) a set of elements devoid of relationships; (b) a set of elements with only limited relationships; (c) multiple relationships between elements, the boundary of a system, its inputs and outputs; (d) subsystems within a system; (e) narrower system, wider system, environment, wider environment.

a distinct system with a boundary. Finally, (e) shows that a system (comprised of a narrower and wider system) has an immediate environment with which it directly exchanges, in this abstract sense, material, information, and/or energy; other factors that may influence the system indirectly via an environment are termed the wider environment.

Any system exists in (or is unique to) the eye of the beholder (be this a person or a group) and is associated with interests, as is suggested by "SOI." The United Kingdom, for example, could be seen as an economy by economists, a society by sociologists, a threatened chunk of nature by conservationists, a tourist attraction by some Americans, a military threat by rulers of the Soviet Union, and the green, green grass of home to the more romantic of us Britons.

Some elemental attributes of systems are known as **state variables** of the system (for example, volumes of water in a series of reservoirs, population sizes of a group of interdependent species, inventories in a warehouse), and thus the system can be described by a **state vector**:

$$\mathbf{x} = \begin{bmatrix} x_1 \\ x_2 \\ \vdots \\ x_n \end{bmatrix}$$

such that each x_i ($i = 1$ to n) of the state vector $\mathbf{x}$ represents one of the system states (for example, representations of the volume of water in one reservoir, the population size of one species, the number of goods in stock of one item). The change in these states over time forms the **state trajectory**, as shown in Figure 1.4. In this figure the state trajectories of (a) a two-state variable system, and (b) a three-state variable system are shown, with x_1, x_2, and x_3 representing, say, volumes of water in three reservoirs. The totality of the space in which the trajectory may move is termed the **state space** of the system. In the systems considered to date, the state variable of the system map on a one-to-one basis (the system is **deterministic**) with their future states:

$$\begin{bmatrix} x_1(t) \\ x_2(t) \\ \vdots \\ x_n(t) \end{bmatrix} \begin{array}{c} \longrightarrow \\ \longrightarrow \\ \\ \longrightarrow \end{array} \begin{bmatrix} x_1(t+s) \\ x_2(t+s) \\ \vdots \\ x_n(t+s) \end{bmatrix}$$

where $x_1(t)$ is the value of that state variable at time t (t is the present time), $x_1(t+s)$ is the value of that state variable at a later time $t+s$ (s might be, say, one month).

In more complex systems the state variables of the system may map on a many-to-one or one-to-many basis (the system is **indeterminate** or **probabalistic**). In some situations, where many factors of complexity are apparent, the fuzziness can be extreme. They can be **poorly structured**, somewhat nebulous and difficult to envisage in terms such as state variables, state trajectory, and state space; and the boundaries are often very difficult to identify. Many real-world manifestations of human activity systems—notional purposive systems that express some purposeful human activity (Checkland, 1981)—are typically poorly structured or "messy." Situations that are well structured lend themselves to quantitative analysis such as are discussed above in systems terms, whereas poorly structured situations require an alternative approach for analysis. This theme will be pursued at appropriate points throughout the book.

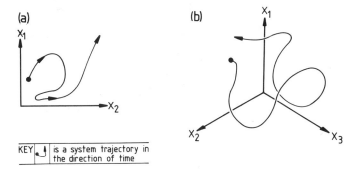

FIGURE 1.4. State trajectory: (a) a two-state variable system; (b) a three-state variable system.

Let us now, however, make some distinctions between structured and messy situations. This will act as an early reference point which will be developed as each chapter is read. The definition comes from Flood (1987a). Features of a situation which may be labeled structured are determined by the nature of the situation itself. The most important are listed below:

1. Measurement, if achieved, can typically be realized in rigorous quantitative terms (statistics and mathematics are therefore permissible).
2. The quality of measurement is questionable only with respect to noise (interference) because the instruments of measurement are known to be measuring the attribute of interest.
3. The major problem concerning measurement, other than noise, is accessibility, that is, can the attribute of interest be measured without destroying the integrity of the situation or parts thereof?
4. As a consequence of (1)-(3), laws rather than theory are normally achievable.
5. A second consequence of (1)-(3) is that system identification (determining what is the system, boundary, environment, and so on, of interest) is relatively straightforward because the elements of the system can generally be agreed upon and, in many cases, parameters defining the structure of the system can be estimated quantitatively.
6. In general, there is agreement concerning the function of the situation under investigation (a unitary rather than pluralist position may be achieved).

In essence, (1)-(6) describe situations typically found in the natural sciences. Messy situations of the social sciences are, at least in part, given some expression by exclusion from (1)-(6). We will now return to defining fundamental concepts.

The important concept of **homeostasis** can be explained in state space terms. Mature organisms, for example, appear to remain more or less unchanged over discrete periods of time (one month, say s). In terms of system representation this suggests little change in the state vector over time: $x(t) \approx x(t + s)$. However, the fact is, an organism exchanges materials and energy (inputting food and water, outputting material wastes, heat, and water, as examples). So at $t + s$ the composition may appear to be unchanged, but the actual materials that make up the organism at time t will be partially or totally replaced by time $t + s$. This idea of dynamic equilibrium, with fluxes in and out, is termed homeostasis. The open system of Figure 1.5 is an example of this. Let us say that each dot denotes a water molecule, and the labels a to o are permanently attached to one molecule for identification purposes. In Figure 1.5a, the cell at time t comprises five molecules, f to j. In Figure 1.5b, the cell at $t + s$ also comprises five molecules d, e, l, m, n, and on general inspection will appear to be like the cell at t, having five molecules. However, the molecules in the cell have been completely exchanged by $t + s$. The change in the system between t and $t + s$ can be recorded as inputs = outputs, or $(d + e + l + m + n) - (f + g + h + i + j) = 0$, or (5 molecules) $-$ (5 molecules) $= 0$ molecules.

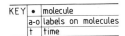

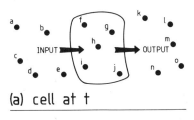

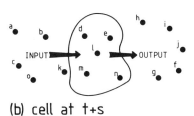

FIGURE 1.5. Homeostasis: (a) living cell at time *t*; (b) living cell at time *t* + *s*.

The five-water-molecule cell is in dynamic equilibrium with its environment. It is a homeostatic system.

The activities of a system are thought of as processes occurring in a **structure**. Structure defines the way in which the elements are related to each other, providing the supporting framework in which the processes occur (refer back to Figure 1.3c or 1.3d). The processes could represent a series of stages in the manufacturing of a product, or more generally, the natural or involuntary operation or series of changes in a situation.

Sequential observations at times $t_1, t_2, \ldots, t_s$ characterize the **situational behavior**, which may appear to be **goal seeking**. For instance, a commercial firm's goal (above other subordinate objectives) might be considered to be increasing profits as a percentage of sales (efficiency). Consider another example. The most obvious basic requirement of any organism is survival (the need for energy and nutrients), and until these needs are satisfied the organism seeks the necessary sources of supply. A third example relates to the activities of national political groupings. These are often seen as being directed toward gaining governmental power and, having achieved it, maintaining that position. To many this goal is "clear," and the associated goal-seeking behavior is by the process of electoral persuasion (in a democracy) or military force (in many autocracies).

A special case of goal-seeking behavior is **adaptive behavior**. Evolution of life forms is, at least in part, an example of adaptation. A commercial firm will also need to adapt to external changes. For instance, adaptation to changes in demand patterns, competitors' actions, technological change, and on occasions to significant changes on the international scene like oil price increases or cuts.

The fact that such adaptation occurs at all, in systems terms, is due to **environmental change**. If an environment remains constant then a system's survival is not threatened (at least, not by exterior forces). Changes in an environment may be acute. Such changes are termed **environmental disturbances**. These will require short-term adaptive behavior via **regulation** and **control**. If the changes are chronic, longer term regulation and control mechanisms will be required to maintain a system's integrity. Thus a system needs a variety of control mechanisms designed to cope with a range of environmental changes (see Ashby's law of requisite variety, discussed later).

Man's attempts to control, service, and/or design very complex situations have, however, often been fraught with disaster. A major contributory factor has been the unwitting adoption of **piecemeal** thinking, which sees only parts of a situation and its **generative mechanisms**. Additionally, it has been suggested that **nonrational** thinking sees only the extremes (the simple "solutions") of any range of problem solutions. The net result of these factors is that situations exhibit **counterintuitive** behavior; outcomes of situations are rarely as we expect, but this is not an intrinsic property of situations; rather, it is largely caused by neglect of, or lack of respect being paid to, the nature and complexity of a situation under investigation.

Adaptation, regulation, and control bring us to the subject area termed **cybernetics**. As already indicated, this is the science of control and communication in animals and machines. It describes the natural laws that govern the communication, computation, and control operations of dynamic situations. Homeostasis (discussed above) is an important concept that applies to cybernetics. Some other important concepts are discussed below. Beer (1981), Robb (1985), and Espejo (1987) provide a number of the definitions.

In cybernetics a system is normally described as a **black box** whereby the whole of a system's generative mechanisms are lumped into a single transfer function (TF). This acts on an input to produce an output; see Figure 1.6a. To ensure that the output is monitored, so that a system may remain homeostatic (the critical variables remain within acceptable limits) or attain a new steady state (according to input decisions, say), the output of the TF is brought back into its input where the difference between the desired and actual levels is identified. This is known as **feedback**; see Figure 1.6b.

Negative feedback is associated with seeking defined objectives via control parameters; and **positive feedback** is either contained replication and growth or uncontained and unstable growth, which may lead to structural changes or death.

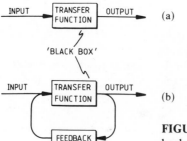

FIGURE 1.6. Transfer function: (a) without feedback; (b) with feedback.

Autopoiesis is linked to the concept of homeostatic behavior. In this case, the variable that is held steady is the system's own organization or the maintenance of an identity over time. Variety is a "measure" of the possible distinguishable states of a system, of which control can be obtained only if the variety of the controller is greater than, or equal to, the signal or system to be controlled—this is the **law of requisite variety** (Ashby, 1956).

Communication and **conversation** refer to the passing of information to others and the sharing of concepts between participants, respectively. These are both important ideas in cybernetics.

In systems terms, **metalanguage** is one that is not contained in the system itself but is imposed, in some way, from an external system superior in the logical hierarchy of systems. Subordinate systems may have no understanding of the metalanguage, possessing only their own object language. This idea is illustrated in the situation representation of Figure 1.7, an example familiar to many of us. Here we see a metasystem, possessing a metalanguage, commanding an object system initially in a higher level metalanguage. Owing to the limited vocabulary and lack of syntax and structure of the object language, the object system is not capable of understanding the higher level metalanguage. In order to effect the desired control over the object system, the metasystem switches from its own metalanguage to the language of the object system, whereupon the commands may be understood and obeyed.

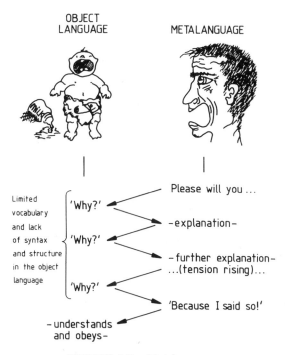

FIGURE 1.7. Metalanguage.

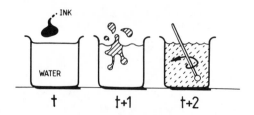

FIGURE 1.8. Entropy.

The concept of **entropy** relates to the tendency of things to move toward greater disorder, or disorganization. An example of this is given in Figure 1.8. Here, at time *t* there is a high degree of order and the ink is organized as a distinct whole. At time *t* + 1 the ink droplet has fallen into a beaker of water, where it immediately tends toward disorder. At time *t* + 2, and after stirring, the ink particles have become randomly displaced and the probability of the ink moving to total order is effectively zero. The second law of thermodynamics expresses precisely the same concept. This states that heat dissipates from a central source and the energy becomes degraded, although total energy remains constant (the first law of thermodynamics). Entropy suggests that organisms, organizations, societies, machines, and so on, will rapidly deteriorate into disorder and "death." The reason they do not is because animate things can **self-organize** and inanimate things may be serviced by man. These are **negentropic** activities which require energy. Energy, however, can be made available only by further degradation. Ultimately, therefore, entropy wins the day and the attempts to create order can seem rather a daunting task in the entropic scheme of things. Holding back entropy, however, is another of the challenging tasks for the systems scientist.

Situations often form levels in **hierarchical** structures. Figure 1.9 represents this type of structure in the case of a multinational company. Here, reduction of the situation (downward) increases the **level of resolution** of analysis. An important part of any systems study is to ensure that an appropriate level of resolution has been chosen and that the WSOI and the environment are appropriately identified. This requires that a systems scientist be both a **holist** (looking at the system as a whole) and a **reductionist** (converting the system into many simpler forms) at the same time (M'Pherson, 1974).

Ascending hierarchical structures reveals an important phenomenon that has provided the words of the systems anthem for many years: "**the whole is greater than the sum of its parts**" or "we can see **emergence**." This has an instantaneous appeal, but on deeper thinking can seem a little mystical and demands an explanation; after all, we are scientists not just believers. However, the fact is that order, together with communication and control between our bodily organs and other tissues (for example), gives rise to a walking, talking, thinking, observing, listening, feeling, smelling, tasting, whole organism as opposed to an aggregation of bodily parts. Bricks, mortar, tiles, plaster, wires, carpets, cookers, furniture, and so on, when put together (in a well-**designed** manner) produce a whole labeled a "house" (with all its inputs and outputs), a controlled environment in which we (whole organisms) have reduced the

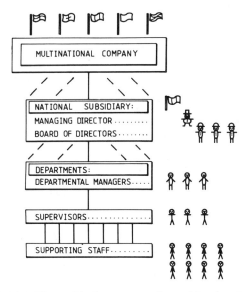

FIGURE 1.9. Hierarchical structure of a multinational company.

uncertainty and thus feel relatively safe. If you take a number of people from their homes, transport them to another larger man-made structure, add many machines (each representable as a system in its own right) then supply a mix of material, information, and energy (inputs), the resultant is a new organized whole, which we label a "factory" (that transforms inputs into outputs).

Now consult Figure 1.10 for a more abstract insight into emergence, and note the relationship between emergence, state trajectory, and systems behavior. In this figure we have a representation of qualitative change of an object, say x, in its state space $s(x)$. Each coordinate axis represents one property of the object, and the trajectory, or behavior, of the system is described by the direction of s. During the first part of the existence of x, point s (which represents x's instantaneous state) moves on the b–c plane until it hits the vertical plane at $t = r$. It loses property c at this time and gains property a,

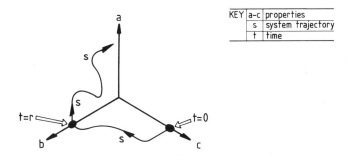

FIGURE 1.10. Emergence (from Bunge, 1977; reproduced by permission).

moving on to plane $a-b$ (Bunge, 1977). This, in real-world terms, appears as a change in the nature of the situation.

Synergy is a term that is also used to describe the emergence of unexpected and interesting properties. **Learning** is also closely associated with emergence, where connections are formed and new powerful wholes emerge out of disparate parts, otherwise termed the "Eureka experience."

Let us now consider the word "system." This has two adjectives, **systemic** and **systematic**. Systemic is concerned with holistic thinking as discussed above. Systematic, however, is concerned with step-by-step procedures, and from the point of view of some systems scientists is important during problem management. The adoption of a systematic approach forms the basis from which methodologies have evolved. Traditional **methodologies** are essentially systematic, although they may incorporate systemic thinking at appropriate steps. Some contemporary methodologies, however, are purely systemic, as will be seen in Chapter 6. Much time has been spent in designing and developing methodologies for so-called **hard** and **soft** situations. A hard situation is essentially well structured (as defined earlier), so it is relatively easy to measure and quantify, and often performs well according to known laws, thus having a high degree of predictability (physical situations typify this). Soft situations, in contrast, are poorly structured, are very difficult to attach numbers to, and usually have a variety of conflicting theories associated with them and no generally accepted laws; and it is difficult to reach a consensus of view on their behavior or function (any situation including human beings would typically be labeled soft).

Finally, it is important to recognize that the discipline of systems science is in fact a **metadiscipline**. The framework of thought can be transferred from discipline to discipline (that is, it is **interdisciplinary**), and from situation to situation. Systems science is not multidisciplinary. It is not concerned with lots of disciplines separately, but rather with disciplines brought together in an integrated fashion; it is an interdisciplinary **metasubject**.

1.4. CONCLUSION

In this chapter we have introduced systems science by identifying its origins and evolution, and then by presenting the fundamental concepts and terms that underly systems thinking, theory, and to some extent application. Chapter 1 is an essential introductory chapter that provides the systems concepts and framework of thought that, we believe, can help us to deal with complexity. Chapter 2 seeks to define complexity and is the second phase of the introduction.

PROBLEMS

1.1. What are the four main development cycles of systems science?

1.2. In what way can the four main development cycles of systems science help to explain its evolution?

1.3. Briefly describe the following systems terms:
1. Element
2. Relationship
3. Attribute
4. Boundary
5. Environment

1.4. What are the main differences between "open" and "closed" systems?

1.5. Do you think that "closed" systems exist only as theoretical constructs, or can you identify a real-world example?

1.6. Briefly describe the following systems terms:
1. State variable
2. State vector
3. State trajectory
4. State space

1.7. By considering a situation of interest to yourself, explain the meaning of homeostasis.

1.8. Explain why "structure," "process," and "systems behavior" are the three basic concepts associated with dynamic systems.

1.9. What effect can a "system's environment" have on a "system's behavior?" How is "environmental change" catered for?

1.10. Is "counterintuitive behavior" a property of situations

1.11. Draw a "black box" with feedback from the output to the input. Explain the concept of "negative feedback" by reference to this diagram.

1.12. Explain the meaning of the concept "metalanguage."

1.13. Explain both in words and using diagrams the concept of "entropy."

1.14. Describe in words an example of a hierarchically structured situation. Now present your example diagrammatically.

1.15. Explain the meanings of the terms "systemic" and "systematic."

1.16. Why should systems science be regarded as an interdisciplinary area of knowledge?

SYSTEMS AND COMPLEXITY

2.1. INTRODUCTION

Having armed the reader with an understanding of the fundamental concepts of systems science, it is now appropriate to start the second phase of the introduction by again posing the question, "What is systems science all about?" A typical answer that a systems scientist might give is that it is about "dealing with complexity." This response, however, will leave most inquirers feeling just as perplexed, and inevitably will provoke the question "what is complexity?" A typical response to this question is that "complexity has many possible meanings" (Klir, 1985b). So where do we go from here?

Well, the task of this chapter is to explore those many meanings associated with complexity and provide a transportable conceptual framework that will contribute to the understanding of complexity in a wide variety of situations. This is essentially a qualitative investigation following Flood (1987b) which, when taken alongside the terms and concepts presented in Chapter 1, provides the reader with a conceptual understanding of systems science that will enrich the reading of the book as a whole.

2.2. COMING TO GRIPS WITH COMPLEXITY

2.2.1. Systems and People

"In general, we seem to associate complexity with anything we find difficult to understand."

This proposition offers us two clues as to how we might proceed to disassemble the concept of complexity. These are as follows:

Clue 1 "we": Complexity is associated with us, people.
Clue 2 "anything": Complexity is also associated with things.

We can, of course, note that people may themselves be considered as "things"; however, the reasons for maintaining the artificial dichotomy identified above will become apparent as the argument progresses.

Let us take the latter clue and consider it further in order to attach a meaning to the word "thing" in the context of this discussion. A "thing" has been defined as "an object of thought" (*The Concise Oxford Dictionary*, 6th ed.), which seems to suggest concreteness and tangibility in the sense that "object" implies a material thing that can be seen or touched. However, Klir (1985b) stated that "it is not operationally meaningful to view complexity as an intrinsic property of objects," and in this vein of thought we will assume that complexity arises from, or exists in, abstractions of the world (situations in thought). This is much less concrete. In fact we can say that systems are situations as perceived by people, as also illustrated in Figure 2.1 (using the concrete object as an example), which implies that even the most concrete situation may be seen from a variety of perspectives.

So Clue 1 associates complexity with people and Clue 2 associates it with systems. We will now progress by taking an in-depth look at systems and people in the context of complexity.

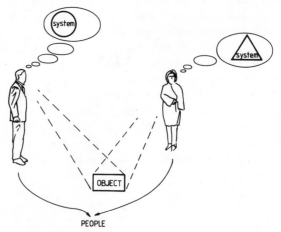

FIGURE 2.1. Systems are objects as perceived by people (Flood, 1987b; reproduced by permission of Pergamon Journals).

2.2.2. Parts and Relationships, Notions and Perceptions

Klir (1985b) noted that commonsense definitions of complexity from *Webster's Third International Dictionary* are as follows:

1. Having many varied interrelated parts, patterns, or elements and consequently hard to understand fully
2. Being marked by an involvement of many parts, aspects, details, notions, and necessitating earnest study or examination to understand or cope with

We have already noted that systems are situations as perceived by people. Now in addition to this, the definitions suggest, we need to include the ideas of (1) the number of parts, (2) the number of relationships between the parts, and (3) notions/perceptions.

The argument so far is summarized in the illustration given in Figure 2.2. We now intend to investigate rigorously the "elements" of complexity at the "third level" of this figure. This will provide the basis by which, we anticipate, the reader will formulate an understanding of the concept "complexity" within the overall framework proposed in the figure.

Perception has been dealt with, to a certain extent, in Figure 2.1. An alternative legend for that figure, however, could be "perception is about the way we build up models in our minds," a phrase frequently repeated by our colleague Derek Cramp. The concept of notion is closely related to the concept of perception and may be considered as our understanding or opinion of the model construction in our minds (our perceptions). Notions and perceptions are also intricately related with individuals' interests and capabilities.

The idea that complexity is directly related to a person's interest has been highlighted by Ashby (1973), as noted by Klir (1985b), when he stated that

> to the neurophysiologist the brain, as a feltwork of fibers and a soup of enzymes, is certainly complex; and equally the transmission of a detailed description of it would require much time. To a butcher the brain is simple, for he has to distinguish it from only about thirty other "meats."

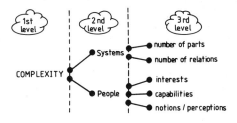

FIGURE 2.2. Disassembly of complexity—I (Flood, 1987b; reproduced by permission of Pergamon Journals).

This point is clear, but what of a person's capabilities in understanding the multipart, multirelationship schema outlined for complex situations?

Research has shown that capability can be measured for a population or an individual. The former case was elucidated by Miller (1967), who stated that the limit of people's span of absolute judgment is not great, "usually somewhere in the neighbourhood of seven... uni-dimensional judgements." This has been described by Uhr *et al.* (1962) as the "inelastic limit of human capacity." From a base of simplicity, very few additional parts and/or relationships would be required before Miller's limit was exceeded, and thus a threshold of complexity reached. Miller also noted that once this threshold has been passed, people reformulate the information into larger and larger chunks, each chunk containing more information but less detail than before. This, however, does lead to stereotyping and other gross simplifications.

An individual's performance may vary from the population mean as concerns the precise number of unidimensional judgments achievable or, indeed, the mental ability to recursively develop information-saturated chunks (this being the key to man's ability, albeit far from perfect, to deal with complexity on a day-to-day basis). Let us now consider, in more detail, the nature of the complexity of the information that we as individuals receive from the real world.

At the third level shown in Figure 2.2, along the "system branch," it is suggested that complexity is concerned with the number of parts and relationships. Pippenger (1978) discussed these aspects by referring to complex situations, such as computers or a telephone exchange, these being interconnected constructs of a large number of simple components. He wrote that

> the most important lesson of complexity theory is the demonstration of the diversity of phenomena that can arise through the interaction of simple components. Today's computers and telephone exchanges present problems beyond our understanding.

An illustrative way of showing how this sort of complexity can arise from the growth in the number of parts and, consequently, the number of possible relationships and states is offered in Figure 2.3. Consider each node as an element (e), and each connection as a relationship (r) between two of the elements. The graph in Figure 2.3 shows that the rise in the number of potential relationships grows at a faster and faster rate as the number of elements is repeatedly incremented by one. Considering the number of possible states, or the variety of a system with n elements (using the formula 2^n, where each element may be in one of two states, ON or OFF) it can be clearly seen that there is a truly rapid growth as n is repeatedly incremented by 1.

In a similar vein of reasoning, Brewer (1973) investigated the number of interactions that occur between a limited number of variables. He considered a mathematical model (a simple representation) of the national economy. The model used is reproduced below (note: any reader experiencing difficulty in following this symbolic representation is advised to read the first part of Chapter 8 on using letters instead of numbers).

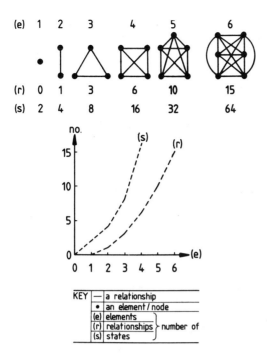

FIGURE 2.3. Elements, possible relationships, and states as a measure of complexity; where (e) are elements, (r) are relationships and (s) are states (Flood, 1987b; reproduced by permission of Pergamon Journals).

$$Y_t = C_t + I_t + G_t \tag{2.1}$$

$$C_t = \alpha Y_{t-1} \tag{2.2}$$

$$I_t = \beta(C_t - C_{t-1}) + I_{t-1} \tag{2.3}$$

$$G_t = \gamma Y_{t-1} \tag{2.4}$$

$$N_t = N_{t-1} + \mathrm{PRN}_{t-1} \tag{2.5}$$

Y is gross national product, C is consumption expenditure, I is investment expenditure, G is government expenditure, N is population size, PRN is net rate of population change, α, β and γ are constant coefficients, and t is time. The equations in this context are important only in the way that they display the coupling, or interactions between the dependant variables. For instance, if the gross national product (Y) varies, then so will consumption expenditure (C) as the latter is a function of the former. Using this model it was shown that, by adding only a few variables or relationships, the number of interactions within the model rose rapidly over a given time span. Witness this below.

The connectedness of the variables from the above set of equations is represented in Matrix **A** (with population unlinked):

Inputs

	Y	C	I	G	N
Y	0	1	1	1	0
C	1	0	0	0	0
I	0	1	1	0	0
G	1	0	0	0	0
N	0	0	0	0	1

Outputs { ... }   Matrix **A**

The connectedness Matrix **B**, unlike **A**, shows population linked to consumption expenditure (*C*), investment expenditure (*I*), and government expenditure (*G*):

Inputs

	Y	C	I	G	N
Y	0	1	1	1	0
C	1	0	0	0	1
I	0	1	1	0	1
G	1	0	0	0	1
N	0	0	0	0	1

Outputs { ... }   Matrix **B**

The square of these matrices (the matrix multiplied by itself) shows the number of interactions between the variables over one time period. Successive powers (multiplications) show the number of interactions accumulating between the set of variables over successive time periods. The total accumulation for any power (time period) is equal to the sum of all the values on the matrix at that time period. For instance, on Matrix **B** above, the sum of all the values equals 11. Some important results of carrying out this operation are detailed in Table 2.1. From this table it can be seen that the number of

TABLE 2.1
The Number of Internal Connections for
Matrix **A** and Matrix **B**

Power (time periods)	Cumulative internal interactions	
	A	**B**
1	8	11
2	14	22
5	76	143
10	1432	2770

internal interactions of the system with population coupled (Matrix **B**) is roughly double that of the population-unlinked system (Matrix **A**) after five time periods, which becomes a sizable difference after ten time periods. This is the result of including only three additional relationships, and note this excludes factors that could act upon the model from its "environment" (if it was open).

2.2.3. Nonlinearity, Asymmetry, and Nonholonomic Constraints

The now familiar (to the reader) idea of multiple parts and interactions of complex situations has been further expanded by Yates (1978). He believes that complexity arises when one or more of the following five attributes are found:

1. Significant interactions
2. High number of parts, degrees of freedom or interactions
3. Nonlinearity
4. Broken symmetry
5. Nonholonomic constraints

Note that 3–5 above can be appended to Figure 2.2, as shown in Figure 2.4, which acts as a summary of the argument so far. These last three attributes of complexity are discussed later, the first in systems terms.

Nonlinear systems (the graph of at least one relationship displays some curved feature) are notoriously more difficult to comprehend than linear systems, that is, they are more complex. Consequently they are also more difficult to control. This is exemplified by the volumes of elegant mathematics that have been developed in the search for optimal control of linear systems. In contrast to this there are significantly fewer publications on nonlinear control theory, and this work has not enjoyed the degree of success that can be accorded to its linear counterpart.

Contrasting the dynamics of linear and nonlinear systems is a further way of exemplifying the greater complexity of the latter type. Referring to Figure 2.5, which shows graphical outputs derived from real sets of equations (highly simplified representations where all inputs were assumed constant), note how

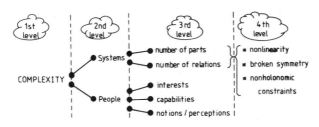

FIGURE 2.4. Disassembly of complexity—II (Flood, 1987b; reproduced by permission of Pergamon Journals).

the final state of the profit *x*, over time *t*, of a small firm represented by a linear model is independent of the initial state. A feature of linear systems is that different starting points lead to the same "end" point and do not make the model unstable. They are relatively easy to understand. Now note how the final state, or direction of response, of the profit *y* over time *t* of the firm represented by a nonlinear model is highly dependent on the initial state. A feature of nonlinear representations is that different starting points will lead to varying "end" points and can cause the model to become unstable. They are generally very difficult to understand and commonly "display" counterintuitive behavior, a characteristic of our inability to comprehend, in this case, complex systems.

Asymmetry, in the context of this chapter, refers to situations that display broken symmetry. Consider a single cell after fertilization which multiplies to two cells, and then four, and then eight, and so on. Eventually this process produces some creature in the mold of its parents. The reason the single cell becomes a distinct creature is due (among other things) to differential growth. Differential growth means asymmetry, and without it the growth process described above would have produced nothing more than a large blob of cells, and a large blob of cells is no more difficult to understand than a small blob of cells. Thus, when asymmetrical processes occur, the rise from a few elements to many elements makes it substantially more difficult for us to reformulate the information into larger, sensible chunks.

The state of development of mathematical theory in relation to some attributes of complexity is a clear measure of our ability/inability to deal with that attribute (as implied in the discussion on linear and nonlinear systems). This notion can be applied to the case of symmetrical and asymmetrical situations. Consider a communications network (perhaps Pippenger's telephone exchange). The network representation in reality would be somewhat intricate and clearly asymmetrical; however, let us assume that the digraphs of Figure 2.6 represent two communication networks. (A digraph is a structured representation of a situation showing which variables/elements directly influence/communicate with other variables/elements. These are discussed in

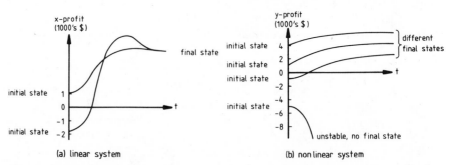

FIGURE 2.5. Contrasting dynamics of (a) linear and (b) nonlinear systems (Flood, 1987b; reproduced by permission of Pergamon Journals).

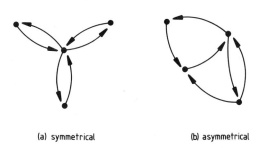

(a) symmetrical   (b) asymmetrical

KEY	•	node
	→	communication

FIGURE 2.6. Two possible structures for a four-node communication system: (a) symmetrical and (b) asymmetrical (Flood, 1987b; reproduced by permission of Pergamon Journals).

detail in Chapter 3.) The symmetrical network of Figure 2.6a is of the form known as an "advanced rosette" (a special class of symmetrical digraph where one node is a component of all cycles, and it is possible to move from any given node to any other node and back again). Mathematical theory for these structures is relatively simple and complete (see Brown *et al.*, 1972). For digraphs with broken symmetry—an example is displayed in Figure 2.6b— theory is difficult to formulate and consequently is currently incomplete. Asymmetrical situations, then, are more difficult to understand as they have a higher degree of complexity.

Nonholonomic constraint relates to laws (*nomic*) of wholes (*holos*). Constraints of laws of wholes, in systems terms, implies integrity of, and communication and control in, a system. So the obverse of this, nonholonomic constraints, implies that parts of the system are temporarily outside central control and can in fact go off and "do their own thing" (our interpretation). Complexity may therefore arise when there is some sort of localized transient anarchy in a system.

Anarchy itself suggests disorder and lack of government; however, our argument is not one of entropy but as follows: In systems terms, anarchy can cause such strains on a system, including positive feedback, that the system itself may go through a transition. In many cases anarchic behavior is the catalyst of system transition, not from one state to another (within a predetermined state space; a one-to-one mapping of the state variables), rather, from one nature to another. That is, some essential qualities are replaced by another set of essential qualities (this idea is exemplified in Figure 1.10). The label of such a situation, however, may well remain the same—France was still France after the revolution (perhaps because of cultural cohesion).

The discussion so far has developed a framework by which we may consider the concept of complexity. There are, however, further dimensions of this concept which we shall now present.

2.2.4. Hierarchy and Emergence

Much of the argument so far (refer back to Figure 2.4 for the current summary) has skirted around the phenomenon of emergence. Let us again recall Pippenger's "diversity of phenomena that can arise through the interaction of simple components," and consider Simon's comment (Simon, 1965) on complex situations (a comment noted by many before and many subsequently) that "the whole is more than the sum of the parts." Clearly, something "additional" can happen when a situation consists of a large number of parts with many interactions (plus any other attribute of complexity). Instead of being merely an aggregation of shaped materials, an airplane can fly. Instead of being a blob of cells, we can walk and talk. When a coherent structure with appropriate communication and control is formed, an aggregation of parts can and does become a viable unit. When a collection of viable units (firms, government, and others) interact, and we observe this activity, we call it a national economy, a viable unit in its own right. So, in systems terms, if we decompose a viable system then a number of other viable systems of a different nature can be found; and if we think of a collection of interacting viable systems as a whole, then a single viable system of a different nature may emerge. Thus, it is clear that communication and control, and emergence and hierarchy are intimately related. Together these contribute significantly to complexity, as, when they are present, analysis becomes that much more difficult. Let us develop these points.

In his discussion on the problems for science posed by complexity, Checkland (1981) modified the classification of science proposed by the nineteenth-century writer Comte, and offered the following classification:

Physics–chemistry–biology–psychology–social sciences

which is often labeled the hard–soft spectrum. About this he wrote:

> In this sequence physics is the most basic science with the most general concepts, such as mass, motion, force and energy. Chemical reactions often entail these and are increasingly explained in terms of them, but when hydrochloric acid gas and ammonia mix, and a white solid not previously present settles out, we have a phenomenon which intuitively is more complex than those of physics. And though a biological phenomenon such as the growth of a plant from seeds entails much chemistry (as well as physics) the reproductive ability of the plant again brings in a new level of complexity. Psychology, and the concept of consciousness, bring in a higher level still and social life exhibits yet higher levels.

The argument that follows goes something like this: A phenomenon set in the classification sequence presented above cannot be explained in terms of the classified sciences to the left without introducing new concepts. Checkland (1981) says that

> the puzzle which remains is that of the apparent existence of a hierarchy of levels of complexity which we find it convenient to tackle through a hierarchy of separate sciences.

Interestingly, Checkland argues that social sciences present considerable problems for the method of science, and introduce "a new kind of difficulty beyond that of mere complexity." The problems Checkland is referring to relate to the innate tendency of human beings to appreciate the "same" situation from differing viewpoints. Clearly this is an emergence at the softest end of the classification for experimental sciences and is a new kind of difficulty above those in the natural sciences. However, at the outset of the current chapter it was noted that complexity is related to anything we find difficult to understand, and indeed our fellow human beings can be exceedingly difficult to understand. We have different sets of beliefs and values and can choose to do the unpredictable (if only for the sheer hell of it). Checkland's special plea for the subject matter of the social sciences as being "beyond mere complexity" centers around people and things that are difficult to understand. According to the argument here this can be regarded as just one, very important, aspect of complexity. The way in which we deal with the different "emergences" from complexity is another matter altogether, however, and one that underlies the thesis of this book.

2.2.5. Aesthetic Measures—An Illustrative Example

An illustrative work, from as far back as the early 1930s, is that of Birkhoff (1933). His main concern was with ascertaining "aesthetic measures," but his approach can be used to draw together many ideas presented above. *Aesthetics*, incidentally, is defined as "many auditory and visual perceptions that are accompanied by a certain feeling of value," that is, aesthetic value.

The work proposed a way of ascertaining an aesthetic measure (M) from the complexity of an object (C) and associated order, or symmetry (O).

Working toward a "psychological meaning of complexity," Birkhoff noted that interest of some kind is necessary for sustained attention. To this he associated the

> feeling of effort always attendant upon perception [which] appears as a summation of the feelings of tension which accompany the various automatic [neural] adjustments requisite to the act of perception.

The psychological meaning of complexity is thus defined: If A^*, B^*, and C^* are various automatic required adjustments; a, b, and c are respective indices of "tension"; and r, s, and t are the times that they take place; then the measure of complexity is the sum of the various values:

$$C = r \cdot a + s \cdot b + t \cdot c \cdots \qquad (2.6)$$

An example of a polygonal tile was given. Perception, it was stated, is nearly instantaneous, the feeling of effort is almost negligible. However, the eyes do follow the successive sides of the polygon, which does give rise to a slight feeling of tension attendant on each adjustment, and the complexity (C) will be measured by the number of sides of the polygon.

This is a clear statement of how complexity is associated to the number of parts, where an object of clearly definable structure is the focus of interest.

It was further stated that sensations from such neural activity, which have been derived from an object, are associated with various ideas and attendant feelings. This constitutes the "full" perception of the object.

An important distinction was made between "formal" and "connotative" associations. The former are those that are easy to define, such as symmetry. The latter associations touch our experience at many points and are not unitary in nature, for example poetry. Within these "distinct" areas, "elements of order" can be found, each having either a positive or negative effect. Examples of "formal elements of order" with a positive effect include repetition, similarity, equality, contrast, symmetry, balance, and sequence. A less obvious example is a center of focus in a painting. Examples of those with a negative effect are ambiguity, undue repetition, and unnecessary imperfection.

Continuing, Birkhoff defined the psychological meaning of order (symmetry) as follows. Assume the associations of various types L, M, and N; which take place with respective indices of tone of feeling l, m, and n, that occur at u, v, and w times, respectively; then we may regard the tone of feeling as a summation:

$$O = u \cdot l + v \cdot m + w \cdot n + \cdots \tag{2.7}$$

which is the psychological counterpart of order, where l, m, and n may be negative, zero, or positive.

The mathematical argument proposed stated that if two objects are in the same class, have the same O and C, then their Ms would be equal. This functional dependence, on O and C only, gives rise to the expression

$$M = f(O, C) \tag{2.8}$$

with a ratio of the form (O/C) seen as appropriate since "it is natural that reward should be proportional to effort."

Observations on this formula, made by Birkhoff, support, either directly or indirectly, much of the argument of the preceding section. These can be summarized as follows:

1. It is restricted in application to narrowly defined classes (would you compare a vase to a melody?).
2. Aesthetic comparison, where M is the determining index, will only have meaning when it represents the normal or average judgment of some selected group of observers—the "idealized normal observer."
3. It is clear that quantitative application of the formula can be effected only when the "elements of order" are mainly "formal."

This does distinguish situations with structure from those that are poorly structured, or the systems from the people branch of Figure 2.4. It does highlight the plurality of connotative associations, a dimension of complexity related in this chapter with social sciences. Lastly, it gives a strong suggestion that (and to reiterate the message of the last sentence of the preceding section) the way in which we deal with different emergences from complexity is an important matter for concern.

2.3. TWO-DIMENSIONAL SCIENCE

Our discussion of hierarchy and emergence has been set in the traditional one-dimensional representation of the spectrum of science, that of the experimental sciences as classified above. The rise in systems science, however, is characterized by investigations of a **relational** as opposed to an experimental nature. A relational study may incorporate aspects of physics, chemistry, biology, psychology, and/or sociology; it may stretch the length of this hard-soft spectrum. This is a second dimension of science (systemic science) and the very stuff of managerial activities as well as a wealth of other interdisciplinary studies. Furthermore, this also implies that we have two forms of reduction, that of the traditional scientific reduction, and systemic (relational) reduction. Explicit general recognition of this new systemic scientific approach, which has evolved as a means of dealing with the new kinds of complexity associated with contemporary man, is difficult to find.

Systemic reasoning, however, is implicitly evident in Western society. It is for this reason that Klir (1985a) stated that

> the significance of this radically new paradigm of science—the two-dimensional science—has not been fully realized yet, but its implications for the future seem quite profound.

2.4. ONE DIMENSION BEYOND THREE RANGES OF COMPLEXITY

There are further aspects of complexity that can help us to identify the role of systems science. Weaver (1948) identified three ranges of complexity: organized simplicity, organized complexity, and disorganized complexity.

Organized simplicity occurs where a small number of significant factors and a large number of insignificant factors appear initially to be complex, but on investigation display hidden simplicity. This type of discovery is typical of seventeenth-, eighteenth-, and nineteenth-century sciences (Klir, 1985b). Disorganized complexity can be said to exist where situations can be represented by many variables that exhibit a high level of random behavior. The behavior of gas molecules exemplifies this (Klir, 1985b).

The commonality between organized simplicity and disorganized complexity is that they are both eminently quantifiable, the former by analytic mathematics, concentrating on specific elements, and the latter by statistical means, calculating average properties of many variables, for example. Each subrange is slim and the two occupy positions at the opposite extremes of

Weaver's range. Between these two wafers is organized complexity. Of organized complexity Klir (1985b) had the following to say:

> Instances of systems with characteristics of organized complexity are abundant, particularly in the life, behavioral, social, and environmental sciences, as well as in applied fields such as modern technology or medicine.

Typical of such situations is the richness, which must not be oversimplified, but equally cannot be dealt with by techniques that work effectively on a large degree of randomness. Klir and others have suggested the use of fuzzy set theory as an appropriate analytic means of inquiry for organized complexity.

There is, however, an underlying difficulty here. While this argument of three ranges of complexity is compelling in the context of "natural systems" and "designed physical systems" (where common notions are achievable), it does present a rather uncomfortable fit for "human activity systems" and (perhaps to a lesser extent) "designed abstract systems" (these four system classes constituting Checkland's systems typology). It is at this point that some sympathy is felt for Checkland's view that aspects of social science are beyond mere complexity. However, we would contend that although social science is beyond Weaver's three ranges of complexity, it can be explained in terms of another dimension of complexity. What characterizes this dimension is that, no matter how analytic our activities are, there will always be many other people who would not subscribe to our findings on the grounds of differing values, notions, perceptions, and/or beliefs. So, perhaps it would be meaningful to think of a dimension of complexity that moves away from Weaver's line of complexity, specifically away from organized complexity, the home of relational systems, to which it is most naturally attached. This is the *Homo sapiens* line. Interestingly, cybernetics has recently developed a "second-order" offshoot—the cybernetics of "observing systems"—which recognizes, to some extent, the existence and importance of this line. Clemson (1984), for example, adds "relativistic organized complexity" to Weaver's original three distinctions. This recognizes the need to study "observing systems" because the nature of perceived reality is inevitably conditioned by our nature as observing systems.

Now it seems that the argument has come full circle, and that we are back to people (the *Homo sapiens* line) and (other) systems (Weaver's line) that constitute both the starting and finishing points of this chapter. These ideas, however, are necessarily expanded upon in Chapter 10.

2.5. CONCLUSION

The view of complexity that we have taken in this chapter is summarized in Figure 2.7. This is a looser arrangement than Figure 2.4, as befits the very nature of complexity. The arguments and ideas presented represent a first pass through this difficult area, but are sufficient to identify the need for a special set of tools designed for identifying, investigating, and enhancing our understanding of situations in terms of relations. This is the role for systems science.

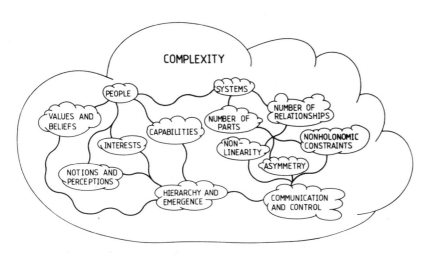

FIGURE 2.7. Disassembly of complexity—III (Flood, 1987b; reproduced by permission of Pergamon Journals).

PROBLEMS

2.1. What are the main attributes of complexity?

2.2. Discuss the main attributes of complexity in the context of a structured situation (for example, a machine, an ecological situation, a biological situation, or an economic situation).

2.3. Discuss the main attributes of complexity in the context of a poorly structured situation (for example, a managerial situation, a political situation, or any social situation).

2.4. List the main differences between your answers to Questions 2.2 and 2.3 above.

2.5. Discuss the relationship between hierarchy and emergence.

2.6. In what ways does the work of Birkhoff (1933) illustrate the attributes of complexity and how we deal with them?

2.7. What is meant by two-dimensional science?

2.8. How appropriate are Weaver's three ranges of complexity to contemporary issues?

Chapter Three

Systems and Modeling I

DIAGRAMS AND IDENTIFICATION

3.1. INTRODUCTION

There are a number of reasons why we may want to distinguish a situation from its surroundings. These include, for example, studying structure, processes, and behavior of the situation through systems methodology, or systemic scientific research. Forming representations, however, is not an easy task, since it is prone to a number of serious difficulties. One particular difficulty (which is discussed in detail below) is, in fact, how we abstract a system from the situation, determining what is system and what is environment, and where the boundary between the two should be drawn. This process is not an easy affair as we the abstractors are part of that process; hence a strong subjective element is included. Beishon (1980) suggested that our attempts to be objective are rarely successful because we are "prejudiced." He consequently suggested that we need some guidelines to help us disentangle potentially meaningful systems from the complexity that surrounds us. Building models and diagrams, Beishon proposed, is one useful approach. Let us first consider models in general.

A model is defined in *Webster's Third International Dictionary* as "a description ... [an] analogy used to help us visualize, often in a simplified way, something that cannot readily be observed." This tells us a little bit about what a model is and gives us some ideas about why we may want to model. As the aim of this book is to investigate the means by which man can deal with complexity (which is not readily observable and certainly requires suitable simplification), models apparently offer us precisely the sort of approach we require.

A model might be iconic, symbolic or analogous. An iconic model is the most familiar, being representative in form, but not necessarily size or detail. For example, a model car is an iconic representation, as are the models of aircraft whose aerodynamics are assessed in wind tunnel experiments. Symbolic models are representations by means of symbols. For example, a mathematical model is symbolic, as are set theoretic representations. An analogous model is one where features of a situation are represented by alternative means in such a way that the emergences, or our understanding of them, are not significantly altered. For example, an analog computer representation can reproduce behavior of structured situations; or an organic analogy of a firm *might* help bring us better understanding of its functions (a view on this latter point is given in Chapter 5).

Diagrams are in fact one of several modeling approaches available and may be iconic, symbolic, or analogous. The use of diagrams as models, in this first chapter on modeling, will therefore become our principal concern. Now let us consider the nature of diagrams a little further.

A *diagram* has been defined as "relational of a situation; the way in which something is placed in relation to its surroundings; helps in the problem of lack of understanding" in *Webster's Third International Dictionary*. This parallels the need expressed above to represent complex situations. We can therefore feel optimistic about the role diagrams might play. This optimism has been confirmed by Checkland (1979), who wrote that

> a diagram is an improvement on linear prose as a means of describing connections and relationships. Looking at a map, for example, we can take it as a whole. Our minds can process different parts of it simultaneously, in parallel, whereas prose has to be processed serially, putting a much greater burden on memory if our concern is with relationships. In addition, and presumably because of this possibility of "parallel processing," diagrams are automatically summaries. Imagine the amount of prose needed to convey all the information contained in a 1 : 50,000 Ordnance Map.

Figure 3.1 has been included for those who are not familiar with Ordnance Survey maps.

We have developed some fundamental reasoning as to why we might well benefit from the use of diagrammatic approaches. We now need to consider the types of diagrams that are available. Returning to a commonsense description is beneficial in helping us to initially identify a number of classes. *Webster's Third International Dictionary* describes a diagram as "a drawing that shows arrangement and relations; as of parts to a whole, relative values, origins and development, chronological fluctuations, distribution." From this description we have distinguished two classes of diagram:

1. Those that show relations as of parts to a whole
2. All other diagrammatic frameworks of reference

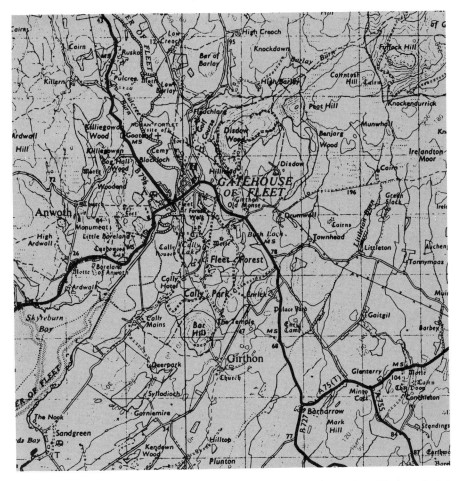

FIGURE 3.1. Sample taken from an ordnance survey map (reproduced by permission of Ordnance Survey).

The first type comprises those that we shall call system diagrams. These are defined as having elements and relations and may be represented (at least in principle) as a network-type diagram with nodes representing elements and lines the relationships (Jones, 1982).

System diagrams can be divided into two groups, providing representations of well-structured and poorly structured situations, respectively. Diagrams in the first group are schematic, in the sense that they correspond to established or formalized conceptions. "Hard" system diagrams conform to this type. Checkland (1979) stated that hard situations are those for which it is not

> difficult to obtain agreement on what constitutes the system in question . . . and this may help to explain the existence of agreed conventions for diagram construction . . . . The task of describing systems relevant to "soft" system studies is rather more difficult given the number and complexity of possible relevant systems.

Soft system diagrams therefore form a second group, although representations of this type are currently extremely primitive.

This chapter will thus focus upon (1) system diagrams, that is, hard system diagrams and soft system diagrams; and (2) other types of diagram useful in systems studies. In addition, as the specification of elements and relationships and the identification of the system boundary are integral parts of developing hard system diagrams, a section is included that discusses these features of diagram development.

3.2. MISUSE AND ABUSE

Before proceeding to consider the classes of diagram set out above, three general but flavored suggestions are offered for the guidance of the reader. These are relevant when (1) developing their own diagrams, or (2) interpreting other people's diagrams.

SUGGESTION 1.   Using an inappropriate type of diagram, not presenting it clearly, and not declaring a key lead to ambiguity and incorrect analysis. These applications are to bad purpose. This is misuse.

SUGGESTION 2.   Unwitting claims, such as claims of general validity for specific cases (inductive) (e.g., this firm works well with this structure, therefore all firms work well with such a structure) are unjustified and invalid claims. This is misuse.

SUGGESTION 3.   Deceiving images wittingly claimed represent a corrupt use of diagrams. This is abuse.

The pitfalls indicated in Suggestion 1 can be avoided by adhering to the following three rules, set out by Checkland (1979), for the process of drawing diagrams:

RULE 1.   Define what type of diagram is appropriate. (Is it to convey structural relationships? Material flows? Information flows? The logical dependencies among activities? Interaction of process parameters? Social influences?)

RULE 2.   Decide on a convention for the diagram's entities and relationships, ensuring that a symbol is selected for each kind of element.

RULE 3.   Provide a key that ensures that different readers will interpret the diagram in the same way.

The pitfalls of Suggestion 2 may only effectively be removed by increasing the awareness that broad sweep homologies (a feature of some of the General Systems Theory school, particularly in the earlier years) may be very dangerous indeed. Suggestion 3 is self-explanatory; we are all familiar with this kind of abuse as it is typical of what we have come to expect from politicians, journalists, and the like.

Now having secured some feeling for the nature of diagrams and some insight into the problems of their use, let us review the types that are available within the classes identified above.

3.3. SYSTEM DIAGRAMS

3.3.1. Graphs

The traditional understanding of a graph is that it is a diagram that shows the relationship between two variable quantities each measured along one of a pair of axes. Interpreting this at a general level we may consider relations between many variables. A graph, therefore, can be a diagram that shows relations between many variables in a network structure. If a relationship is shown as an arrow, representing the direction of influence, the network is then termed a **digraph** (see Figure 2.6). A digraph can represent the level of sophistication necessary for system identification, as discussed in Section 3.6.

One further sophistication is to add signs to directed relationships. A positive (+ve) sign states that given a rise (fall) in the targeting variable, the targeted variable will also rise (fall). Such a relationship is augmenting. A negative (−ve) sign states that given a rise (fall) in the targeting variable, the targeted variable will fall (rise). Such a relationship is inhibiting. A **signed digraph** is a compact, structured representation of a less structured conceptual model, which may be sentential or merely a set of thoughts or ideas. The structuring capacity of the method is apparent when converting the information contained in the signed digraph (back) to spoken or written language where a strict grammatical format is attained. For instance, "a rise (fall) in plasma volume will cause a rise (fall) in arterial pressure." See Figure 3.2 for signed digraph conventions.

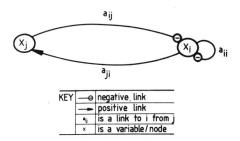

FIGURE 3.2. Conventions used for signed digraphs.

A loop in a signed digraph can be identified by following logical flows through the network and finding one (or more) that trace back to their starting points. Identifying these aspects of the microstructure is soon learned. A loop can be classified as +ve (either all arrows are +ve or an even number of arrows are −ve on a loop). A +ve loop is a growth-producing part of the microstructure and if left unchecked will cause the model to "blow up." Alternatively, a loop can be classified as −ve (an odd number of arrows are −ve on a loop). This is a stable part of the microstructure which, in an unstable model, will at least in part be counteracting the effects of any +ve loops. For a model to be stable it is necessary that the −ve loops can, at some time, damp out the growth loops. Figure 3.3 is an example of this approach. The figure represents the effect of land on urban growth; D is labor, goods, and services demanded; PBI is population, business, and industry in the city; FL is the fraction of land occupied; and CLA is the city land area (from Roberts *et al.*, 1983). The positive loop suggests that as demand for labor, goods, and services rises, so too will population, business, and industry. The effect of the +ve loop is reduced by the inhibiting effects of the increasing usage of land.

The time scale (or length) associated with the operation of a loop can be approximated by initially attaching, say, an S, M, or L to each signed directed relationship (S for short, say days; M for medium, say months; L for long, say years) and then calculating the length. So, if *loop A* is

$$S^2 + M^4 + L^2$$

that is, $S = 2$, $M = 4$, and $L = 2$ (there are eight relationships in the loop, two that are short, four that are medium, and two that are long), then the order (O) of the loop is L and the approximate length (Le) of the loop is something over L^2. The order often corresponds to the longest of S, M, or L which is present in the loop. A second five-relationship *loop B* might be

$$S^1 + M^0 + L^4$$

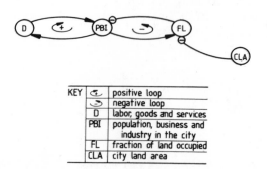

KEY	⟲	positive loop
	⟳	negative loop
D		labor, goods and services
PBI		population, business and industry in the city
FL		fraction of land occupied
CLA		city land area

FIGURE 3.3. Example of signed digraph approach: Effect of land on urban growth (example taken from Roberts *et al.*, 1983; reproduced by permission of Addison-Wesley).

with approximate length L^4 and order L. The following comparisons can be made:

$A \underset{O}{=} B$, the order (O) of A is equal to the order of B; and

$A \underset{Le}{<} B$, the length (Le) of A is less than the length of B.

The strength (or weighting) of the relationships (and consequently the loops) can also be assessed in a similar way and hence the relative effect of two or more loops on a shared variable can be assessed in a qualitative fashion. An ordinal (ranked) scale (explained in Chapter 4) has to be selected. A scale from 1 to 10 might be chosen, with 1 referring to a weak impact and 10 a strong impact. The strength of impact thus rises in an ordinal fashion from 1 sequentially up to 10. The information can then be translated into tabular form. A hypothetical example of this approach for *loop A* is given in Table 3.1. Here, in the top left-hand corner, the loop A has been classified as positive. The table shows that the total sum of the short relationships $(\sum s)$ is 2, but only one of those will have a significant impact. Utilizing this type of information it is possible to make qualitative assessments. If we had selected one (or more) variable that was perceived as central to our purposes (interest), and let us say that this variable was placed on both *loops A* and *B*, then it would be possible to assess the overal impact of each loop on the shared variable by considering the information documented in the tabular form. This qualitative information is useful in a wide variety of situations, from pure research to strategic management.

An influence diagram is a special type of signed digraph, which is used in the system dynamics modeling methodology for socioeconomic systems (Wolstenholme, 1983a). The essential difference between signed digraphs and

TABLE 3.1
Tabulated Consolidation of Qualitative
Information concerning *Loop A*

A (positive)	S	M	L
1	1	0	2
2	0	2	0
3	0	1	0
4	0	1	0
5	0	0	0
6	0	0	0
7	0	0	0
8	0	0	0
9	1	0	0
10	0	0	0
$\sum$	2	4	2

influence diagrams is the strict logical rules of the latter for relating the elements. Figure 3.4 explains the logic as follows: R is a rate, the amount of something that flows in given time period (per unit time); L is a level, the accumulation of rates added to an initial condition; A is an auxiliary variable. Levels and rates are necessary to describe a situation; however, auxiliaries are used to break down rate equations into manageable parts. This is particularly useful when writing sets of equations from the diagram. Influence diagrams also have a set of rules that should be strictly adhered to. These, taken from Coyle (1977), are described below:

1. A level in a loop can only be preceded by a rate.
2. A level may be followed by an auxiliary or a rate.
3. An auxiliary may be followed by another auxiliary or by a rate.
4. A rate must be followed by a level.
5. A level may not directly affect another level.

An example of this approach is given in Figure 3.5. The diagram is intended to be the basis of a system dynamics simulation model. Averaging periods have been omitted for convenience. Note that the loops are all structurally coherent. Profit is used to control production, which both increases stock and has a cost associated with it. Stock has a value associated with it, so total costs are (production cost − increased value). In the model, profit is determined by ([sales] × [unit price] − total cost). Unit price also determines the value of increased stock. Sales rate determines income from sales and depleted stock. An increase in production rate implies that the stock level rises (assuming SRATE is constant), which causes an increase in stock value that should be greater than the increased production cost (assuming that UNIT is greater than PCOST for a unit, which is likely to be the case). Thus total costs drop, and profit rate increases by a required amount. In order to maintain the increased profit, stock must continue to increase (that is, accumulate unsaleable stock). The profit, according to the model, is an accounting artifact rather than being real. This is not a viable way of increasing profits. Clearly, much qualitative information can be drawn from this representation. The management policy link could thus be brought into action to assess desirable control over this model.

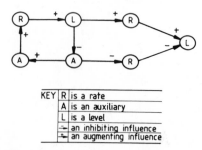

KEY	R	is a rate
	A	is an auxiliary
	L	is a level
	−	an inhibiting influence
	+	an augmenting influence

FIGURE 3.4. Conventions used for influence diagrams (Coyle, 1977; reproduced by permission of John Wiley & Sons).

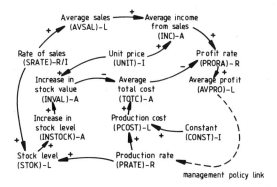

FIGURE 3.5. Example of influence diagram approach: A financial model.

The ideas of graph theory, including ideas of connectedness and centrality of elements, are unfortunately far more wide ranging than is possible to cover here. The interested reader is directed to Wilson (1979) for an excellent introduction to graph theory. Other more sophisticated graphical analyses include the methodology of Puccia and Levins (1985), which focuses on loop analysis and time averaging. The successes of these graphical approaches are a direct result of the ability to convert graphical representations into matrix form and then investigate the model (in that matrix form) with a computer using some simple well-developed mathematical techniques.

There are a number of advantages to using sophisticated graphical approaches (such as those of Puccia and Levins) rather than more traditional mathematical representations. These points (presented below) are well expressed by Kohn and Chiang (1982) and Kohn and Letzkus (1983) among others. Model control properties may not be self-evident from the solution of parametrized equations, although sensitivity analysis will quantitate the control features (see Chapter 9 for a brief insight into sensitivity analysis). Expanding this idea, Kohn and co-workers observed that a complete catalogue of the degrees of sensitivity of a model's behavior to the values of the parameters may give far more information than is needed. Furthermore, the effects relating to local regulation are jumbled with the synergistic outcomes that arise from the presence of each element in a larger representation. The argument is that, for some situations, only qualitative information is required to identify the important sites of regulation and control and the sequence of events underlying the observed behavior to the structural features of the situation.

Graph theory is an excellent tool for analyzing structured situations for a variety of purposes, including problem management. There are many such problems in engineering and design that can and do benefit from graphical analysis. Graph theory can also be used to investigate things with structure that it is impossible, or unethical, to investigate by direct numerical measurement (*in vivo* human physiology, for example).

Now let us briefly consider block diagrams, another diagrammatic approach that lends itself to the investigation of hard structured situations, before moving on to soft systems diagrams.

3.3.2. Block Diagrams

Block diagrams are quantified diagrammatic representations of variables and relationships and are usually drawn to represent a set of equations. The mathematical concepts are explained in Chapter 8. Block diagrams are presented here for consistency. The conventions are presented in Figure 3.6.

The main advantages of a block diagram as opposed to a set of equivalent equations are as follows:

1. The signal flow can be traced with ease through the set of equations.
2. The positive and negative loops can easily be identified.
3. The nature of the model can easily be assessed, that is, whether it is nonlinear or linear and so on.

It should be noted that a block diagram is generally used as a quantitated signed digraph, that is, a parametric signed digraph with explicit quantitative relationships. They can be used as nonparametric representations when summarizing controversial ideas or areas of weak knowledge. An example of the approach is given in Figure 3.7. Here we see a simple representation of population (P) dynamics with k_1 and k_2 as constants and d/dt the differential form.

There are, however, some messes that defy even the best intended efforts to apply structured diagrammatic approaches. An alternative approach is to use soft system diagrams.

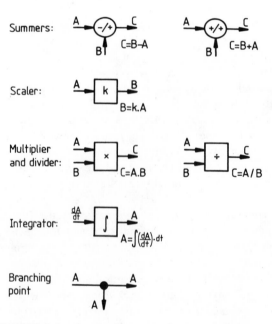

FIGURE 3.6. Conventions used for block diagrams.

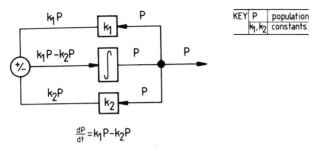

$$\frac{dP}{dt} = k_1 P - k_2 P$$

FIGURE 3.7. Example of block diagram approach: A simple population model.

3.3.3. Soft System Diagrams

As has previously been stated, soft system diagrams are at a primitive stage of evolution, and the best we can do is to review the benchmark paper of Checkland (1979) on diagrams in soft systems practice.

Checkland pointed out that diagrams attempting to represent soft situations, usually human activity systems, often include, for example, "the same kind of arrow [which] represents now a physical flow, now the expression 'is a part of.'" Later he states that "no doubt the creators and users of these promiscuous models understand them, but they are unreadable to an outsider."

Checkland also opposes the use of a set of symbols and rules for developing soft system diagrams because they would, at the outset, impose limits on what could be represented and thus prestructure the process of system conceptualization.

The type of representation he prefers employs the idea of sentences broken down into phrases. Some of the phrases constitute the start, end, or inner section of one or more sentence(s). Figure 3.8 shows the conventions of soft system diagrams. This approach is exemplified in Checkland's model of any religion, which he constructed from a statement by Professor N. Smart. It may be considered as a set of beliefs and practices having six dimensions (namely, institutions, doctrines, myths, rituals, experiences, and ethical values; see Figure 3.9.).

The lessons of carrying out this exercise, Checkland noted, are as follows: Professor Smart commented that he found the representation to be free from

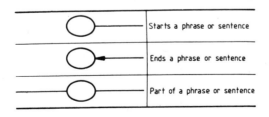

FIGURE 3.8. Conventions used for soft system diagrams.

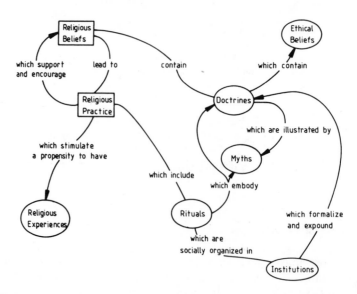

FIGURE 3.9. Example of soft system diagram approach: Any religion may be considered as a set of beliefs and practices having six dimensions (Checkland, 1979; reproduced by permission).

ambiguity, but the diagram represents only one out of many possible interpretations of the relationship between the six elements. The latter point was seen as extremely important by Checkland as it "was significant in the realization that any real-world equivalent of what a human activity system tries to model can never be described in a way which will command universal assent, but only in ways which reflect the differing viewpoints and purposes of different observers."

This disclosure led to the idea that any diagram of a social situation should be based on one *Weltanschauung* (world view) and that normally a systems analyst should construct several models, each expressing a relevant viewpoint of the situation being considered.

3.4. OTHER USEFUL DIAGRAMS

3.4.1. Unit Diagrams

A unit is a whole made up of like or unlike elements, especially when it is part of a greater whole. A unit diagram is therefore different from the systems diagram which sets out to display relationships between pairs of elements. It is useful when defining major subsystems and activities with feedback and control from hard situations. Two types of unit diagram are the subsystem and cybernetic unit diagrams. The conventions of each type are shown in

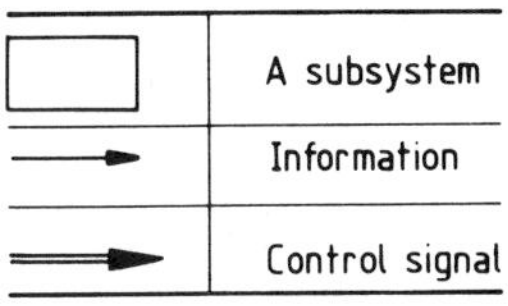

□	A subsystem
→	Information
⇒	Control signal

FIGURE 3.10. Conventions used for subsystem unit diagrams.

Figures 3.10 and 3.11, respectively. In the latter type the cybernetic units are defined as follows:

CONTROL UNIT. Compares actual to desired output, and when a discrepancy is found ($i <> o$) sends control signals to the activating unit in order to bring about change in the controlled process.

ACTIVATING UNIT. Receives control signals from the Control Unit and responds by making the desired changes to the controlled process in order to match actual output to the desired output.

CONTROLLED PROCESS. That which is being controlled.

INFORMATION SYSTEM. Measures the actual output and relays this information to the Control Unit, including deviations caused by environmental disturbances.

An example of a subsystem unit diagram is given in Figure 3.12 (see Table 9.13 for an explanation of the symbols). This represents the structure and interconnections, at the subsystem level, of fluid volume maintenance in man. This example forms the basis of a case study on modeling in Chapter 9. Figure 3.13 is an example of a cybernetic unit diagram. This example of an aircraft flight may be read as follows: A pilot has details of the flight path, destination, and expected time of arrival. These three items of knowledge can be continually

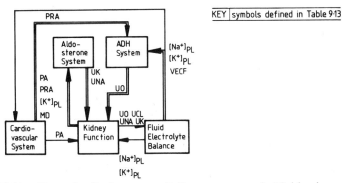

FIGURE 3.11. Example of subsystem unit diagram approach: Fluid volume maintenance in man.

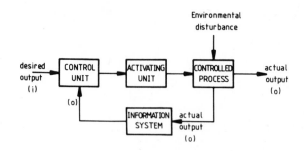

FIGURE 3.12. Conventions used for cybernetic unit diagrams.

compared with the aircraft's progress via measurements from navigator and instruments. Given some deviation from the flight plan, the pilot may make adjustments to wing and tail flaps and/or engines in order to change speed, direction, and consequently the temporal-spatial position.

3.4.2. Rich Pictures

An approach by which subjective interpretation and understanding of messy situations is achievable, and consequently transferable for other peoples' subjective consumption, is the rich picture approach of Checkland (1981). A rich picture is one that expresses, in as rich a manner as possible, a person's general appreciation of a perceived problematic situation. The idea developed as an integral part of Checkland's soft systems methodology (see Chapter 6). However, we have applied the approach to a wide range of situations, including medical (social systems) and ecological (without human activity) situations to great effect.

Essentially, the development of a rich picture parallels brain storming, but represents the ideas in pictures rather than words. It is like a gigantic cartoon representation of a situation in nonsystem terms. In our experience, we have seen groups of students developing rich pictures in a "laboratory" exercise, working on a chalkboard, drawing pictorial representations of ideas, arguing and debating over them, and relating and structuring them in a way

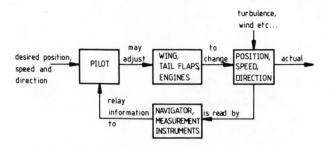

FIGURE 3.13. Example of cybernetic unit diagram approach: An aircraft flight.

that seems to make some sense. Although it has been the case that no two rich pictures of the set task have evolved in an identical manner, it is evident that the groups of students have been able to communicate (with mutual understanding) their appreciation of the problem with other groups through their own rich pictures.

There are no conventions as such for rich pictures; however, annotations and explanations are essential. An example is presented in Figure 3.14. This is a representation of vice in central London, and constitutes one part of a research program being carried out by Superintendent P. Gaisford and R. L. Flood. The aim of the project is to ascertain whether there is a problem (some do not perceive this to be so), and if there is one, whose is it? Can, or ought, it be alleviated? The rich picture clearly shows that these questions are not going to be easy to resolve. Nevertheless, it offers one step in a lengthy learning exercise.

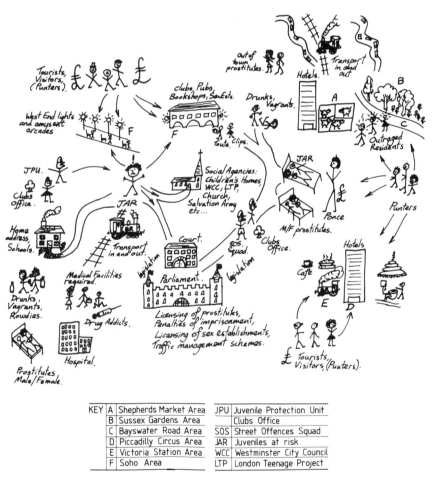

KEY	A	Shepherds Market Area	JPU	Juvenile Protection Unit
	B	Sussex Gardens Area		Clubs Office
	C	Bayswater Road Area	SOS	Street Offences Squad
	D	Piccadilly Circus Area	JAR	Juveniles at risk
	E	Victoria Station Area	WCC	Westminster City Council
	F	Soho Area	LTP	London Teenage Project

FIGURE 3.14. Example of rich picture approach: Vice in the West End of London (Unpublished research, R. L. Flood and P. Gaisford).

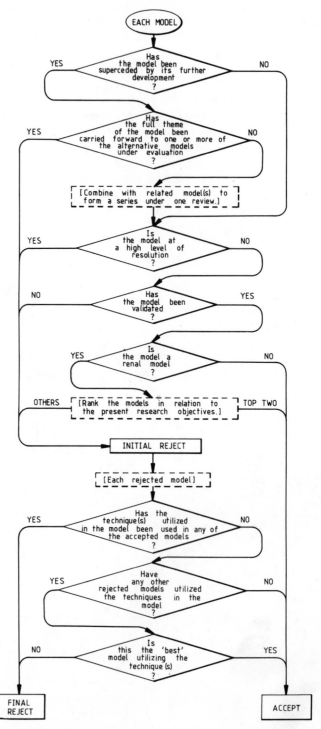

FIGURE 3.15. Example of decision flow diagram approach: Selecting a representative and manageable set of models, found by literature search, for a critical review.

3.4.3. Decision Flow Diagrams

In Chapter 1, decision making was briefly introduced as a subset of systems problem "solving." Decision flow diagrams can be applied usefully in such situations. They have the advantage of rationalizing the procedure, while also making explicit the criteria used. This type of diagrammatic form is useful when an end point is known in advance (that is, the decision to be made is *a priori* identified), although an actual "solution" depends on the alternatives selected for consideration. This methodological theme is pursued in depth in Chapter 6.

The decision flow diagram of Figure 3.15 is clearly methodological in nature. In this example we have documented the reasoning we used when confronted with over 100 models of the fluid balance in humans following a comprehensive literature search. Our interest was to draw together other researchers' efforts in this area, in order to discover the modeling approaches that had previously been adopted. Renal models made up a large percentage of the set and consequently they passed through a special filter. The knowledge contained in the "accepted" models would be, we anticipated, suggestive and directive for our purpose of modeling the fluid dynamics in man as the basis of decision-making tools for clinicians. The subsequent research program is documented in the case studies of Chapter 9.

3.4.4. Hierarchical Representations

Hierarchy was introduced in Chapter 1 as an important systemic concept and this point was reiterated and expanded upon in Chapter 2. Representing a situation via associated levels of resolution can sometimes be useful (see Figure 1.9). Another useful representation is that of hierarchical control, a cybernetic concept that, for example, is central to Beer's organizational cybernetics approach (Beer, 1981) as presented in Chapter 5.

Additionally, hierarchical structures are used to show structured objectives (company objectives, for example) and intent structures, using the Interpretive

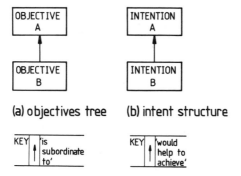

FIGURE 3.16. Conventions of interpretive structural model diagram: (a) an objectives tree and (b) an intent structure.

Structural Modeling technique (ISM, Warfield, 1976). These diagrammatic representations are a special class of graph that lump any feedback loops. As with other graphical representations they are convertible to matrix form and are thus easily dealt with by computer.

The conventions of an ISM diagram are shown in Figure 3.16. Here structure (a) is the convention used for objectives trees where a number of objectives are "ranked" in order of importance and are related to superordinate objectives which they contribute to the achievement of. Structure (b) groups together sets of related intentions so that they are related in a logical hierarchical

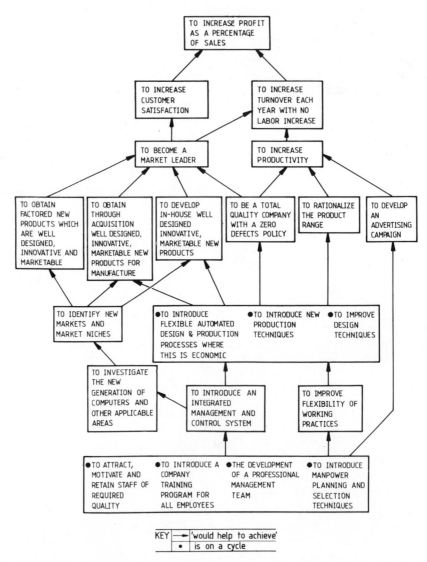

FIGURE 3.17. Example of interpretive structural model diagram approach: Intent structure developed for a commercial company.

sequence. These approaches, when used in conjunction with "triggered" questions that help to generate "the objectives" or the "intentions" of a group, are used to define strategies and make "mission" statements.

An example of an intent structure is shown in Figure 3.17 (used by permission of K. Ellis). Here, a group of people have generated and structured a number of intentions relating to the future course of a commercial company. The relationships are transitive so that achievement of any intention, which can be reached from some preceding intention, will be helped by the achievement of that preceding intention. Additionally, all intentions within one box represent a lumped cycle.

3.5. HARD SYSTEMS DIAGRAMS AND MESSY SITUATIONS

We intend to highlight some difficulties of using hard systems diagrams for messy situations, although we shall not totally exclude their use, by concentrating on the cybernetic unit diagram approach as an example.

This type of description is difficult to apply to soft systems where it may not be possible to form a consensus for many of the block labels. This is a similar finding to that of Checkland with regard to soft system diagrams, and it again points to the necessity of developing a set of relevant diagrams. Checkland does (as previously noted) reject conventions for soft system diagrams; however, convention based diagrams may have some use when identifying difficult aspects of soft problems (for example, when identifying relevant feedback and control mechanisms that monitor transformation processes).

We have chosen to illustrate the problems and possibilities of using cybernetic unit diagrams to describe, or summarize, aspects of soft systems with a discussion of the concepts from Figure 3.11. The general lessons of this illustration equally relate to other hard diagrams that attempt to represent aspects of soft situations.

Let us consider the ancient term *cybernetics* and its Platonic meaning, the art of steersmanship of a government. One control (survival) function of a sovereign government is to maintain order or prevent anarchy. If disorder increases, say during a period of high unemployment, then the government may choose to create more jobs to increase civilian satisfaction, or they may choose to increase the size and powers of the police force to quash the disorder, depending on how they perceive the situation. At least two possible activating units associated with these decisions have therefore been identified.

Another difficulty arises when attempting to detect disorder. How should this quality be measured? In other words, what are the sources of information, the instruments of measurement, and their strengths and weaknesses? Furthermore, the differences between the desired and the actual values are inevitably not subject to simple numerical calculation where the soft situation may be seen to deviate from a set point control parameter(s). More likely, in this instance, a number of qualitative societal attributes could be identified and monitored, and we would rather envisage a set range for those attributes, although an interpretation of this sort would be highly subjective. Furthermore, it is not always possible to form a consensus on what the controlled process is. This may be because the controller performs many functions, or because people's political ideas just do not overlap.

Associated with the last point is a common error that arises when applying the cybernetic unit diagram approach to soft situations. It is the use of the "should" approach, for example, "this is the way a government should maintain order." However, even when adopting the "is" approach, people will interpret soft situations quite differently. For example, any government that chooses to enforce order may be seen by some as desiring to create an undemocratic police state, and by others as desiring to suppress a dangerous minority, thus ensuring that democracy is maintained for the people. Clearly, a number of diagrams representing relevant views are required.

In summary, interpretation or use of diagrams has to be carefully undertaken when applied to soft situations. A diagram (if professionally drawn) will look clear, crisp, and concise (as opposed to the messiness of soft situations) but may be displaying only the author's ("pure") beliefs or theory (which if made explicit is quite useful). A systems analyst, however, has to be clear-minded enough to appreciate plurality and developed diagrammatic models of all relevant views, and clear minded enough to appreciate and document all inherent assumptions.

3.6. ELEMENT, RELATIONSHIP, AND BOUNDARY IDENTIFICATION

3.6.1. Introduction

A wide range of diagrammatic approaches have been presented in this chapter. They encompass useful ways of summarizing substantial amounts of information that may substantially help us to understand complex situations. What we have assumed so far is that (for the system diagrams) the elements, relationships, and boundaries have been identified *a priori*. We now need to consider the problems of system identification.

In some instances, the task of identifying a system may appear straightforward; for instance, an organism can easily be represented in terms of boundary, inputs, and outputs. Here, the elements and relationships that are represented will be directly related to the investigator's interests and/or purposes. In this instance, however, difficulties may arise in attaining a parsimonious description of the organism. In other words, when is an element or a relationship so significantly involved in the dynamics of interest that it warrants inclusion?

Other situations are "messier" than the example of the organism. "Human activity systems" display no clear-cut structure. Here the difficulty of system identification is considerable. Again, we can state that different people might identify different systems from the mess according to their interests and/or purposes. The crucial consideration (as we have previously noted) is that, even with the same interests and purposes, the set of systems identified by researchers would not necessarily overlap in totality. This all stems from the individual perceptions of what is going on in the situation, which is also intricately related to beliefs, values, and ideas. If people can differ on these fundamental issues (and they do), then attempts to define a specific technique for system identification is either pointless, dangerous, or both. These and other fundamental methodological issues are the theme of Chapter 6.

A meaningful contribution, however, in the context of system diagrams as such, can be made by offering a number of insights, guidelines, and rules of thumb.

3.6.2. Data Filtering for Information Production

Irrespective of their messiness, most situations can be viewed as a giant and dynamic source of data. To achieve any kind of understanding about a situation requires that access to the data is secured. The important process of data acquisition is the art of measurement, and Chapter 4 is dedicated to this. However, data are only data until transformed into a useful form, at which point data have been converted into information. This defines our current concern.

Data filtering (during modeling exercises) may be undertaken via expert consultation or process consultation, and the important task of achieving parsimony may be realized through technique or human interpretation (Flood, 1985; see Table 3.2).

Expert consultation is the process by which the modeler is the ultimate filter of all data available or gathered. The constituents (which make up the whole), the composition (the structuring of the constituents in the whole), and the interactions (the processes introducing the dimension of time) of the system representation are exclusively determined by the modeler(s). In process consultation, the modeler(s) also acts as a filter. However, process consultation

TABLE 3.2
Transforming Data to Information: Expert and Process Consultation,
and Human and Technique Interpretation[a]

Conceptualization		
Expert consultation (EC)	Process consultation (PC)	Selection of variables
EC/HI	PC/HI	Human interpretation (HI)
EC/TI	PC/TI	Technique interpretation (TI)

[a] Source: Flood (1985).

differs in that the constituents, composition, and interactions of the developing model are determined (to varying degrees) by people in the situation of interest.

A modeler(s) may also employ mathematical, statistical, computational, and/or heuristic tools during the data filtering process in further search of a parsimonious representation. These may be formally developed interpretive techniques such as pattern recognition (Attinger, 1985) or qualititative heuristic interpretations such as root-definitions and rich pictures (Checkland, 1981). Some filtering is done intuitively, often owing to a paucity of data, when the modeler(s) is forced to make personal judgments about constituents, composition, and/or interactions.

Whether expert or process consultation is adopted, and whether human or technique interpretation is used, depends on the modeling situation, that is, the nature of the situation, the resources available, the purposes of model development, and the modeler(s)'s viewpoint(s). These points are elaborated in Chapter 9.

3.6.3. System Identification

There are two distinct and fundamentally different approaches to system identification. This point has been expressed effectively (in the context of international relations) by Reynolds (1980). He suggested that

> a basic difference in the method of conceptualization appropriate to ... various questions arises from the choice of starting point. In endeavoring to conceive a system which will parsimoniously represent that part of reality which one is interested in studying, one may start by endeavoring to identify and define the significant units and then proceed to try and identify the significant interactions that take place among these units. Most analysts who have applied systems analysis to the study of international relations have gone about the matter in this way.

What is evident here is the dominant wisdom of the hard systems school (also see Chapter 6 on this matter). That is not to say that hard systems protagonists have pervaded international relations; rather, it suggests an underlying argument as to why hard structured reasoning has been excessively used. Structured situations are more obvious than messy ones and thus became the first "systems of interest." The approaches to investigating structured situations are well developed (they have a relatively long history) and are extremely useful (when applied to such situations). What has become apparent more recently is that there are many more situations if only we could find a way of coming to grips with them. Reynolds continued, saying that

> there is a totally different way of conceiving international systems. This involves starting from the interactions and not from the units. One might for instance observe that across state boundaries many interacting transactions take place which relate to, or arise from, the production and distribution of wealth. One might call such transactions economic. One could then say that one was interested in all international economic transactions. An international economic system could be conceived, the defining feature of which would be the economic nature of the interactions. The starting point for definition of the system would be a definition of a particular kind of interaction, not identification of particular units which interact in various ways.

The abstraction from reality that would be being made would be of a particular kind of behaviour, and it is obvious that in an international system so conceived many different kinds of unit would be members.

(This story continues, in the context of international relations, in Chapter 7.) Reynolds has actually distinguished a **structural** modeling approach from a **behavioral** one. The structural approach is where a set of elements is assumed in advance of any search for processes. The behavioral approach is fundamentally different in that structure is not assumed *a priori*. Rather, a particular type of interaction of interest is chosen, and this is then used to identify structure. The outcome of such an approach is a "purer" behavioral system. The former is applicable to the relatively small class of clearly structured situations; the latter is more applicable to the huge class of messy situations. In more general terms, the former is suitable for an objective expert consultation approach, while the latter demands an essentially subjective process consultation approach (although an expert component is not unusual). This seems to be totally consistent with the view of Checkland that hard situations are a subset, or special case, of soft situations.

The first step of system identification, then, is to choose between a structural or behavioral approach. The logical extension of the above argument, however, is that a behavioral approach will work for all situations (even if only producing a similar set of theories to a structured approach for a structured situation), whereas a structural approach will work only for a minority of situations (the structured ones). For systems that can be tackled with a structural approach, parsimony is relatively easy to achieve as the essential elements are either known *a priori*, or can be identified using an appropriate methodology. The selection of a structural approach should, however, be fully justified.

That established, let us now consider four rules of thumb, three in the form of questions for identifying systems, as given by Beishon (1980).

RULE 1.   Be suspicious of recognized boundaries or apparently obvious ones.

To a large extent this point has been made above; however, Beishon additionally notes that "existing" boundaries may be historical, accidental, or even irrelevant (from our point of view).

RULE 2.   Is the potential component connected in any way to other parts of the system? If so, how strong is the connection? Does or can the system affect the potential part? Can the potential part affect other parts of the system?

If the answer to the above questions concludes that there are strong connections between a proposed element and a number of other elements, then the "part" should be included with the appropriate connections made.

As we suggested in Chapter 1, a system and subsystems can tentatively and visually (qualitatively) be distinguished from their surroundings and other systems by looking for clusters of rich interactions in network representation. This second rule suggests we systematically search for relationships between a set of proposed elements (structural); or, having possibly identified an element with interactions of interest (behavioral), then we search for richness of similar interactions with other likely elements. If the diagram is drawn clearly then the clusters will manifest themselves.

RULE 3.   Does the potential component contribute to the system's ability to achieve the aim(s) we have set (or identified)?

For the structural approach this rule "relates back" the elements to the behavior of interest. If an element is a member of a set of elements that together exhibit the emergent properties or behavior of interest that meet our aims, then the proposed element should remain included. For the behavioral approach, this rule ensures that the inclusion of possible elements on behavioral grounds relates to a situation of interest and not some other (similar or even associated) behavioral situation.

RULE 4.   Can the system or the components exert any control over the functioning or activity of the potential component?

This rule is clearly a boundary searching rule. If any aspect of the system as it stands can control the potential element, then it is included. If not, and it contributes only inputs to the system (or receives outputs), then it is part of the environment. If anything other than these outcomes results, then the potential component can at best have only an indirect link from a wider environment.

   The difficulty here is interpreting the word "control". In the context of boundary setting we need to clarify whether influence is synonymous with control. If not, and an element exists that may only be influenced (assuming influence to be weaker than control), then it would sit in the environment. However, a consequence of this would be the existence of a feedback loop between the system and its environment (this point is important in the discussion below).

   In the context of social situations Checkland (1981) stated that a proposed element should be considered within the system if it can (in principle) be engineered by the decision maker, whereas it should be considered to be in the environment if it may only be influenced by the decision maker. However, this is not universally accepted. Jones (1982) wrote:

> Certainly I find the line between "engineerable (in principle)" and "may be influenced" a hazy one. If an aspect of the environment is seriously considered to be a target for influence, then why not include it, and the paths of influence, within the system? If not, leave it out.

Jones then proposed three guidelines for boundary setting in the domain of social situations:

GUIDELINE 1.   Certain behavior of certain elements and subsystems in the system description should be identified as constituting the "behavior of interest" for the purpose of the study. All such elements and subsystems should be considered to be within the system (not in its environment).

GUIDELINE 2.   All elements in the system description whose behavior is wholly or partly under direct influence of the client should be considered within the system.

GUIDELINE 3.   Any element that lies on any chain of influence from an I to a B, however long and involved, should be considered to be within the system.

In the above, I is the subset of elements that have a property or properties deemed to be under direct influence or control; and B is the subset of elements that display behavior deemed to be of interest for the purpose of the study.

These guidelines state that feedback loops should not exist between the system representation and its environment, and that all transactions across the boundary are of the form input or output. For many, this idea is (at least, initially) a difficult one to grasp. For instance, switching back to real-world thinking for a moment, if a firm is not able to influence its environment, for its own purposes say, then why is so much money spent on advertising? This is where the concept of wider system of interest comes in. Jones drew on Beer's idea of a system being embedded in a metasystem that can monitor the environment to help cope with unforeseeable change. This metasystem then attempts to bring some environmental factors under its influence, thus reducing uncertainty. Flood (1987a) developed this idea (see Figure 3.18). Here the "sombrero" shows a narrower system of interest (NSOI), which includes the portion of elements that are under control of the metasystem's (MS) components. The MS, however, may attempt to influence elements outside the NSOI. Where this is successful, these elements are termed the wider system of interest (WSOI). The (whole) SOI = WSOI + NSOI + MS. If the MS has no success in influencing the environment (WSOI = O), then SOI = NSOI + MS. With this approach the boundary of the wider system of interest may be drawn to include, for example, representations of the customers.

3.7. CONCLUSION

The first part of this chapter reviewed a variety of diagrams that are central to our ability to cope with complex situations. The second part of the chapter introduced the reader to the art of identifying (abstracting) systems from situations, although it should be pointed out that learning this art can be achieved only by practical experience. Differing opinions on boundary setting have been presented. The important process of data acquisition (an essential

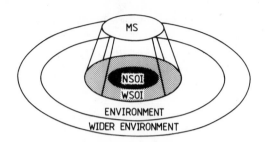

KEY	MS	metasystem
	NSOI	narrower system of interest
	WSOI	wider system of interest

FIGURE 3.18. Defining a system's boundary: The "sombrero" (Flood, 1987a).

step that either precedes, or forms an integral part of, system identification) was briefly mentioned and declared to be the art of measurement. This topic is the concern of the following chapter.

PROBLEMS

3.1. What is a model? How can we classify models?

3.2. Discuss the fundamental reasoning as to why we might benefit from the use of diagrammatic approaches.

3.3. What are the essential features of systems diagrams that distinguish them from all other diagrammatic frames of reference?

3.4. In what ways can diagrammatic approaches be misused and/or abused?

3.5. How can we avoid the pitfalls associated with Question 3.4 above?

3.6. Draw a signed digraph of a structured situation (for example a machine, an ecological situation, a biological situation, an economic situation).
1. Identify the loops in the diagram, and label them as either positive or negative.
2. Assess the overall stability of the model qualitatively (use the ideas of time scale and impact in your analysis).

3.7. Draw a set of soft system diagrams that represent the most relevant viewpoints you identify for a poorly structured system (for example, a managerial situation, a political situation, or any social situation).

3.8. Draw a cybernetic unit diagram of a structured situation (for example, a machine, an ecological situation, a biological situation, an economic situation).

3.9. Discuss the main problems that you would expect to confront when using "hard" systems diagrams for poorly structured situations.

3.10. What is meant by "system identification" in the context of diagrammatic modeling?

3.11. In what ways can data be transformed (by filtering) into information?

3.12. Compare and contrast the strengths and weaknesses, in "system identification," of a "structural" and a "behavioral" approach.

3.13. Use a "system identification" approach, as outlined in Section 3.6.3, to draw a systems diagram of, in this case for example, an economic situation, a managerial situation, a political situation (if you have any difficulty here, reflect on your answer to Question 3.9).

3.14. Use the "sombrero," Figure 3.18 to explain the control component of your systems diagram from Question 3.13.

SYSTEMS AND MEASUREMENT

4.1. INTRODUCTION

It was noted in Chapter 3 that structured and even messy situations can be viewed as giant and dynamic data sources, and that to grasp any kind of understanding about them requires that access to the data is achieved. This is the art of measurement. Subsequent transformation of the data into a useful form for decision making (that is, into information) is discussed in Chapters 3, 6, and 9.

Measurement is the process by which numerals, numbers, and other symbols are assigned to attributes of the real world in such a way as to describe them according to clearly defined rules. It is worth restating here (also see Chapter 1) that it is the changes in the attributes of interest that are of prime concern, so it is the attributes we wish to measure.

The aim of this chapter is to present the nature, scales, and associated difficulties of measurement. This is achieved by considering some concepts of measurement, the scientific method of measurement, and measurement via an experiential approach. The works of Finkelstein (1973, 1974) and Nachmias and Nachmias (1981) provide a concise account of much of the subject and were found generally useful when preparing this chapter.

4.2. THE NATURE OF MEASUREMENT

4.2.1. Numerals, Numbers, and Other Symbols

A numeral has no quantitative meaning unless explicitly specified. Numerals and symbols are often used to label things. For instance, some books have chapters with Roman numerals, I, II, V, X; and many mathematical equations label attributes of elements (variables) with Greek symbols, α, β, γ, δ. A number can also be used to label things. For example, a building site is segmented into n plots with each plot being labeled with a number from 1 to n, and a fishing lake has various fishing spots each labeled with a "peg number."

Numerals that are used in a quantitative context are then considered as numbers. Unlike numerals, numbers can effectively be manipulated using statistical and mathematical techniques. The appropriate techniques for a given purpose(s) (description, prediction, and/or explanation; see Chapter 9) must be considered with full understanding of the measurement scales (described below) and the nature of the situation. The use of quantitative techniques and qualitative manipulation is part of the interpretation process that transforms data into information.

4.2.2. Assignment

In measurement, the process of assigning a numeral, symbol, or number to real-world attributes is synonymous with the idea of mapping. Figure 4.1. shows diagrammatically the concept of mapping in the context of measurement. Here S maps onto 1, 0 maps onto 2, and * maps onto 3. The rules of this mapping process do not assign a number to the attribute P.

4.2.3. Rules

Rules define precisely how numerals, symbols, and numbers are to be assigned to attributes of the real world. Different rules produce different

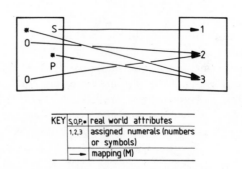

KEY	S,O,P,*	real world attributes
	1,2,3	assigned numerals (numbers or symbols)
	—▶	mapping (M)

FIGURE 4.1.   Expressing measurement as a mapping process.

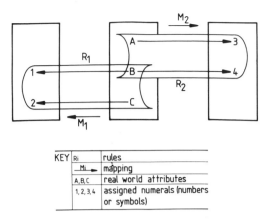

KEY	R_i	rules
	M_i	mapping
	A, B, C	real world attributes
	1, 2, 3, 4	assigned numerals (numbers or symbols)

FIGURE 4.2. Different rules (R_1 and R_2) produce different mappings (M_1 and M_2).

mappings (see Figure 4.2). If the rules are not clearly defined then the quality of the measurement is indeed suspect, that is, the empirical correspondence with reality is in doubt.

Homomorphism (a necessary requirement), in the context of measurement, suggests that there is an identical structure in the numerals, symbols, or number systems with the attributes being measured. This causes few problems when hard situations are being measured, where the relation between the attribute under observation and the numerals, symbols, or (more likely) numbers is direct. Measurement of soft situations, however, is less direct, consequently far more difficult, and unfortunately the measurements are far less manipulable. It is necessary, therefore, to identify levels of structuring. These levels are known as the scales of measurement.

4.3. SCALES OF MEASUREMENT

4.3.1. Introduction

As suggested earlier, the mathematical and statistical techniques that it is permissible to perform on a measured set of numerals, symbols, or numbers are directly related to the scale of measurement defined by the adopted rule. The scales can be ranked in order of "strength," that is, the stronger the scale the more techniques there are to manipulate the numerals, symbols, and numbers. Consequently, with the strongest scale more rigorous types of investigations can be made, greater and shared understanding can be achieved, and the more likely it is that laws (consensus) can be agreed upon from theory (theory being ideas shared by some and disputed by others). The four scales, from weakest to strongest, are nominal, ordinal, interval, and ratio. Each scale has its distinct set of logical properties as discussed later.

It is important to note that a statement about measurement is meaningful if its truth is unchanged by a permissible transformation of the scales of measurement. For instance, it is meaningful to consider the ratio of two masses, as their ratio is invariant when units are changed. However, it is not meaningful to consider the ratio of hardnesses on Moh's scale (ranking by material's ability to scratch other material), as that ratio could change under any transformation of the scale. Similar types of observation can be made between interval and ratio scales and so on. Application of numerical systems and statistics that are not isomorphic to the structure of empirical properties (where attainable) will not contribute to knowledge. Furthermore, the following rule of thumb exists: Attributes that can be measured on stronger scales can also be measured on weaker scales, but not vice versa.

These explanations have clear implications for hard and soft situations. If we consider the classification of experimental sciences (hard to soft), discussed in Chapter 2, in relation to the scales of measurement, the following observations can be made:

1. The nominal and possibly ordinal scales are permissible for soft situations, but the ability (and validity of trying) to achieve homomorphism must be very carefully assessed if intending to use a stronger scale, for instance in the social sciences, where theory is the norm.
2. The four scales of measurement are permissible for hard situations, for instance in the physical sciences, where laws are the norm.

In essence, the scales act as an arbiter. To meet the requirements of that arbiter we must consider the data we have (or may acquire) and attach them to one of the scales. Following this we must not perform unpermissible transformations on the data; nor must we make statements or observations on the data that are inappropriate; for example, we cannot make interval statements on ordinal data.

4.3.2. The Scales

Nominal Scale

With such a scale, numerals, symbols, or numbers are used to label an attribute in a classificatory or nominal manner. Attributes are compared with standard samples and those that match the standard are assigned the same numeral, symbol, or number as the standard. The logical properties are as follows:

1. Reflexivity either $A = A$ or $A < > A$
2. Symmetry of equivalence: if $A = B$, then $B = A$
3. Transitivity: if $A = B$ and $B = C$, then $A = C$

In essence, attributes of any nominal group share an identity. For example, competitors at the Olympic games may be classified as athletes. Alternatively, they may be classified as male and female athletes, or athletes from particular states.

There are few techniques available by which nominal groups may be investigated. Statistical techniques that leave the measurement unchanged may be appropriate, for example, commonness of occurrence.

Ordinal Scale

Where the relation "is greater than" ($>$) applies, an ordinal scale can be used to relate attributes of the real world. An ordered standard series of attributes can be selected and assigned numerals, symbols, or numbers in such a way that the order of the attributes and the order of the numerals, symbols, or numbers assigned are the same. When measuring, attributes are systematically compared with members of the standard series in a similar way as in nominal measurement, and if equal to a standard attribute they are assigned the numeral or symbol of the standard. If an attribute is not equal to any of the standards, it is then necessary to determine between which two standards the measured attribute lies. It is then assigned a numeral, symbol, or number lying in between the two standards. The logical properties are as follows:

1. Irreflexive: A is not $>A$
2. Symmetry of equivalence: if $A = B$, then $B = A$
3. Asymmetry of order: if $A > B$, then B is not $>A$
4. Transitivity: if $A > B$ and $B > C$, then $A > C$

Thus, the attributes of any ordinal grouping are ranked. The classical example is Moh's scale of hardness of minerals, where A is ranked harder than B if A can scratch B, but B cannot scratch A. Another example is the ranking of national teams at the Olympics using the criterion of the number of gold medals each team wins.

Permissible techniques for investigating rankings are those that do not alter the order of the ranking. This is acceptable because the spacings between the rankings are not considered as equal.

Interval Scale

Such a scale relates to the situation in which attributes of the real world are ranked and the interval between each ranking is known precisely according to a scale of intervals. The choice of zero on an interval scale is arbitrary.

The logical and arithmetic properties are as follows:

1. Symmetry of equivalence: if $A = B$, then $B = A$
2. Asymmetry of order: if $A > B$, then B is not $> A$
3. Commutation: if A and B are real numbers, then $A + B = B + A$ and $A \cdot B = B \cdot A$
4. Association: if A, B, and C are real numbers, then $(A + B) + C = A + (B + C)$, and $(A \cdot B)C = A(B \cdot C)$

5. Substitution: if $A = B$ and $A + C = D$, then $B + C = D$; and if $A \cdot C = D$, then $B \cdot C = D$
6. Uniqueness: if A and B are real numbers, then $A + B$ and $A \cdot B$ produce a single real number, respectively

The operations of arithmetic can therefore be applied to the differences between the numbers of a set of attributes assigned to an interval scale. Manipulation of an interval scale is permissible if the ranking and relative differences are preserved, for instance, by a linear transformation (multiply by a constant). All common statistics are appropriate.

A typical interval scale can be found on a thermometer where the zero is arbitrary and the equally spaced intervals do not have comparable magnitudes determined by the number of times one contains the other; for example, 50°C is not twice as hot as 25°C.

Ratio Scale

This scale applies where measures of a real-world attribute have both ranking and interval properties. Additionally, the scale has a natural zero so that any two intervals on the scale have comparable magnitudes determined by the number of times one contains the other, for example, 50 meters is twice the distance of 25 meters and half the distance of 100 meters.

The logical and arithmetic properties are essentially the same as for interval scales, with the additional property of ratio comparability. Therefore, measures on the ratio scale can be investigated with any mathematical or statistical technique. Attributes that can be measured on a ratio scale can also be measured on interval, ordinal, and nominal scales.

An example that relates all the scales of measurement is incorporated in the details of a league table. Nominal measurement is apparent from the labeling of each team, whereby a player is ascribed as a member of one team. Ordinal measurement is apparent when considering only the ranking, or position of the team in relation to all other teams in the same league. Interval measurement is apparent in the cumulative scores of each team whereby, say, 2 points may be awarded for one type of score and 3 points may be awarded for a different type of score. Here there are point intervals; however, 10 points is not necessarily seen as twice as good as 5 points if goodness is the criterion of measurement. A ratio measurement is extractable from the data because, for any one type of score, one team may achieve twice as many of them in comparison to the opposing team.

4.4. PROBLEMS ASSOCIATED WITH MEASUREMENT

4.4.1. Introduction

Assigning numerals, symbols, and numbers to attributes gives rise to a range of associated problems. Measuring instruments may not be totally reliable, and consequently the assignment process may introduce an error in the measurement process. The assigned numeral, symbol, or number may not represent reality as a consequence of some discrepancy.

69

Systems and Measurement

reliable, and consequently the assignment process may introduce an error in the measurement process. The assigned numeral, symbol, or number may not represent reality as a consequence of some discrepancy.

In the hard sciences, the measurement instrument may well be measuring the intended process; however, the instrument may also be picking up signals other than that of the process of interest, which it is not able to "filter" out. For example, when measuring low levels of radioactivity of a substance, the measuring instrument (Geiger counter) must be able to filter out the natural background radiation (if significant to the overall "signal"); otherwise the measured process would be distorted by this background noise. It is also essential to recalibrate measuring instruments at regular intervals to ensure that they are not introducing errors. This is commonplace for medical instruments that measure, for example, concentration and which are recalibrated with solutions manufactured at standard concentrations.

In the softer sciences these problems are more acute. Social scientists, for example, can never be absolutely sure that the property being measured is indeed that intended by the investigator. Social scientists who adopt scientific methods of measurement have this fundamental problem to deal with, in addition to the worry of reliability of their imprecise measuring instruments (questionnaires, for example). The following considerations of validity have therefore been developed (and may also offer some lessons for the harder sciences).

4.4.2. Content Validity

Content validity is usually encountered as face or sampling validity. **Face validity** relates to the situation in which a group of experts or referees assesses whether the measuring instrument relates to the attribute of interest. If there is a consensus among the judges (which is subjective and not necessarily repeatable), then the measuring instrument can be said to have face validity. **Sampling validity** relates to the statistical concept of sampling. A representative sample of the attribute being measured can be achieved only if a representative set of statements, questions, or indicators (from the assumed infinite set of these) is achieved *a priori.*

The construction of a questionnaire (as an example of a soft measurement instrument) is therefore an iterative process that is first judged by experts and then tried and tested on the attribute of interest. Following any changes in the questionnaire that are deemed necessary after assessing the sampling validity, it is instructive to reassess face validity.

4.4.3. Empirical Validity

It has already been noted that calibration of measuring instruments in the harder sciences is essential. This does assume that a standard exists and that after calibration the correlation between the instrument and the standard is effectively total.

In the social sciences, however, criteria have to be selected by which to evaluate a measuring instrument. In the United Kingdom, for example, A-level results are used as a measure of assessing a student's potential as an undergraduate university student. The actual results can be correlated (statistically) with academic achievement on graduation, and this validity coefficient can be used as a method of assessing the empirical validity of A-level results as a measure of academic potential. If the validity coefficient was found to be low, then some change in assessing potential would seem to be a necessary requirement.

4.4.4. Construct Validity

Construct validity examines the relationship between a measuring instrument and a theoretical framework. The closeness of the instrument to the framework is assessed. One approach is described in the following paragraph.

Initially, it is proposed that the instrument measures an attribute, *A* for example. The proposition is then included in the current theory associated with attribute *A*. The theory is then used to delineate between attributes that are, or are not, related to the instrument. Empirical data are then selected that either confirm or refute the predicted relations. If confirmation is achieved, construct validity of the instrument can be assumed.

4.4.5. The Experiential Approach

There are clearly a number of significant difficulties associated with adopting scientific methods of measurement in the social sciences. There is a body of researchers who in fact totally reject the adoption of such methods. The main criticism is that an objective approach assumes that there exist real and tangible social systems in an external real world. Plurality associated with human interaction suggests that it is wholly unacceptable to make such an assumption, as we know about the social world only via our experiences and the sharing of them. In such circumstances, we have said, we cannot make statements about the external world with any confidence.

Given this view, it would clearly be nonsense to go about measuring things that we cannot categorically say exist. An organization, for instance, is only a notional construct. This does not preclude investigation but does strongly suggest an alternative subjective approach. Such an approach necessarily requires that the investigator becomes a part of the activities of interest so that concepts and theories are developed by experiencing what is going on around the observer, and by sharing those experiences with other observers. This equally does not totally preclude the ideas of measurement since the concepts are nominal. Labels can be attached to shared experiences, either in agreement or disagreement. This is equivalent to the mapping of names to experiences. Such a view of the social world is called "nominalism," one possible philosophical position on "what is."

Measurement of notional systems is typically carried out alongside other activities. It becomes a part of an ongoing learning process where notions are recursively updated. There are no final unequivocal measurement "statements," as one would expect with the scientific method. Measurement thus acquires a strong methodological flavor and does not lead us to making "what is" statements or to expressing categorically our knowledge of the world.

Action research provides the basis for an appropriate methodological approach for those with the "experiential" view of social situations. In essence, action research proposes that a researcher is involved in an action process and a change process. This approach underpins soft systems methodology, which is presented and discussed in Chapter 6. The fundamental differences between those who employ scientific methods and those who adopt an experiential approach are expanded upon and elucidated in Chapters 5, 6, and 10.

4.5. CONCLUSION

Measurement is a necessary bridge between the real world and our ability to investigate its attributes. Traditionally numerals, symbols, or numbers are assigned to the attributes in accordance with set rules. Sets of measurements relate to levels of structuring known as scales of measurement. The stronger the scale, the more manipulable the measurements and the more likely it is that laws can be formulated from theory. There are a number of difficulties associated with measurement that relate directly to the reliability and validity of measuring instruments. These include the ability to filter noise, accuracy, and whether the instrument is measuring the attribute of interest. Tests of reliability and validity are available and may be systematically employed on measuring instruments; however, this does not overcome the fundamental problems of plurality in the social sciences. An experiential school of thought rejects such scientific measurement in the social sciences and proposes a nominal methodological approach. This argument can be followed as the text progresses.

PROBLEMS

4.1. In the context of the measurement process, briefly discuss:
1. Numerals, numbers, and other symbols
2. Assignment
3. Rules

4.2. Briefly describe the four scales of measurement and write out their associated logical properties. In what way are the four scales of measurement related to each other?

4.3. Discuss the main problems associated with measurement in the natural sciences.

4.4. How appropriate is a traditional scientific approach to the measurement of so-called social situations?

4.5. How appropriate is an experiential approach to the measurement of so-called social situations?

SYSTEMS VIEW OF MANAGEMENT AND THE ORGANIZATION

5.1. INTRODUCTION

In this chapter we aim to provide an insight into the process of management in the context of both people and organizational structure, concentrating on various systemic viewpoints that have emerged. Initially, the focus is upon the general contribution of systems thinking to the evolution of management theory. However, we rapidly turn to detailing the essentially cybernetic nature of management and organization theory.

5.2. EVOLUTION OF MANAGEMENT THEORY

5.2.1. Introduction

Let us first briefly consider how management theory has developed over the course of this century. The aim is to adopt a systems view of this process. In the following section we will consider a cybernetic interpretation of the management theory presented here.

5.2.2. Traditional Management Theory and Industrial Psychology

Traditional management theory is taken to include the "scientific" management of Taylor and his followers and the "administrative or classical theory" inspired by Fayol.

Taylor, generally regarded as the father of scientific management, set out to change the understanding of managers about the process of industrial shop floor management from an experiential base to that of a science "resting upon clearly defined laws, rules, and principles" (Taylor, 1947). Fayol (1949) produced a theory of administration and a set of management principles (which are still in use today) and which are relevant to managers at all levels in the organization. Fayol's major contribution was in delineating the elements of the management process: planning, organizing, commanding, coordinating, and controlling.

The industrial psychology school, on the other hand, was concerned more with the individual in an organizational setting, carrying out research into fatigue and health at work, and employee selection. The movement claimed to be humanitarian in nature. There are those, however, who considered industrial psychology as a surrogate "Taylorism" in that it accepts deskilling as a central part of industrial management.

5.2.3. The Birth of Human Relations Theory

The Hawthorne studies (Roethlisberger and Dickson, 1939) are regarded by many as the most significant piece of research ever conducted into organizational management. Burrell and Morgan (1979) assert that "The Hawthorne model emphasises that employee attitudes and work behaviour can ... be understood in terms of a complex network of interacting elements ... within and outside the work situation and ... within the individual." They go on to argue that the systems model developed by the Hawthorne researchers is "open" insofar as social conditions in the environment are said to influence the social and physical conditions of work and the personal history of the individual.

The studies have been criticized by many for the methodological approach used, for adopting a paternalistic view of workers, and for failing to consider the endemic nature of conflict in the organizational setting. However, this does not detract from the achievement of Roethlisberger and Dickson in applying, for the first time, a fully developed systems model to the work situation. The Hawthorne studies represent a landmark in management theory producing, among many other things, a scheme for interpreting complaints and reduced work effectiveness.

The importance, however, of this early "systems approach" appears not to have been fully recognized. The Hawthorne researchers' only immediate influence lay in their so-called discovery of social man, which gave an important impetus to the human relations movement. For example, the work of Maslow, Herzberg, and others, which following from Roethlisberger and Dickson came to constitute the core of human relations theory, did not use a systems model.

5.2.4. Sociotechnical Systems

The Hawthorne systems model was not really developed further until the work of Trist and Bamforth (1951; the Longwall coal mining studies), which attempted to view the relationship between social (work group) elements and production technology elements as interdependent. Within the sociotechnical systems tradition, such work led to recommendations for improvements in job design, which resulted in the emergence of the "Quality of Working Life" approach to management in the 1970s (Davis and Cherns, 1975).

5.2.5. Equilibrium Theories

Chester Barnard considered that a major responsibility of management was to maintain organizational equilibrium as a means of survival. This equilibrium was to be achieved by adjusting the environment, the organization, and individual behavior. Clearly we can see systems thinking within equilibrium theories in that Barnard appeared to regard organizations as homeostatic in nature. These early "cybernetic" theories of Barnard offer rewarding reading (see Barnard, 1938, "Functions of the Executive").

Herbert Simon (1957) developed an approach that "integrates the motivational and structural approaches to organisation within the context of a theory of equilibrium" (Burrell and Morgan, 1979). Simon proposed a theory of administrative behavior centered on the choice, or decision making, of human elements within a host organization. The model has been developed by Cyert and March (1963) to the point where "it sees the firm as an information processing and decision making system ... [coping] ... with various conflicts both from within and outside its boundaries" (Burrell and Morgan, 1979).

5.2.6. Structural Functionalism

The notion of a "rational organization" put forward by the traditional theorists has been criticized by Selznick (1948), who has argued that the formal rationality of organizations is subjected both to internal informal and environmental pressures. Selznick goes on to argue that an organization must be considered as a functional system of relationships between resource availability and allocation, and as an adaptive social structure, and suggests a structural functionalist model analogous to a biosystem.

5.2.7. Open Systems

Developing from the structural functionalist and equilibrium models came open systems models of organizations, reinforcing many systems concepts such as that of emergence.

In this vein of reasoning Rice (1958), from the Tavistock Institute and a leading light in the sociotechnical systems movement, considered a company to be "a living organism which is 'open' to its environment." The company takes in information, money, and materials from the environment and transforms them into products or services, which are returned to the environment. Katz and Kahn (1966) identified five subsystems that are contained within an open organizational system (drawing upon their terminology). These are as follows:

1. Production or technical
2. Supportive
3. Maintenance
4. Adaptive
5. Managerial

This work further emphasizes the importance attached by open systems theorists to the environment and to the use of organismic analogies.

5.2.8. Empirical Studies

The empirical studies of Woodward (1965), and the Aston school of organizational theorists (Pugh and Payne, 1977) into the relationships between organizational structure, size, and use of technology were a return to the objectivist thinking of Taylor. The systems notions contained in the Hawthorne studies tended to be neglected, while the empiricists concentrated on measuring, in a scientific manner, organizational phenomena and characteristics in "true objective" style.

The empirical studies contributed greatly to the birth of the contingency model of the organization.

5.2.9. Contingency Theory

The contingency model usually represents the organization as containing four "subsystems":

1. Strategic control
2. Operational
3. Human
4. Managerial

Contingency theorists contend that "the effective operation of an enterprise is dependent upon there being an appropriate match between its internal organisation and the nature of the demands placed upon it by its tasks, its environment and the needs of its members" (Burrell and Morgan, 1979).

As well as empiricism, contributions to the contingency model include structural functionalism and open systems theory. The coming together of these disparate ideas has had a major impact on the systems view of management (see, for example, Lawrence and Lorsch, 1967).

5.2.10. Summary

The main schools of thought in management and organization theory have been presented. The aim has been to draw out the systems component of each theory. Building on this presentation it will be argued that a cybernetic basis can be established for many of the schools of management and organization theory. The following section develops this theme.

5.3. A CYBERNETIC VIEW OF MANAGEMENT AND ORGANIZATION THEORY

5.3.1. Introduction

It is possible to argue, on the basis of the previous section, that much of management and organization thinking has an inherent cybernetic quality. Robb (1985) went further when he noted that cybernetic concepts provide a bridge between the theories that have evolved so far. In his paper, he reviewed management theory under three schools of thought: classical management theory, scientific management theory, and organizational theory. Following this, a review of how cybernetics relates to these theories was given. In this section we intend to review a part of that work, as it offers an explicit account of how cybernetics (a subset of systems science) has pervaded much of man's thinking about his own activities, here, specifically in the context of man and resource management.

5.3.2. Three Schools of Thought

The study assumed that there were (roughly) three schools of management thinking. This is a further (somewhat unorthodox) classification of the theory presented in the previous section. The three schools are briefly described below.

Classical Management Theory. The main concerns of this school are the ways in which an organization may be structured and communication networks realized. The theorists promoted deskilling and believed that improved performance would follow from extending the principles of division of labor. Similar investigations undertaken by Weber (1947) concentrated on the sociological study of bureaucracy, which is considered to have the following features: a set of legal rules, a salaried administrative staff with specialized functions, an archive of written records, and authority vested in the position held. Classical theorists paid particular attention to sources and delegation of authority. Individual initiative was not trusted. To counteract such initiative it was deemed necessary to provide clearly defined instructions and report on the results of the execution. For a manager, performance is measured in accounting terms. Management by objectives (and the many ideas on this theme) emerged out of this thinking. The traditional professionals in management, such as accountants and engineers, were educated in this school of thought. Finally, the shift from owner and shareholder to the professional manager, as advocated by the classical theorists, reflects the desired move toward the separation of ownership and control.

Scientific Management Theory. Division of labor and internal feedback marks the early scientific management theory. Taylor (1911) advocated that there should be a specialized workforce deskilled as far as possible to enable workers' tasks to be easily measured so that performance can readily be assessed. He proposed time and motion study. This enabled alternative methods of work to be evaluated so that the optimum way could be chosen. This defined the manager's role as one of minimizing cost and maximizing efficiency, and led naturally to the production line that Ford made famous in the early days of car manufacturing. The approach, however, neglected the difficulty of motivating the manager and the managed, and the relationships between the firm and its surroundings.

Organization Theory. An emphasis on the human factor is apparent in the work of theorists under this heading. The idea that to provide improved work conditions was not only humanitarian, but also good business, was proposed by Rowntree (1921) following the earlier ideas of Mill (1859). Amenities were perceived as desirable. Pension schemes and similar benefits improved productivity since concern over job security was reduced. Around the 1950s industrial psychologists and welfare and medical officers were to be found in management. In essence, the social and physical environments were each perceived as part determinants of behavior. Company identity and culture became prominent. This thinking has also extended beyond the firm to the market place, where results of motivation and attitude research (Dichter, 1960) and demographic characteristics of consumers were used to generate attitude change in the market.

The three preceding paragraphs offer only the barest of pictures of the three schools of thought as identified by Robb. We shall now consider some major commonalities between cybernetics and these schools.

5.3.3. Cybernetics in the Three Schools of Thought

The ideas are offered below under the same three headings.

Classical Management Theory. Both classical and cybernetic theorists consider the idea of communication networks. The classical theorists have done this by identifying formal channels of responsibility (and authority). Cybernetics, although not ignoring formal networks, suggests that an informal communications structure will also be present such that complex conversations at a number of levels between two or more individuals exist. Cybernetics therefore builds on the classical concern to provide an appropriate organizational setting in order that adequate communication channels can be realized.

Scientific Management Theory. Feedback is the most obvious commonality between scientific management and cybernetic theorists. The nature and function of the feedback loops is the major concern of cyberneticians. Quantitative feedback cannot necessarily be assumed. Qualitative feedback only may be achievable; nevertheless, such feedback relating to management decision making is considered vital. In cybernetic terms, a closed feedback loop enables a metasystem (with its metalanguage) to learn about, and understand, behavior of an object system (in its object language) such that a higher level of control can be exerted where necessary. Robb did note, however, that in large organizations effective closed feedback may be difficult to attain since there are various convergent factors at work. These reduce the variety of the information that is fed back, for instance the tendency to feed back supportive information and to effect a reduction in dissonance (Festinger, 1962). Thus incremental management may be impossible so that large changes must eventually be effected. This is generally undesirable because oscillatory behavior often results.

Organizational Management Theory. Organizations are represented as open, interactive systems involving human beings and with a variety of interlocking systems at a number of levels. This stresses the need to consider the human factor in any management scheme and thus identifies the major commonality between the two theories at hand. Any person's loyalty will be torn between the different situations in which a role is held or strong influence is felt. For this reason, the social–psychological research of the organizational theorists is highly relevant, in that, if a manager is to influence the managed to get work done, he must raise the organization's profile (culture and purposes) in an employee's scheme of thinking, thus achieving a high level of dedication. The systemic aspect of the individual's predicament is therefore a concern of both cybernetic and organizational theorists.

5.3.4. Summary

The preceding three paragraphs offer only a brief insight into the holistic view that cybernetic bridges exist between the three schools of thought. The study does, however, identify the following:

1. The authoritarian nature of control
2. The humanity of the people in the organization being managed
3. The validity of measurement (in certain circumstances)

For a further and supporting account of the links between management theory and cybernetics, the interested reader might consult Strank (1982). We now intend to take forward this set of ideas and integrate them into what has been termed "administrative" management. Administrative theory is built around the "elements" of the management process first identified by Fayol.

5.4. ADMINISTRATIVE MANAGEMENT

5.4.1. Introduction

In this section we will consider the activities of planning, organizing, directing, and controlling. It is only meaningful to consider the activities separately in order to draw out the essential factors that, when integrated together, form the administrative theorists' view of management—the dominant approach in Western culture. As with other review components of this book, the terminology associated with the theories in question have been used. These activities are discussed below.

5.4.2. Planning

Planning is fundamental to administrative management. If the effort expended by an organizational group is to be effective, then the group members must know what they are required to achieve. That is, managers need to conceive a procedure by which they determine how things are to be done in advance of them happening.

Organizations exist in a dynamic and complex environment in which change is endemic. Such change, alongside other factors like economic growth, presents opportunities for perceptive managers, although change also holds many risks. This latter point is particularly the case in contemporary life where much of man's activities center around management of scarce resources and competition for finite markets. An effective manager will plan in order to minimize risk, for example, in accessing scarce resources, while maximizing opportunities, for example, by diversifying the manufacturing output.

Planning thus implies the need to organize, direct, and control. Hence, planning is the primary managerial function that "precedes" all others. The systemic relationship between planning and the other functions of management is shown in Figure 5.1.

Effective planning, this theory proposes, arises most commonly from a rational systematic approach, and a self-explanatory planning sequence of this type is shown in Figure 5.2. This figure suggests that planning is a continual process with features such as feedback within the process and inputs from the environment (external risks and opportunities). Thus planning will necessarily involve the establishing of organizational objectives (which helps to explain the good reception given by managers to Warfield's, 1976, ISM). Planning also defines a need to prepare and design an organizational structure capable of achieving those objectives.

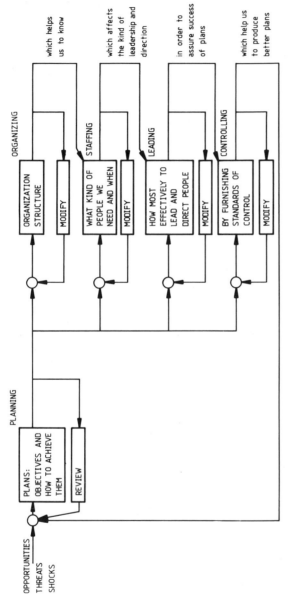

FIGURE 5.1. Systemic relationships between planning, organizing, staffing, leading, and controlling. (Upublished research, K. Ellis, 1987.)

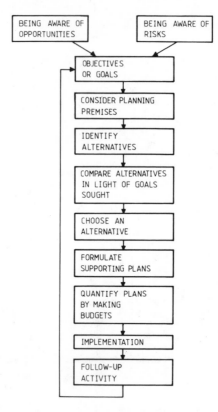

FIGURE 5.2. Planning sequence (adapted from Koontz *et al.*, 1984).

5.4.3. Organizing

Organizing, as stated above, naturally follows from planning activities. We have also noted that organizations exist in a complex and changing environment. This, therefore, implies that the structure of an organization is not static. Organizing can be considered as a continuous process. Effective organizing is responsive to risks, opportunities, and shocks from the environment, the last of which may drastically alter an organization's trajectory.

Let us consider the process of organizing by referring to Figure 5.3. The inputs to the process include the objectives derived from the planning process and the external inputs of threats, opportunities, and shocks. The structure reflects the organizational objectives and plans (plus the external inputs) as energetic and resourceful (enterprise) activities are derived from these. The grouping of the required activities (for example, production, finance, sales, and so on) will of course be subject to available resources. An "administrative" approach would suggest that the resulting organizational structure should ideally incorporate the necessary authority via vertical and horizontal coordination to allow enterprise managers to function effectively. The structure would

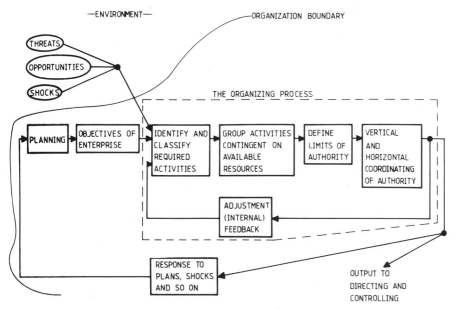

FIGURE 5.3. Process of organizing (adapted from Koontz *et al.*, 1984).

be capable of adapting to changes associated with (internal) process requirements as well as those originating from the environment. The structure would,
therefore, be systemic and dynamic rather than mechanistic and static.

The output of the organizing process leads to the directing activity, and within
this process are considered the kinds and numbers of people required to staff
the structure.

5.4.4. Directing

The special features of this element of management are staffing and
leading.

Staffing

An organization's structure determines the numbers and kinds of managers
and staff required. As an initial step in the process, requirements are compared
with the currently available resources in an analysis of the present and future
needs. Sources, either internal or external, are identified such that the discrepancy between current resources and needs can be eliminated by recruit-
ment, selection, and production. Managers and staff are subject to appraisal,
development, and training on a regular basis such that personal and organizational goals are achieved in a congruent fashion. All the elements of the
staffing subsystem are influenced by personnel policies and the "reward system," as is the organization's structure, which may vary from organization to
organization.

The process of staffing is adaptive in that it responds to internal requirements and changes in structure, and external changes in the environment.

Leading

The objectives of the organization will only be realized, the administrative
viewpoint suggests, by people committed to, or influenced to work toward,
achieving them. The individuals that make up the organization, however, have
their own needs and objectives, which may not be congruent with those of the
organization. This dichotomy can cause particularly difficult problems for
organizational managers. People, and the individualism they display, pose the
most complex problems in organizations. (This observation on plurality by
administrative thinkers is indeed interesting.)

Management theorists over the years have derived models designed to
assist practicing managers in dealing with such complex problems. Schein's
(1980) work, concerning people in organizations, was based on four sets of
assumptions:

1. Rational-economic: man's behavior is controlled by economic factors.
2. Social: social forces within the work group control behavior.
3. Self-actualizing: behavior is controlled by self-motivation.
4. Complexity: a complex motivational pattern controls behavior.

Alternatively, McGregor's Theory X and Theory Y models, set out in *The
Human Side of Enterprise* (1960), address the question of how managers view
those who work for them. The results of this study suggest that managers
cannot create and maintain an appropriate working environment, which promotes cohesion and the willingness to work toward common objectives, without
holding an awareness of what motivates people. Motivation of subordinates
can, however, be problematic. With this approach, managers should recognize
that people are motivated by a desire to satisfy a need. The resulting activity
is goal directed, and it would be argued by administrative theorists that even
organizations, with all their complex fuzziness, are purposive and goal seeking.
Many theorists, Maslow, Herzberg, Porter and Lawler, and Fiedler included
among them, have considered motivation and leadership. Their work,
documented extensively elsewhere, is beyond the scope of this chapter (see
Koontz *et al.*, 1984).

It is our belief, however, that to date no true administrative model of the
leading aspect of directing has emerged, although work by the contingency
theorists offers some promising models (see, for example, Fiedler, 1967).

5.4.5. Controlling

Once the activities of planning, organizing, and directing are at least
satisfactorily achieved, then the process of controlling may effectively be

exerted. Without such a base of healthy conditions, even the best-conceived controller may fall foul to managerial failures.

The essential elements of administrative control are to (1) establish standards, (2) measure performance against standards, and (3) take corrective action on discrepancies.

Standards specify performance criteria. These are usually applied as benchmark points in an *a priori* planned program of activity. They are measures of performance. This allows corrective action to be applied within the program should deviations be detected.

Setting performance standards implies the need to measure in such a way that deviations from a plan can be located and counteracted in sufficient time. This is not always possible to achieve as time lags in information processing are inherent in managerial control, for example, accounting methods such as profit and loss. The work of Beer (1981), discussed later, considers these aspects and introduces a novel approach. Where (and when) a deviation(s) from a plan is detected it is the task of managers to take appropriate action to eliminate the deviation in order to return to the planned activity program. The cybernetic diagram shown in Figure 3.11 is a general example of this approach.

The management activity of control is then, by definition, cybernetic in nature. Managerial control classically involves feedback mechanisms designed to correct errors. Figure 5.4 further illustrates this process. The feedback process is inertia-based in that time lags often prevent corrective action within an appropriate time scale. This can lead to reactive management and/or oscillations in performance. Proactive management control should be preferred, the theory tells us, if at all possible.

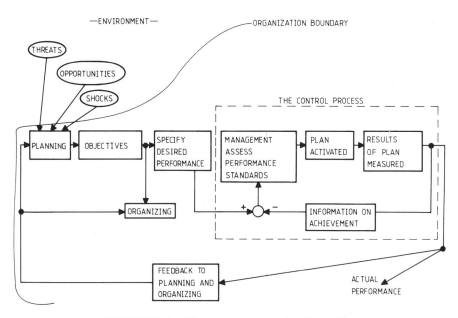

FIGURE 5.4. Management control cybernetics.

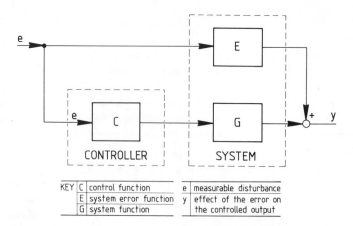

KEY

C	control function	e	measurable disturbance
E	system error function	y	effect of the error on
G	system function		the controlled output

FIGURE 5.5.   Feedforward control (adapted from Flood, 1985).

Feedforward control mechanisms therefore offer many advantages. Feedforward control is used to initiate action to prevent an undesired state from occurring, or to bring about a desired future state. This is illustrated in systems terms in Figure 5.5 (the general model coming from Flood, 1985). Here we can see that in response to a predicted, or "measured future," disturbance e, a controller C responds to eliminate the effect of the disturbance E on system G. The effect of the error on the controlled output is y, which equals $(E + G \cdot C)e$. The effect of the error can, therefore, be removed if $C = -E/G$. This clearly requires some means of qualitative or quantitative prediction. Beer's approach (to be discussed later) provides a good example of how prediction and feedforward control could be incorporated into management thinking.

5.4.6.   Summary

The four elements of management—planning, organizing, directing, and controlling—form an integrated, interlinking management complex that is universal in nature. The ideas are systemic, as they are manifestly cybernetic in nature, demonstrating dynamic control. This approach provides the basis of an administrative framework within which, many have suggested, the complexity of managing people and scarce resources within organizations may be effectively tackled.

5.5.   THE VIABLE SYSTEM MODEL: A STRUCTURALIST ALTERNATIVE

5.5.1.   Introduction

In the previous section reference has been made to Stafford Beer's ideas on control in organizations. These constitute only one part of a major piece of work in which Beer developed a complete cybernetic model of the organization (Beer, 1979, 1981, 1985). The model was developed from analogy with the human brain and neural control, following cybernetic first principles. It provides a radically different view from that found within traditional Western (orthodox) theory. In particular, Beer demonstrates a more "structuralist" orientation, being concerned to uncover the "mechanisms" that promote the retention of viable organizational structure, processes, and functioning. The Viable System Model (VSM), which constitutes the cornerstone of these ideas, and some of the reasoning behind its development, provide the content of this section.

5.5.2. The Need for Change

Central to the orthodox approach is the organizational chart. This indicates how parts are interrelated and determines where responsibilities lie. The chart is supported by job descriptions. In essence, Beer suggests, the chart specifies anatomy while the job descriptions specify physiology.

The orthodox manager is presented as someone who sees or **describes** in the conventional sense

1. Structure of basic divisions of production, sales, and so on
2. Functions of basic divisions of line and staff relationships

The orthodox manager is seen as one who **prescribes** with limited concepts (taken from an insufficiently rich framework of thought) and physical equipment (for example pencil and paper producing two-dimensional sketches), and some management theory principles. The conventional job description is also criticized. Beer is concerned that the boss defines in his own mind what he thinks an employee ought to be doing and then translates this onto paper, considering only the person who will perform to the specifications. Thus, the conventional structure does not allow for an impersonal job description since history has "now determined" that no employee can be found to fit it. It is suggested that as a consequence of this defect in orthodox management, jobs have evolved only with the employee in mind and not the job they are to perform.

This description, according to Beer, has been set by management culture and does not best deal with the difficulties arising in transforming input to output. It does not answer the question "how shall input be optimally converted to output?"—the dimension of control itself. Three main reasons were given for rejecting the orthodox approach:

1. The brains of the managers were once the only medium for information handling, and in an era of low information output this was successful. Today, however, the requirements are high and managers do not have the required capacity.

2. The language of management is too simple to deal with the complexities that exist today. This is not a direct attack on the vocabulary; rather, it refers to an insufficiently rich conceptual framework.

3. Today's pressures have forced certain roles to be performed, which, given the orthodox model, have led to friction. For example, cost accountants have a problem of line-staff confusion. They try to interrelate the parts of the whole for control purposes.

Rather than merely criticizing the current state of affairs (so typical of many critics) Beer proposed a radically new approach. He suggested that we should use a control model as the basis of our activities. The idea he put forward was to learn from the structure of control in complex situations, particularly where control is recognized as being highly successful. Beer proposed that we learn from the body (the firm) and the brain (its controller). The neurocybernetic model was used as an example that we could usefully consider.

5.5.3. The Model

Model development included both horizontal and vertical command axes. Five hierarchically arranged systems were drawn up, as shown in Figure 5.6. A brief description of each system is given as follows, with some reference to that which is being represented:

System One

1.   This lies on the lateral command axis.

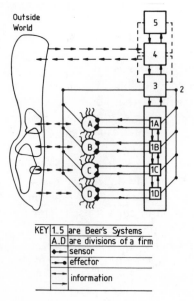

FIGURE 5.6.   A viable system model (Beer, 1981; reproduced by permission of John Wiley & Sons).

2. There is transduction of information from the lateral command axis to the vertical command axis.
3. Where computers are involved, transduction is performed by terminal entry, which may have some delay. If appropriate, sensors on machinery would remove the delay.
4. This system is typical of a subsidiary of a firm, whether it is a whole company or a department.

System Two

1. This lies on the vertical and lateral command axes.
2. As the controller of System One it receives instructions down the vertical control axis and compares these to the transduced information from System One.
3. It has an initial plan for the assemblage of subsidiaries, and each segment of System Two has an initial plan for its related subsidiary.
4. Reflex control action is governed by a set of transfer functions and is concerned with negative feedback.
5. There is also a role for feedforward control.

System Three

1. This is wholly alert downward (reflexes) and necessarily sleepy upward, preventing policymakers from receiving an inundation of information.
2. It controls the internal stability of the internal environment of the firm by providing necessary feedback.
3. It prevents isolation of each subsidiary on the lateral axis by forming a cohesive set of controllers.
4. It monitors System Two by giving an overall direction.
5. It uses a higher language than System Two as it has to "discuss" the latter's behavior.
6. It receives information from the subsidiaries and from System Two control centers. The former (parasympathetic) information is watched for excess "strain" and "slows down" activities where necessary, whereas, the latter (sympathetic) information is watched for signs of "lethargy" whereupon activities are "revved up."

System Four

1. Receives initial information for management by exception and arouses System Five when significant deviations occur.
2. Monitors and switches the general output of the vertical axis.
3. Re-sorts System Five's decisions and relays command downward.

System Five

1. Formulates policy, assessing ongoing implementation of plan and modifying where necessary.
2. Receives arousal information from System Four via many routes from many origins.

A summary of the requirements common to all five systems is given below:

1. An initial plan
2. Constant updating of plan on central command axis
3. Immediate recognition of the state of affairs to plan the needs of the organization as a whole (and prevent oscillation)
4. Means of commanding subsidiaries to update plans

The major task of the firm, Beer states, is to bring into accord (1) stability of the internal environment and (2) stability of the interaction with the external environment.

5.5.4. Operationalizing the Model

System One

The aim is to find some means of measuring performance in order that information may be transferred to the vertical command axis. Traditionally, Beer argues, short-term measures are used. For instance, cost accounting in the form of cost and sales prices and the direction and route of cash flows. This leads to minimization of cost and maximization of profit, which, he argues, ignores long-term control instruments like latent capabilities. Ratio measures are favored. The general relationship advocated is (actual)/(possible) = (productivity). This is further developed in Figure 5.7. Potentiality is what could be achieved by developing resources and removing constraints; capability is the possible achievement using existing resources within existing

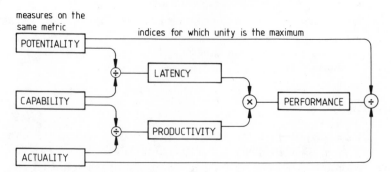

FIGURE 5.7. Measuring system performance using normalized ratio measures (Beer, 1981; reproduced by permission of John Wiley & Sons).

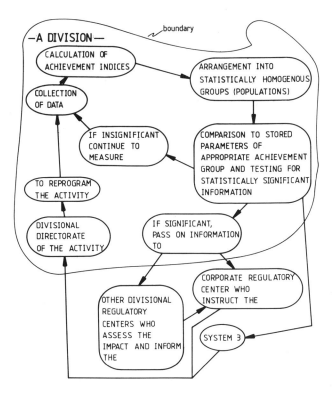

FIGURE 5.8. Beer's System One: The control cycle.

constraints; and actuality is the current achievement with existing resources and constraints. Two ratios can be derived from these: (latency) = (capability)/(potentiality); and (productivity) = (actuality)/(capability). Performance is then the product of latency and productivity. Operations research is seen as essential in developing the complex models of capability and the simpler models of potentiality. The key factor with this approach is to look for patterns. This can be achieved by use of a control cycle such as that we have presented in Figure 5.8.

System Two

This is an elaborate interface between Systems One and Three. It is seen as the only means by which uncontrolled oscillation between the division can be prevented. If the outcome of Figure 5.8 is that "significant deviations from stored parameters have been identified," then the following activities come into action:

1. The divisional directorate has to find out what went wrong and devise measures to put it right.
2. Other divisions have to assess the impact and report to the corporate regulatory center.

3. The corporate regulatory center takes corrective action through (a) the regulatory machinery and (b) System Three when management perogatives are involved.

Beer argues that, in orthodox organizations, the corporate level is not informed until oscillations have set in, whereupon human attitudes degenerate into suspicion and defensiveness, and divisions do not operate within the intention of the whole organization.

System Two provides local homeostasis and takes no account of the environment. It is a divisional controller and interdivisional interaction controller. It has no knowledge about the adaptation and growth of the total organization.

System Three

This is the receiver of three types of information as described below:

1. Information about the internal environment is handled in three ways:
   a. As a metasystemic controller acting downward
   b. As a senior filter of somatic news upward
   c. As an algedonode (raising the alarm according to regulation of a nonanalytic mode)
2. Information upward from System Two of which System Three is the only receiver
3. Information from the subsidiaries

System Three controls the organic homeostasis, taking into account environmental factors. This implies a novel, heuristic, and evolutionary approach.

System Four

This deals with information switching and handling information ascending the central axis and from the outside world. It should monitor managerial action which is considered to be the generator of oscillations. Figure 5.9 provides a concise representation of Beer's view. Here we can see the idea of feedback control, with a feedforward component included. The control settings are defined as follows: A, product improvement acting on existing products; B, product innovation acting on new products; C, potential operating efficiency acting upon performance; X, responsiveness of market acting on technological change (x_1) and economic change (x_2); Y, power to borrow money acting on investment capital. The company activity is defined by the function $f(s)$, and a model of this, $f'(s)$, is used to predict the future state by simulation methods. Corporate planning is defined by $F(s)$, which feeds back control information to the parameters. Input i, error e, and output o are also main concerns of this approach.

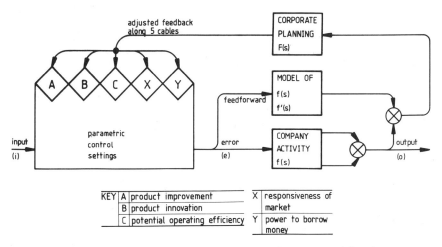

FIGURE 5.9. Beer's System Four: Monitoring managerial action.

The following phenomena, it is suggested, should be studied with models (this may be achieved by using the system dynamics approach, for example):

1. The differences that are bound to exist between the time constants of the three investment channels *A*, *B*, and *C* (see Figure 5.9)
2. Sluggish (long time constant) output response to certain kinds of rapidly varying input
3. Amplifiers that increase the amplitude of dangerous oscillations

It was noted that all the units that made up System Four exist in firms (to varying degrees) but lack a means of communication with either the board or the operations directorate. Failings of a typical extant System Four are as follows:

1. They are seen as an enemy, interfering with what management is trying to do.
2. Their reports are not read.
3. The informal route of interaction is most successful but is open to accusations of a political nature.

System Five

This is alternatively termed the multinode, an elaborately interactive assembly of elements (or managers). Owing to a high degree of "redundancy," the probability of arriving at the wrong answer is almost nil, unlike the low probability that good decisions can be achieved from organizational chart structures, a conclusion that Beer highlighted using concepts of reliability theory. To help achieve the proposed "mass interaction," we are asked to accept

1. That any boss is a colleague of a group that includes his subordinates

2. That the "one-man, one-boss" principle may work in some contexts but that protocol must not preclude rich interactions throughout a group

3. That there is necessarily more communication between people at the same level in the enterprise than there is between seniors and juniors

Normally, Beer says, such an operation is called politics, and success goes to the politically skilled because of the immense complexity of the communication paths. The solution can be found, we are told, with the new cybernetic model and the concepts of redundancy and flexibility—the robustness of real multinodes. Multinode activity begins with a plethora of possibilities and operates to reduce the variety to one. This requires (1) a paradigm of logical search and (2) an actual metric (a rule and a scale) for measuring uncertainty.

The idea is to clump and nest. Logical variables are clumped together within dimensions, giving a relatively small unidimensional reduction. Variables in different dimensions are then nested together giving a large reduction in dimensions. The use of logarithms to base 2, where $\log_2 2^n = n$, is promoted as a logical binary base ideal for maximizing and attaining yes/no decisions.

A key feature of the VSM is multiple recursion so that Figure 5.6, as well as representing a particular "division" of concern, can be used to represent a wider situation of which that division is a part, and each "subdivision" (in this case; *A*, *B*, *C* and *D*) making up the division of concern.

We shall now consider one attempt to implement the VSM described above.

5.5.5. The Chilean Experience

Beer became involved with the government of Chile in July 1971 following the rise to power of Dr. Salvador Allende, whose administration represented the first democratically elected Marxist government in Latin America. Allende became president of Chile and head of the Unidad Popular Coalition. Beer received a letter from Fernando Flores of the Unidad Popular Coalition which informed him of mass nationalization of banks and companies. The nationalization involved the means of production, distribution, and exchange. Beer was asked whether, with his cybernetic ideas, he was interested in some involvement in the complete reorganization. On November 4, 1971 Beer arrived in Santiago and on the 13th of that month he returned to London with the initial plans drawn up. A brief summary of the main projects outlined or undertaken follows:

CYBERNET.   The development of a national network of industrial communications to a center in Santiago, providing consultation and access from all to all. This network was based upon multiple recursions of the economy modeled according to the VSM.

CYBERSTRIDE. The development of a suite of computer programs providing statistical filters for all homeostatic loops. Work on this was given to Arthur Anderson and Company in London.

CHECO. The development of a model of the Chilean economy with a simulation capability.

OPSROOM. The design of an operations room that provided an environment for decisions, and was dependent on the previous three "Cs."

CYBERSYN. A program for the dissemination of information and presentation of data to the system.

PEOPLE PROJECT. Essentially the government–people arrangements, that is, that part of the organization of the state that is not economic but societal.

The following dates are significant. In May 1972 Beer was appointed scientific director. In June 1972 the first printouts/runs were realized from the CHECO project. On January 10, 1973 the operations room was running. On September 11, 1973 President Allende was assasinated and the whole project was terminated.

Three significant factors should be noted alongside the above thumbnail sketch.

1. The sophisticated program was to be achieved over a very short time period.
2. There was an almost total lack of technology.
3. The success of the project was always in question because, given the political nature of the coalition, external forces were at work.

For a full documentation of the Chilean experience, the reader is referred to Beer (1981).

5.5.6. Summary

This section documents one major piece of cybernetic thinking. A cybernetic model of the organization has been presented that offers an alternative to the orthodox approach that is typically based on the organizational chart. The model is a "hierarchically" structured control system model with five levels and multiple recursions. The main features resemble the neuro-cybernetic structure and process found in man. The process of putting the model into operation was discussed and one large-scale application sketched out.

5.6. MANAGEMENT AND ORGANIZATIONAL CYBERNETICS

5.6.1. Introduction

The idea that the cybernetic model can be usefully viewed in the separate contexts of management and organizations was introduced by Jackson (1986). Jackson's idea distills and expands upon the cybernetic component of management and organization theory presented up to this point. Jackson's purpose in proposing such a dichotomy was to examine the criticisms that have been made of the cybernetic model, and these issues will be considered in due course. Our immediate task is to draw out the distinctions between the two versions, which, to date, have been considered as a single approach. This will provide a structure through which the origin of the "successes" and "failures" can be explicitly assessed.

5.6.2. Distinctions

The distinctions between management and organization cybernetic theory can be identified by adopting a historical approach.

Cybernetics is possibly one of the few ancient systems terms, having been used in the context of steering a government (as one would steer a ship) by Plato and his *kybernetics*; as the art of government in the social sciences by Ampère (1884), and for example more recently by Deutsch (1963) in his book *The Nerves of Government*. At a more mechanistic level Maxwell (1864) used the word to describe feedback in mechanical governors, and Wiener (1948) extended the idea to incorporate both control and communication in animal and the machine.

These approaches tended toward either mechanistic and/or organismic analogy. For example, Plato's idea of a government steering the state, as a helmsman would steer a ship via a rudder, is mechanical. It takes no consideration of the people of the state. Using this approach, Plato defined a blueprint of precisely how society should be structured and run. The guardians, the workers, and the soldiers each had their duties, jobs, and role in society (Ellison and Flood, 1986). This authoritarian nature of control has continued to dominate much of cybernetic reasoning.

Advanced mechanistic, cybernetic control has more recently been applied successfully in quantitative disciplines such as mechanical engineering (also see Section 8.6 on "Quantitative Cybernetics"), but has been criticized in its neglect of human purpose and well-being within organizations. Even the organismic analogies took as their starting point the black box (input–transformation–output) idea, which again neglects the internal human aspects in favor of the view that the generative mechanisms are somewhat deterministic (Platonic).

Transferring such ideas to the management of scarce resources incorporating feedback control, led to the view that organizational goals are set from the outside. This is not surprising because cybernetic thinking was structured as shown in Figure 1.6b; the desired state is clearly set outside the black box transformation process. Such a structure, with information feedback suggests that regulation is then achievable. Feedforward control also assumes an exterior position with a deterministic view of the black box.

We have so far described, from our viewpoint, the features that Jackson (1986) associated with "management cybernetics." To summarize: mechanical and organismic analogies are used; the organization is viewed as a black box with essentially deterministic components, control over which is effected through external goal setting and, preferably, self-regulation, by drawing upon feedback and feedforward ideas of control.

For "organizational cybernetics," we shall adopt Jackson's proposal to concentrate on the later ideas of Stafford Beer (1979, 1981, 1985) as they "encapsulate the most important features of organizational cybernetics." A discussion of the most notable distinctions between Beer's work (reviewed in the previous section) and management cybernetics are as follows.

First, management cybernetics treats organizations as if they were machines or organisms, whereas organizational cybernetics was developed in *Heart of the Enterprise* (Beer, 1979) from cybernetic first principles, as Beer clearly states. In other words, cybernetic laws were introduced without reference to mechanical and biological analogies in the latter case.

As with management cybernetics, feedback and feedforward control are advocated in Beer's work. A distinction does arise here, however, in that the organization is not viewed by Beer merely as a black box. Rather, the internal "components" are explicitly considered and in principle could act as part of the information and decision-making component and could well be involved in goal setting (depending on how the model was applied). In essence, "organizational cybernetics" implicitly incorporates ideas from the organizational management school of thought identified by Robb (1985), which has been discussed earlier. This recognizes the human factor, particularly the social psychological elements, while leaving room for the political and coercive features of human behavior.

Associated with the idea of control is the categorical rejection by Beer of the organizational tree which supports the "power allocation, power maintaining" elitist structure favored in Western culture. In principle, Beer's approach leaves room for democratic processes where the goals themselves may be changing.

To summarize: the distinctions lie in the use of cybernetic (first) principles, the nature of the control loops, acceptance of the human component, and rejection of the organizational tree.

We are now in a position to consider the criticisms that have been leveled against the cybernetic model, and make some comments on the "successes" and "failures" of its use in management and organizational thinking.

5.6.3. The Cybernetic Model on Trial

Eight criticisms of the cybernetic model were grouped under three headings by Jackson (1986). These are presented as follows in a modified and reduced form, which, we hope, still captures the flavor of the original text.

Methodological

1. The cybernetic model is often accused of adherence to misplaced mechanical and biological analogy.
2. The concept of variety has been criticized as (a) a poor measure inappropriate for scientific work, and (b) deficient as it is employed in cybernetics as an absolute, observer-independent measure of complexity.

Epistemological

3. The cybernetic model is held to give an impoverished, or subset, picture of organizations.
4. The cybernetic model emphasizes stability at the expense of change.
5. It is dangerous for the organization to function on a set of *a priori* identified goals in a dynamic (to varying degrees) environment.
6. The cybernetic model underplays the purposeful role of individuals in an organization.

Utility

7. Following (6), there are clear autocratic implications when the cybernetic model is used in practice.
8. The cybernetic model is difficult to apply in practice.

Our views of how these charges may be answered are as follows (and do not necessarily follow those of Jackson):

1. Management cybernetics is guilty as charged, although it is up to the individual to consider the seriousness of the charge. Organizational cybernetics, however, cannot be criticized here on methodological grounds since the VSM is derived from cybernetic first principles. If the outcome is viewed as either biological or mechanical, then this is a result of the cybernetic principles and not first-stage ontological assumptions that organizations are mechanical and/or biological in nature.

2. Variety is one of those ideas that remain very much a part of systems theory, but for which it is difficult to imagine a real-world use (we suggested in Chapter 1 that this was the case for some systems theory). Awareness of this concept, however, adds to the systemic power of reasoning. Nevertheless, we have found pointless the idea of designing a measurement instrument that will at least attain the necessary theoretically desirable ordinal representation, as we feel sure that the degree of uncertainty over what would *actually* be measured would be so high, and consequently disputed, that to all intents and purposes the exercise would be fruitless. The question is, though, how central is the idea of variety *in practice* to either cybernetic version? We feel that awareness is the key and the charge misplaced.

3. Management cybernetics appears to capture only a subset of that which is present in an organization. Because of the initial mechanical assumptions,

the management cybernetics model is clearly more appropriate for machine structures, which, in some industries, do represent a major portion of the overall activities. Even in these cases, however, there are people in the black box. Neglecting them will certainly give an impoverished picture of organizations. Beer's approach, on the other hand, provides, in principle, the basis by which the human factor may be included. No longer do we have a black box with unknown generative mechanisms. In its place, there are clearly defined internal processes, which, assuming appropriate application, will allow for richness of human involvement. Management cybernetics is pretty much guilty whereas organizational cybernetics is incorrectly charged, although the people who apply the approach can do so in whichever way they so desire, and consequently it is the way the model is used that warrants interrogation.

4., 5. The idea of a set point approach by which a single trajectory is tracked with great affinity, being displaced on occasions by environmental disturbances, is appropriate for many machines even though this may be in hyperspace (more than three state variables). Extending this approach to the organism we find that the set point approach has to be relaxed a little to allow for the fact that many internal organismic units function within set ranges and do not necessarily "return" to one desirable set of values. Management cybernetics, based on mechanical and biological analogies, clearly seeks a high degree of stability, whereas, organizational cybernetics allows for democratic processes which inherently permit dynamic changes of goals. This allows for an evolving organizational structure according to environmental changes, whereas in a machine this would imply entropy and, if significant, in an adult organism could imply disease processes (also entropic). Again, we see the failure of management cybernetics to meet the charges, whereas, organizational cybernetics seems in principle to stand firm against the criticisms.

6. Without question, Beer's organizational cybernetics caters (in principle) for the purposeful role of individuals in an organization, although, as pointed out by Jackson, it could benefit from an explicit incorporation of what makes satisfying work and how autonomous work groups could be organized. The case for management cybernetics, however, is a poor one, the trial having been rehearsed earlier in this section where the black box material-matter-information transformation approach was clearly seen to ignore the human factor.

7. Autocracy has been suggested as desirable by some cyberneticians and inevitable by others. For those who stand against autocracy, management cybernetics poses a real threat and is guilty as charged. Organizational cybernetics, however, recommends only such control as is necessary to prevent anarchy and enhance efficiency and effectiveness. On this basis individuals might willingly exchange some of their freedom for perceived personal benefits. This is clearly distinct from autocratic, elitist control.

8. Jackson noted that the recommendations for management cybernetics are likely to be difficult to implement since little is offered except more efficient control, but what of organizational cybernetics that has apparently passed on all the previous seven accounts? The real test is in practical attempts to apply the ideas. Beer's Chilean experience can be seen as a failure in the sense that

ultimately the government was overthrown. Yet, as Beer also noted, the more successful organizational cybernetics became within Chile, the greater became the threat posed by external forces opposed to the Marxist government. There appears to be a scarcity of other well-documented practical attempts to apply Beer's model. Consequently, and with some reservations because we might be accused of being anecdotal, we offer the following. Over the past few years at the Department of Systems Science in the City University in London, we have presented Beer's model as one alternative view to the more traditional views of management. Stemming from our Engineering and Industrial Training Board (EITB) Fellowship, for young promising engineering-managers in industry, one fellow has attempted to apply Beer's model within his domain in industry. His experiences are sobering for VSM advocates. The problems appeared to be twofold. First, there was a major hurdle encountered in attempting to educate those in his "immediate working vicinity." Second, and potentially the terminal factor in such projects, was the "nationalistic" ambience which confronted him. This included aspects of culture such as company history, language, rules and norms, and the internal legal system (which supports the overall company structure and control). If this is representative of what is likely to be found in industry, then it seems that there are only two options open for VSM supporters. There is the long-term approach of education and incremental change based on the ideas of "diagnosing the system." Alternatively, given a young, relatively small organization, the VSM could be used as the basic design for the organizational structure. The process of change, if it were ever to happen, clearly would be one that requires much patience and plenty of time.

The VSM has shown that it offers real potential, and yet there is one, as yet not touched upon, doubt (Flood and Jackson, 1988). Our standard of comparison for the VSM has been functionalist organization theory. If we consider the VSM within the interpretive paradigm, however, it does seem to capture only a subset of that which is generally accepted as normally present in organizations. For Checkland (1980), working within the interpretive paradigm, the VSM takes the organization to be like a machine set up to carry through some purpose. However, at best, this is only a partial representation of what an organization is. It is a representation, moreover, that misses the essential character of organizations—the fact that their component parts are human beings who can attribute meaning to their situation and can therefore see in organizations whatever purpose they wish and make of organizations what they will. Because of this, it is as legitimate to regard an organization as a social grouping, an appreciative situation or a power struggle, as it is to see it as a machine (Checkland, 1980).

5.6.4. Summary

In this section we have reviewed Jackson's (1986) separation of the cybernetic model into "management cybernetics" and "organizational cybernetics." Distinction between these has been made in an explicit manner. The two versions were then "put on trial." This resulted in a rejection of management cybernetics, but gave a very favorable verdict on organizational cybernetics within the terms of the functionalist paradigm. One major difficulty, however, appears to be penetrating organizational cultures, which appear to have tremendous resilience and stability against change. A second and more fundamental problem arises when considering the model within the interpretive paradigm when an impoverished view is associated with the VSM. This provides the theme for the following section.

5.7. THE INTERPRETIVE ALTERNATIVES

5.7.1. Introduction

We have spent much time considering the systems view of organizations and management within the "functionalist" paradigm. Functionalism, as Burrell and Morgan (1979) suggest, takes an "objective" position on how theory should be developed in the social sciences and offers a regulative account of the nature of society. In these terms the management and organization theory so far presented, as well as Beer's more structuralist orientation, must all be regarded as essentially functionalist in character. This apparent bias toward functionalism is easily explained by the fact that social systems theory generally exists almost exclusively in that paradigm. A second tradition does exist in the social sciences, however, and it is possible to detect a new mood in social systems theory whereby some of the tenets of this interpretive paradigm are being endorsed. This is despite the so-called practical achievements of the functionalist approach. This brief section is thus included to reflect the rising interest, although the paradigm is more prevalent in methodological studies, underpinning the work of Checkland and others (discussed in the following chapter).

5.7.2. The Fundamental Tenets of the Paradigm

We found the review of Burrell and Morgan (1979) generally useful when preparing this section. The interpretive approach criticizes the use of thinking from the natural sciences being applied to social situations. It is proposed that general laws in the social sciences, which are far less tangible, cannot be established as there is the phenomenon of man's freedom of will to contend with. The alternatives put forward within the interpretive paradigm hold to the view that the primary concern of social sciences should be to understand the subjective experience of individuals. Attention is focused on the complex and problematic nature of human behavior and experience. Social reality is seen as an emergent process, an extension of human consciousness and subjective experience. Some interpretive positions are also of a Gestalt nature, in that appreciation of the intuition of total wholes is proposed.

There is, however, at least one strand of commonality between the interpretive and functionalist paradigms. The overlap lies in the concern for regulation. In this chapter we have clearly shown that this is the case for the cybernetic approach. In addition to this, the interpretive view is said to be "concerned with the ways in which social reality is meaningfully constructed and ordered from the point of view of those involved, for instance the way actors negotiate, regulate and live their lives within the context of the *status quo*" (Burrell and Morgan, 1979).

5.7.3. The Empirical Dilemma and Other Issues

Moving away from pure reasoning to consider empirical research in this area, Burrell and Morgan reviewed the works of Bittner (1965), Zimmerman (for example, Zimmerman and Wieder, 1970), and Silverman (for example, Silverman, 1970; Silverman and Jones, 1976). These researchers are representative of what has been labeled ethnomethodology, which concentrates on the way in which individual actors account for and make sense of their world. By comparing and contrasting both their theoretical pronouncements and their empirical research, Burrell and Morgan identified what they labeled ontological oscillations. This refers to a move from theoretical stress on subjectivity, which denies the existence of social structures, to attempts to operationalize ideas within an empirical context, which often led them to admit (unintentionally) a functionalist viewpoint on what constitutes reality.

Phenomenological symbolic interactionism is the label given to an area of the interpretive paradigm that concentrates on social contexts in which interacting individuals employ a variety of practices to create and sustain particular definitions of the world. Here, "reality" and "facts" are essentially seen as social creations, negotiated through the interaction of various competing themes and definitions of reality. Burrell and Morgan again noted the ontological problems and highlighted the dilemma that phenomenological sociology faces when ideas of pure subjectivity are taken forward into the empirical world.

A number of criticisms of contemporary organization theory have emerged from this background. Some of these have been included in the earlier section, which includes "The Cybernetic Model on Trial." One major attack is on the apparent managerial bias, where, it is said, managerial concepts underpin much of the functionalist reasoning. Nevertheless, it is also suggested that the interpretive paradigm can contribute to the functionalist paradigm by transferring to it the recognition of the role of individuals. It is fair to say, however, that Stafford Beer's work (among others) does go some way to satisfying this suggestion.

As a final note, the reader should be aware that other research is being carried out under the umbrella of social systems theory, but outside of the two paradigms discussed so far. Within a paradigm of radical humanism, Jackson (1985), for instance, proposed a "radical therapy" from critical social system theory. Essentially this approach considers, in parallel, philosophical, theoretical, and practical issues. Deep-rooted social change by human emancipation is the underlying theme of this approach. The social situations that, it is proposed, are appropriate for such treatment, are characterized by inequalities of power and resources among participants, and by conflict and contradiction. Radical humanism, therefore, departs from the theme of regulation shared by the interpretive and functionalist paradigms, proposing radical change.

5.7.4. Summary

In this section we have presented only the barest sketch of some alternative views on organization and management theory which contrast with the more traditional functionalist approach of social systems theory. Some of the ideas of this section will necessarily emerge again, for instance in the contexts of methodology in Chapter 6 and of philosophical issues in Chapter 10.

5.8. CONCLUSION

The aim of this chapter has been to investigate the systems view of management and the organization. The findings clearly identify the functionalist paradigm as the dominant approach in Western society. This approach adopts many of the methods that underpin scientific inquiry and reasoning typically found in the natural sciences. There is a strong perception among a majority of theoreticians and practitioners that the functionalist paradigm has scored many successes of a practical nature. However, the approaches that have been adopted have been criticized for holding a managerial bias, promoting the authoritarian nature of cybernetic control, and neglecting the role of the individual. To some extent the criticisms have been answered through the VSM of Stafford Beer. Nevertheless, there remains a fundamental philosophical difference between the work of functionalists and the paradigm of pure subjective reasoning promoted by the interpretive theorist. A new mood can be detected within social systems theory which endorses many interpretive tenets. However, to date interpretive sociology has suffered from ontological contradictions between theory and practice. Perhaps one of the most successful interpretive systems reasoners is Peter Checkland with his work on methodology. A deeper look at his work constitutes an important component of the next chapter.

PROBLEMS

5.1. List and briefly describe the main theories that have surfaced from the development of management theory.

5.2. Give a brief summary of the holistic view that cybernetic bridges exist between these main schools of thought.

Chapter Five

5.3. Discuss, from a systems viewpoint, the essential features of administrative management.

5.4. Describe Stafford Beer's Viable System Model (VSM).

5.5. How does the VSM, described in your answer to Question 5.4, differ from orthodox management of organizations?

5.6. List the distinctions, made by Jackson (1986), between organizational and management cybernetics.

5.7. What are the main criticisms of the cybernetic model in the context of management?

5.8. How well do management cybernetics and organizational cybernetics stand up to the criticisms from Question 5.7?

SYSTEMS VIEW OF PROBLEMS
AND PROBLEMATIC SITUATIONS

6.1. INTRODUCTION

Much of man's activity has focused on dealing with "problems" in a variety
of forms. The many problem types include knowledge acquisition (essentially
traditional science, but more recently systemic science); the implementation
of knowledge (most obviously encountered in everyday life in the form of
technology); the consequences of technology in society (pollution such as
effluent and noise, and the effects of technological change); and difficulties
arising from, or within, societal organizations themselves.

The sole concern of this chapter is in investigating the various methods
of inquiry that man has developed in order to deal with "problems." Before
looking specifically at such methodologies, however, we propose to spend a
little time in sketching a picture of the basic ideas and major controversies
that have arisen.

6.2. SETTING THE SCENE

In fact, there appears to be a never-ending source of problem generation,
but what do we mean by a *problem*? We need to clarify our understanding of
this concept. There are two clear views on this matter. The following is a broad

definition that suits the hard systems view: a *problem* is a "doubtful or difficult matter requiring solution; something hard to understand or accomplish or deal with" (*Oxford Dictionary of Current English*). On the soft side, Checkland (1981) has defined a real-world problem as "one which arises in the everyday world of events and ideas, and may be perceived differently by different people. Such problems are not constructed by the investigator as are laboratory problems." These opposing views lead to significantly different approaches, and indeed use of words. The hard school happily talk about problems as if they are there, and we can know what the problem is. The soft school, which accepts plurality in human interaction, generally discusses problematic situations rather than problems since different people perceive the "same" situation differently. Furthermore, the hard school often adopts the term *problem solving*, as if once the knowable problem has been dealt with it will have gone; whereas the soft school rather discusses intervention in problematic situations with the aim of reducing dis-ease. It is also common for authors to use the word system to describe real-world things. Since much of this chapter is a review of systems methodologies, the terminology adopted in the articles that are being reviewed, that is, during the review, will be adopted. It would be unfair to do otherwise. In more general comparative discussions, at the front of the chapter, the word "problem" will be used as shown here in double quotes. Outside of these the current authors will adopt terminology as seen appropriate.

Many complex "problems" have been, and continue to be, tackled using a piecemeal, nonrational approach. This approach has often led to a failure to deal effectively with the "problem issues," so that inevitably the totality of the "problem" is not considered. In these cases, some crucial elements may be excluded from the formulation of "a solution." Furthermore, if a nonrational approach is adopted then a reasonable range of alternatives or perspectives will rarely be considered. In such cases extreme solutions are often chosen as they are most obvious.

A systems approach to "problem situations," however, displays systemic (holistic rather than piecemeal) and/or rational systematic (step-by-step rather than intuitive) features. Systems methodologies are thus systematic in the way that a "problem" is tackled and/or systemic in that, at appropriate points (or throughout), holistic thinking is adopted. Let us explore these ideas further.

Systems **methodologies** have evolved alongside **philosophies**. At times methodologies point to the need for **techniques**. Such words, however, are used in a variety of contexts and thus have rather loose interpretations. To add clarity in the context of this discussion, the following operational definitions (based on Checkland, 1981) are offered:

1. Philosophy: a broad nonspecific guideline for action.
2. Technique: a precise specific program of action that will produce a standard result
3. Methodology: lacks the precision of a technique, but will be a firmer guide to action than a philosophy.

A methodology thus follows the systemic and/or systematic and iterative guidelines of a related philosophy. A methodology, however, has a constitution for "things" that should be done (constitutive rules) and sets a strategy for "things" that could be done (strategic rules) (Naughton, 1977). This allows the investigator(s) to stamp a personality on the process by adapting the strategy according to current (group) perceptions.

Although those working in systems science (the systems movement) are in agreement on the need for this kind of well-thought-out methodological approach, there is an apparent conflict in the ideas that produce the precise form of each methodology, that is, what in fact should the constitution and strategy of the approach be?

The difficulty appears to be associated with "problems" in social situations and is a result of the way in which "problems" occurring in such situations are viewed. A hard view, proposed by Daellenbach *et al.* (1983), suggests that for a "problem" to exist there must be an individual or group of individuals (decision makers) who have needs to be satisfied or objectives to be achieved. Additionally, a decision maker must have at least two alternative courses of action that have a significant probability of achieving the objectives, and have some doubt as to which course of action is best in terms of achieving those objectives. Alternatively, adopting a soft approach, a "problem" situation is seen as "a nexus of real-world events and ideas which at least one person perceives as problematic: for him other possibilities concerning the situation are worth investigation" (Checkland, 1981). Checkland, rejecting the hard view, believes there are many "problems," soft "problems" that "cannot be formulated as a search for an efficient means of achieving a defined end: a problem in which ends, goals, purposes are themselves problematic."

A logical response would appear to be that situations of different natures (or perhaps classes) are likely to require different methodologies for their investigation. However, the uncovering of classes of situations has only effectively been put into the context of real-world "problems," for example, as recently as 1985 by Klir in his book *Architecture of Systems Problem Solving* and by Jackson and Keys (1984) in their paper "Towards a System of Systems Methodologies," although these are both different in class definition and the methodological approaches recommended/offered.

These and other propositions are deferred for discussion until later in the chapter. Now, having set the scene, we shall present a detailed look at both hard and soft methodologies.

6.3. HARD SYSTEMS METHODOLOGIES

6.3.1. Introduction

Hard systems methodologies, which set out to select an efficient means of achieving a known and defined end, can conveniently be considered under the headings systems analysis (developed primarily by RAND Corporation) and systems engineering (developed in military and space applications and promoted by A. D. Hall and G. M. Jenkins, among others). Checkland (1978) defined these as follows:

1. Systems analysis is the systematic appraisal of the costs and other implications of meeting a defined requirement in various ways.
2. Systems engineering comprises the set of activities that together lead to the creation of a complex man-made entity and/or the procedures and information flows associated with its operation.

Operations research can also be classified as a hard systems methodology, being typical of the means–end approach. This approach emerged as a means of tackling the vast logistical problems that were encountered during World War II. A whole variety of formal quantitative techniques have been developed for use in operations research studies.

Jenkins (1969), in a comparative discussion of operations research and systems engineering, highlighted their similarities. He pointed readers to two comments by Roy, in Flagle *et al.* (1960), that

> in a certain sense operations research and systems engineering are the same [although] the operations research team is more likely to be concerned with operations *in being* rather than with operations *in prospect* [and] systems engineers are more likely to be engaged in the design of systems yet to be rather than in the operation of systems in being.

Jenkins pointed out that several other authors had proposed these distinctions, and stated that he believed them to be artificial since systems engineering is "just as concerned with redesigning existing systems as in designing new ones." In conclusion, Jenkins noted that semantic discussions resolve nothing and that "operational research and systems engineering, and systems analysis have a great deal in common."

The aim of this section is to present an example of each approach, and to investigate their commonalities and highlight their differences. Comparative observations are consolidated in some remarks at the end of this section.

6.3.2. Systems Analysis

The approach documented here is one adapted from Atthill (1975). The decision-making sequence is tackled in four steps: problem analysis, generation of alternative solutions, evaluation of the alternatives, and selection of the optimal alternative. This is followed by action on the decision. This sequence is summarized in the decision-making loop shown in Figure 6.1.

Step 1. Problem Analysis. The idea here is to define the problem and cost the current system, thus providing an economic measure by which alternatives may be compared. The following two questions aid this process:

S1.1.   What are the limitations of the present system?
S1.2.   What is the cost of operating the present system?

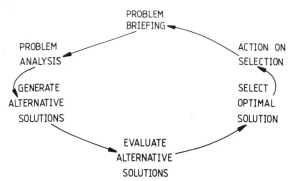

FIGURE 6.1. Systems analysis decision-making loop (Atthill, 1975; reproduced by permission of BP Educational Services).

Issues arising from these questions include the identification of efficient features of such a system and the features of the current system that are worth retaining.

Step 2. Generation of Alternative Solutions. This step requires that the analyst generates alternatives to the present system and then explores the major features of each. Two relevant questions here are as follows:

S2.1.   What alternative systems are there?
S2.2.   What would be the operating costs of the alternative systems?

It is necessary to consider which factors could influence the choice of system, whether any features of the current system should be retained, and, in a general sense, what are the advantages and disadvantages of the alternatives. Economic considerations include a comparative operational costing of the alternatives and testing the feasibility of trading off costs within each alternative.

Step 3. Evaluation of the Alternatives. The emphasis in this step is on assessing the capital costs involved in introducing a new system or improving the present one, and making comparisons between the various alternatives taking both operating and capital costs into account. Two pertinent questions here are the following:

S3.1.   What are the capital costs of continuing with the present system, and of changing to alternative systems?
S3.2.   What comparisons can be made between the various systems, taking all costs into account?

This step includes comparative capital costing and should embrace inquiries into factors such as the rate of return that can be obtained on any money invested. It is therefore important to consider some basic principles of capital investment, such as: What is a reasonable return on investment and over what time period should the investment be considered? To this end, a variety of methods that are available for calculating the return, and their advantages and disadvantages, need to be considered. Additionally, an appropriate method of taking inflation into account when considering future costs is of importance.

Step 4. Selection of the Optimal Alternative. It is now time to select the best available system by considering not only economic criteria but also operational, marketing, environmental, and human factors. The following directive questions should be asked:

S4.1. What is the most economical solution?
S4.2. Is the most economical solution the best "all-round" solution?

Here lies the most sensitive area with real potential for conflict, particularly between the quantifiable economic factors and those that are not readily quantifiable, the latter including such contemporary issues as pollution and the quality of human working conditions. In accordance with these observations, a "best solution" is not always the most economically efficient one; a number of alternative solutions that reflect the major viewpoints should be considered. A "right" answer can only be right in the sense that a course of action is adopted that reflects the company's objectives at the time of the decision (including the company's attitude towards sensitive issues).

These four steps detail one representative way of viewing systems analysis. Presented below is one representative way of viewing systems engineering.

6.3.3. Systems Engineering

The methodology chosen (and summarized) for this subsection is that of Jenkins (1969). The reason for this selection is twofold. First, Jenkins is one of the more sophisticated adherents of systems engineering. Second, the Jenkins methodology was the starting point in the evolution of Checkland's soft systems methodology (described in the following section).

The methodology essentially passes through four basic stages: systems analysis, systems design, implementation, and operation. These stages are shown in Figure 6.2. The methodology is described later.

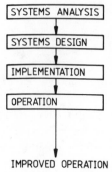

FIGURE 6.2. Systems engineering methodology (Jenkins, 1969; reproduced by permission).

Phase 1. Systems Analysis

P1.1. Recognition and Formulation of the Problem. To obtain a clear picture of the scope of the problem, and the likely benefits that would result from its solution, a dialogue is set up that necessarily includes questions of the form: How did the problem arise? Who are the people who believe it to be a problem? And, if relevant: Who decided to implement a planning decision and what is the logic of the chain of argument leading to the making of the decision? Is the problem the right one and the solution important? Will it save money? Would the money be better spent elsewhere?

P1.2. Organization of the Project. It is important to group together the right sort of systems engineering team. This ideally would consist of members from a systems department supplemented with personnel drawn from other departments with specialist knowledge, for instance, a team leader, a user, model builders, designers, computer programmers, mathematicians, economists, accountants. The systems team requires an opportunity to view the problem anew and therefore should gain the widest possible terms of reference. The team should also ensure that work carried out is performed logically and systematically, and that the implementation is achieved according to a planned end point.

P1.3. Definition of the System. The system to be studied should be defined in precise terms by breaking it down into its subsystems and identifying the interactions between those subsystems using a flow-block diagram representing money, energy, materials, information, and decisions (each type clearly labeled).

P1.4. Definition of the Wider System. A separate flow-block diagram should be constructed to display clearly the role that the system plays within the wider system of which it forms a part.

P1.5. Definition of the Objectives of the Wider System. By using the block diagrams of the system and the wider system, sets of objectives of the wider system may be formulated. These are important, as any change in the wider systems objectives will have a direct effect on the systems objectives.

P1.6. Definition of the Objectives of the System. Initially, objectives are defined in broad terms and are dictated by the needs of the wider system. To identify and reconcile conflicting objectives, a comprehensive list is produced and the objectives positioned ordinally according to their anticipated order of importance. The objectives should, if possible, be definable in economic terms as the end product of this step is the formulation of the criterion (usually economic) that measures the efficiency with which the system is achieving its objective.

P1.7. Definition of the Overall Economic Criterion. A criterion that measures the efficiency by which the system can achieve its objectives is defined in precise terms. The more precise the objectives, the easier it is to set up quantitative criteria. The overall economic criterion should be related to objectives, simple and direct, and clearly agreed on and accepted (even if qualitative). Resolving conflicting objectives requires some compromise, either by attaching a weighting factor to each objective, or by imposing constraints (subjective or objective) on variables set within the economic criterion.

P1.8. Information and Data Collection. This is an extensive stage of systems analysis. Data are required for future modeling of the system as well as forecasting future environments. Efficient information gathering requires clear thinking, an ability to communicate, and a grasp of statistical techniques (to look for significance).

Phase 2. Systems Design

P2.1. Forecasting. This is the first important step in the design of any system; particularly forecasts of demand, the firm's activities, and environment in the short, medium, and long term. Accuracy (estimated) is very important so that risk assessment may be undertaken.

P2.2. Model Building and Simulation. This highly creative activity (explained in detail in Chapter 9) allows the analyst to predict performance over a relevant range of operating conditions and real-life environments.

P2.3. Optimization. After simulation comes system optimization (identifying the most favorable model performance), using the (economic) criterion chosen for the study. To this end, a vast variety of techniques are available.

P2.4. Control. Control is important so that unpredicted system disturbances can be counteracted after real-world implementation. An effective control system helps to provide the most profitable design conditions. A systems approach is perceived as being essential in order that localized control loops are also considered in the wider context of the system.

Phase 3. Implementation

P3.1. Documentation and Sanction Approval. A report that highlights the proposals for action should be prepared. Before issuing the report, the content and form (preferably simple, direct, and logical) should be discussed with those whose backing will be needed to implement the results of the study. Normally, a separate document highlighting the recommendation and a critical path schedule should be prepared. These aid the critical stage of decision making.

P3.2. Construction. Particular aspects of this phase include the scheduled building of special hardware and software before installation to allow control and optimization algorithms to be implemented on time. The construction of the system itself is undertaken.

Phase 4.   Operation

P4.1. Initial Operation. The importance of liaison between the systems team and the system users at this stage is crucial in ensuring a smooth handover. Integral to this is adequate documentation and training (preferably at least one user is on the systems team, and is conversant with the design philosophy). Investment in good systems thinking will reduce start-up problems.

P4.2. Retrospective Appraisal of the Project. This prevents the isolation of users, allowing for some reoptimization, and teases out the lessons of the study, which may then be consolidated.

These four phases detail one representative way of viewing systems engineering. Of the many alternatives, the reader is directed to M'Pherson (1981), who details a far more sophisticated (and up-to-date) systems engineering methodology. This involves identifying and comparing the system worth (involving utility functions and so on) of alternative systems among other things. Continuing, we present below one representative way of viewing operations research.

6.3.4.   Operations Research

The methodology put forward by Daellenbach *et al.* (1983) is described in concise form later.

An operational research program essentially passes (in an iterative manner) through five major steps or phases: formulating the problem, constructing a mathematical model to represent the operation studied, deriving a solution to the model, testing the model and evaluating the solution, and implementing and maintaining the solution. A distinguishing feature of this operations research program is the formal construction of mathematical models, consisting of functions, equations, and inequalities, and the techniques available to find optimal solutions to such models.

In a less formal way than Jenkins, Daellenbach and co-workers initially discuss the importance of the team when adopting such an approach, and the function of team dynamics, enabling the best use to be made of complementary specialized knowledge. They strongly advocate the inclusion of at least one person intimately involved with the operation being studied, thus providing a necessary and reachable source of physical and technical know-how about the operation. The five phases are as follows:

Phase 1.   Formulation of the Problem

The components of a problem are perceived as being the decision maker, the objectives, the alternative courses of action, and the environment. To formulate the problem it is first necessary to identify these components.

A **decision maker** is someone who has control over the choices of action to be performed. Decision makers, however, may be spread over several hierarchical levels within the organization, and the operations researcher will need to gain a thorough understanding of the span of control vested in each level. This helps identify that which may or may not be changed and thus helps define the scope of the project. The method of investigation should include viewing the organizational chart and should involve interviewing and questioning people within the organization.

The **objectives** associated with each level should also be identified. From these, conflicting objectives (both on and between levels) may be found and dealt with during the program.

Alternative courses of action are taken as given by those features of the system that are controllable by the decision maker. In contrast, the environment consists of the uncontrollable features. (The reader might find it interesting here to reflect on the discussion in Chapter 3 concerning system identification and boundary setting.) Ascertaining relevance to the problem by finding a distinction between controllable and uncontrollable aspects is aided by asking the following two questions posed by Churchman (1968): (1) Can I (the decision maker) do anything about it? (2) Does it matter relative to my objectives?

If questions 1 and 2 produce a "yes," then problem relevance and system ownership have been ascertained. If the answer to the first question is "no," but to the second is "yes," then this feature is part of the environment. (An in-depth discussion on this matter is presented in Chapter 3.)

Phase 2.   Constructing a Mathematical Model

Many important considerations relating to parsimony are involved in constructing a mathematical model, for instance simplification, aggregation, approximating relationships, and so on. (This topic is covered thoroughly in Chapter 9.)

Phase 3.   Deriving a Solution to the Model

Having formulated the problem mathematically, we now need to derive a solution. The solution is based on fundamental economic principles of marginal analysis for the case of increasing marginal costs and decreasing marginal returns. The value of the decision variable is increased until marginal costs are equal to marginal returns. The mathematical basis for marginal analysis is based on classical calculus and generally achieved using numeric and computational methods (examples are given in Chapter 8). Often "good" rather than "best" policies are sought using heuristic methods, and the performance of specific decision rules may be evaluated by simulation. Finally, as many decision problems involve a relatively small number of courses of action, complete enumeration may be effectively achieved. A widely adopted technique that helps to achieve this is the decision tree approach (presented clearly by Daellenbach and co-workers; see also Chapter 9 on logical models).

Phase 4. Testing the Model and Evaluating the Solution

Any model, being an abstraction of reality, is prone to errors in the way it represents that reality. It is therefore necessary that a systematic evaluation of model responses to changes in input and parameters should be carried out. By performing sensitivity tests (solving the model for various combinations of change in input and parameter values), control ranges can be established over which the best solution remains near-optimal. Additionally, the marginal value of scarce resources may be calculated.

Also of importance is the empirical testing of the model against actual historical data and forecast future behavior. If successful, the former increases confidence in model performance. The latter also allows comparisons to be made between the present and proposed management rules against a set of future scenarios. (Validation is discussed in Chapter 9.)

Phase 5. Implementing and Maintaining the Solution

This involves putting the tested solution to work. The mathematical solution is translated into a set of easily understood operating procedures or decision rules for the people involved in using or applying the solution. It is necessary to train those people in the proper use of the rules. In addition, the transition period between use of the current system and conversion to the desired mode of operations must be planned and executed. Instituting controls to maintain and update the solution is also necessary. Finally, checking of the initial performance should be carried out until such time as the new mode of operation becomes routine.

As the environment of an organizational solution is dynamic, change requiring adaptation has to be expected. Where environmental parameters or relationships change, there may only be the need to adjust the values of the decision variables. If, however, structural relationships change, in the form or nature of environmental parameters or relationships, the optimal solution may no longer be valid. This may necessitate reformulation of the model. A simple rule can help in making this decision. If the improvement in the benefits that can be gained by adjusting the solution exceeds the cost of making the adjustment, then a significant change has occurred and reformulation of the model is appropriate. Establishing controls over the solution is therefore necessary. This may be achieved as follows: listing for each variable, parameter, constraint, or relationship (within or excluded from the model) the range of values for which the present solution remains (sub)optimal and the type of qualitative change that invalidates the current form of solution; specifying how each variable and parameter is to be measured, which relationships are to be checked, and the frequency of the controls and checks; determining who is responsible for each item and making that person notifiable if significant changes occur; specifying how the solution has to be adjusted for significant quantitative changes and what action has to be taken to deal with qualitative changes in the environment.

6.3.5. Summary

In this section we have presented three so-called hard systems problem solving methodologies representative of three main strands of the hard approach. Let us now summarize what has been discussed.

The most obvious similarity between the three hard systems approaches is the explicit belief that any problem can be solved by setting objectives and then finding from a range of alternatives the one solution that will be optimal in satisfying those objectives. Thus, a systematic approach is adopted, one that incorporates the means of optimization, and that includes some systemic thinking by holistic modeling (system, subsystems, wider system, environment, and so on). Classical operations research and systems analysis have "broadened out" to their current versions in which such an approach is adopted.

The general use and applicability of the methodologies to operations in being and operations in prospect has been a topic of much discussion. It does appear, however, that all three approaches are being used in both cases. Their relative applicability must to a large extent remain in the eye of the user.

This latter point also acts as a trigger for us to move on to soft systems methodology. It was the perceived inappropriateness (by a number of systems thinkers) of means–end, objective-seeking approaches in problematic situations, particularly of soft situations, that gave rise to the methodology reviewed below.

6.4. SOFT SYSTEMS METHODOLOGY (SSM)

6.4.1. Introduction

A soft approach to ill-structured, or messy, situations has been proposed by R. L. Ackoff, C. W. Churchman, and P. B. Checkland. We will review the well-tried and tested methodology of P. B. Checkland as one example.

Checkland's SSM originated from the use of a Jenkins-type approach (described earlier) in situations of purposeful human activity, that is, in human activity systems. In the early phases of Checkland's involvement in such problematic situations he found that systems analysis and systems engineering were unable to progress beyond their early stages as no "objectives" or "needs" could be easily ascertained. These methodologies were apparently not able to cope with messy situations of, for instance, complex organizational issues. Learning from the use of the Jenkins approach in soft situations, Checkland redefined, and by further use refined, the methodology (see Figure 6.3). The output was SSM.

Probably the most important of Checkland's observations, relevant in the context of problematic situations, is that there are always many possible versions of the situation (as discussed in Chapter 3) such that boundaries and objectives are often difficult to define. Checkland subscribes to the view of

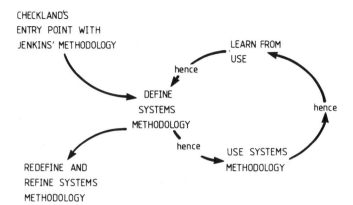

FIGURE 6.3. Methodology development cycle (adapted from Checkland, 1981).

Vickers (1970) that social systems are not usefully thought of as goal seeking, and that a consultant is concerned more with relationship maintenance.

The following description (necessarily presented via examples) of SSM is drawn from Checkland (1981) (where a much expanded description and discussion may be found). These are supplemented by notes and observations taken from a tutorial event (plus the comments of the participants) organized by the Operations Research Society, entitled "Soft Systems Methodology," given by Professor Checkland at Manchester Polytechnic in July 1986. Further comments are taken from some of our own exercises using this methodology.

6.4.2. The Methodology

The original version of the methodology was described in Checkland (1972), with a modified version appearing in Checkland (1975, 1981). The latter is summarized in Figure 6.4. The logical sequence 1–7 is one that

> is most suitable for describing it but which does not have to be followed in using it!... Backtracking and iteration are also essential; in fact the most effective users of the methodology have been able to use it as a framework into which to place purposeful activity during a systems study, rather than a recipe in a cookery book. In an actual study the most effective systems thinker will be working simultaneously, at different levels of detail, on several stages.

Figure 6.4 shows that the methodology consists of both real-world and systems thinking activities. The former activity involves people in the problematic situation, whereas in the latter case the conditions of the study *may* involve those people, although this is not necessarily so. Also for the latter case, real-world complexity is unraveled and understood as a result of translation into the higher-level language (or metalanguage) of systems.

Stages 1 and 2. A key factor here is to achieve a representation of the problematic situation in as *neutral* a way as possible. This is achieved by building a rich picture (as rich as possible; also see Chapter 3). This contributes

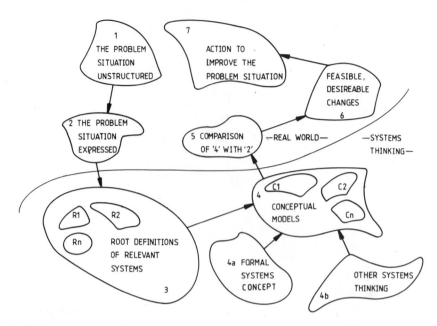

FIGURE 6.4. Soft systems methodology (Checkland, 1981; reproduced by permission of John Wiley & Sons).

substantially to the following development of a set of viewpoint(s) (non-neutral), each offering a distinct angle from which the problematic situation may be investigated. Each viewpoint gives rise to one perceived relevant system. A relevant system chosen at this time will not necessarily be the most revealing, so that, given a situation where future progress is not satisfactory, it might be desirable to step back and consider other relevant systems. In essence

> the function of Stages 1 and 2 is to display the situation so that a range of possible and, hopefully, relevant choices can be revealed, and that is the only function of these stages.

Emphasis is placed, for these stages, on examining structure and process and their interrelationship. The latter is what Checkland terms the "climate" of the situation, the climate often being a "core characteristic" of problematic situations. A variety of themes may be drawn out of the rich picture which relate to what the situation is actually about as perceived by observers of the situation.

Stages 3 and 4. Taking forward some insights concerning the structure, process, and climate of a relevant system promotes the development of a more explicit account of the names of the notional systems which seem relevant to the problematic situation. To achieve this a **root definition** is developed (see later). Again this is not a once-and-for-all process, as the availability of other viewpoints is maintained and their use is encouraged if unsatisfactory progress

> to propose a particular definition is to assert that, in the view of the analyst, taking
> this to be a relevant system, making a conceptual model of the system, and comparing
> it with present realities is likely to lead to illumination of the problems and hence
> to their solution or alleviation.

Checkland notes that the most effective systems thinker will be forward-looking
and will, even now, be considering the conceptual models, their comparison
with that which exists in the real world, and thus the possible changes that
are likely to emerge.

To help elucidate this phase an exercise, carried out at the Manchester
tutorial, is summarized below. The participants were introduced to a problematic situation relating to unease about information flows reaching the management committee of Oxfam. Participants were asked to "identify" relevant
systems of that organization. The following were proposed:

1. A begging system
2. A relief provision system
3. A mail order system ⎱ Retail system
4. A clothes recycling system ⎰
5. An education system
6. A lobbying system

Linking and possible lumping of relevant systems that show commonalities is
advised at this juncture. For example, a mail order system and a clothes
recycling system could be lumped into a retail system.

An important concept in this example is that described by the German
word *Weltanschauung* (W), the flavor of which in English, and in the context
of problematic situations, is "What **view of the world** makes this situation,
meaningful?" Ws of purposeful activity are linked to "culture," that is, they
are biased to "cultural viewpoints" (see Figure 6.5).

Checkland's Oxfam list was as follows:

1. Relief provision
2. Aid provision
3. Fund raising
4. Retailing
5. Political education

These too suggest different Ws with respect to Oxfam.

These embryonic root definitions of this type are functional and are often
found in an organization as departments and are termed **primary task** root
definitions. There are also other factors that are concerned with purposeful
activity that are seen to be issues and are termed **issue-based** root definitions.
Continuing the same example, Checkland proposed two issue-based factors:
(1) activity and information defining and (2) conflict on resources use resolving.

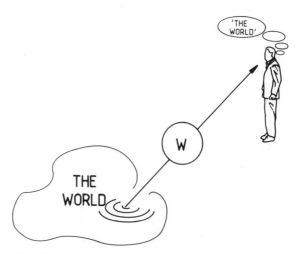

FIGURE 6.5. W: Weltanschauung—from CATWOE.

It appears that issues create managers who do primary things; however, managers do not necessarily create issues.

So far it has been ascertained that a root definition is a core description of purposeful activity taken from a specific point of view. A fully developed root definition, however, is more comprehensive than it might appear from the discussion above. A root definition needs to reflect the aspects of CATWOE, a mnemonic, and can be assessed by considering the questions set out below:

C: "Customer"—Who would be victims or beneficiaries of this system?
A: "Actor"—Who would perform the activities?
T: "Transformation"—What input is transformed into what output?
W: "*Weltanschauung*"—What view of the world makes this system meaningful?
O: "Owner"—Who could abolish this system?
E: "Environmental constraints"—What in its environment does this system take as given?

Having already dealt with W, it is logical and beneficial to progress next to T. T may best be considered via a typical cybernetic model (see Figure 6.6). It is important that the actual output is directly related to the input, so that the input is still there in some altered form. Generally speaking, for a physical/abstract input a physical/abstract output would be required. It is always useful to try both physical and abstract inputs.

FIGURE 6.6. T: Transformation—from CATWOE.

One group at the Manchester tutorial came up with the following Ts for an English pub:

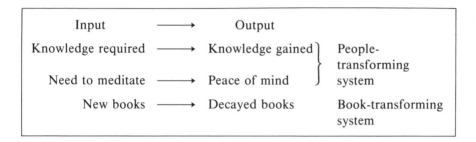

Input		Output
Owned beer and consumables	⟶	Sold beer and consumables
Sober people	⟶	Less sober people
People who needed to be socially satisfied	⟶	Socially satisfied people
Landlord with £x	⟶	Landlord with £x + n

As the group's activity was not set in the context of "a definite problem," it was possible for them to produce particularly cogent answers that personally satisfied individuals. This is also an effect of Ws. In a problematic context, however, the Ts will need to relate to the relevant systems under consideration and a high degree of cogency may be difficult to achieve.

Another example discussed was that of a library. Some Ts and relevant systems were described as follows:

Input		Output	
Knowledge required	⟶	Knowledge gained ⎱	People-transforming
Need to meditate	⟶	Peace of mind ⎰	system
New books	⟶	Decayed books	Book-transforming system

Note that commonalities can be found so that lumping of Ts may be appropriate. For example, a library may be considered as a people- and a book-transforming system.

Additionally, considering how T could fail enables managers to think about monitoring and controling purposeful activity (expressed in terms of input–transformation–output). The question "How could T fail?" ensures that, if necessary, action may be taken to prevent the potential failure (Checkland, 1986). Checkland continued by stating that, in general, there are three ways by which T can fail:

1. T could be the wrong activity to be doing; a measure of effectiveness.
2. The way chosen to do T might not work; a measure of efficacy.
3. T might not be being done with minimum resources (including time as a resource); a measure of efficiency.

If good measures of effectiveness, efficacy, and efficiency can be achieved, purposeful activity can be observed. Control action may be exerted if these measures do not result in a healthy condition.

A full root definition also incorporating C, A, O, and E is then formulated. Care has to be taken here to ensure that A and O are fully considered. Checkland has noted that in 50 of the early SSM studies, 45 did not contain either A or O, that is, the root definition was only primary. Thinking had not penetrated outside the functional units, so that issue-based root definitions were effectively neglected. This may have been a legacy of the earlier (related) systems analysis and systems engineering approaches.

An example of a **root definition** of the sea rescue service is given as:

> a multiownership system (charities and Her Majesty's Government) that should exist and coordinate volunteers and professionals who attempt expedient rescue of endangered people at sea.

A CATWOE **analysis** is

C: Endangered people at sea
A: Volunteers and professionals (lifeboat, coast guard, helicopter services, and so on)
T: Endangered people into safe people
W: It is beneficial to society that such an organization should exist
O: Charities and government
E: The sea and changing weather conditions

If the root definition appears at least satisfactory, then construction and testing of a conceptual model may be appropriate ("accuracy" is not an issue as changing and/or refining of any stage is possible/necessary at any time by forward/backward thinking). The key point is to construct a model that represents that which is contained in the root definition and nowhere else. If this is not achievable then the root definition may need to be changed. When a conceptual model is realized, then "an account of the activities which the system *must do* in order *to be* the system named in the definition" has, to some level of satisfaction, been achieved (Checkland, 1981).

When constructing a conceptual model of the system, it is desirable to select elements as verbs. The minimum number that are necessary to define the root definition are structured in a logical order, reflecting sequences of activity in the system. A conceptual model of the sea-rescue service is given in Figure 6.7. In another study, a manufacturing company had its T defined as "a customer satisfaction transformation system." The following verbs were drawn out of a root definition that had been developed: to compete, to develop, to satisfy, to employ, to be aware, to supply, to produce. It was noted during logical ordering that these fell into two interactive activity cycles, one being a manfacturing cycle and the other effectively a research and development cycle. The initial conceptual model drawn up from these is shown in Figure 6.23 (see the case study in Section 6.7.4).

The conceptual model should then be compared to Checkland's formal system model. This is a generalized model of any human activity system from

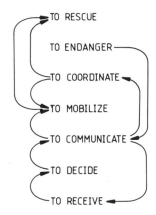

TO RESCUE

TO ENDANGER

TO COORDINATE

TO MOBILIZE

TO COMMUNICATE

TO DECIDE

TO RECEIVE

FIGURE 6.7. Example SSM conceptual model: The sea-rescue service.

the point of view that it is taking purposeful action in pursuit of a goal. This tests the basic adequacy of the conceptual model.

It is important that complex time-consuming model building at Stage 4 is avoided because during the comparison stage (Stage 5). It is possible/desirable to step back and make appropriate additions, or changes.

Stage 5. After the learning process has progressed to a point where at least one of the perceptions taken gives a strong indication that some real insight into the problematic situation has been gained, then comparison of the conceptual model with reality may properly be tackled.

The comparison of the Stage 2 output, a "neutral" perception of the problematic situation, and the systems thinking that culminates in conceptual models, is carried out with concerned participants in the problematic situation. The objective is to generate a debate about possible changes that might be introduced in order to alleviate the problematic condition.

A useful way of preparing for such a debate is to construct an agenda. Activities in the conceptual model may be compared to the real-world situation. Comments may be made on whether conceptual model activities are present in the real world, whether they are present but with differences; and comments on who carries out the activity and why, or why the activity is carried out in the way it is (any specific reasons) may be recorded. Alternatively, comments on comparisons between predicted conceptual model operation and real-world operation may also be usefully recorded. Finally, a decision can be made on the appropriateness of including the findings on a particular activity on the agenda for debate. Now refer to Table 6.1 for the suggested method of recording all these observations. The reader should note that changes to earlier phases may be required at this stage.

Stages 6 and 7. Culturally feasible and systemically desirable changes to structure, process, or attitude may emerge from the discussions. The first two are standard in that they represent aspects of an organization that are

TABLE 6.1

Example of an SSM Agenda Structure

Activity in conceptual model	Present in real-world situation?	Comments	Include on agenda?

relatively easy to manipulate. This may require the use of hard systems methodology and/or techniques.

Let us consider further the case of changes in attitude. This includes "such things as changes in influence, and changes in the expectations which people have of the behaviour appropriate to various roles, as well as changes in the readiness to rate certain kinds of behaviour, 'good' or 'bad' relative to others" (Checkland, 1981). This kind of activity is clearly one of ranking and is related to ideas of the ordinal scale of measurement. These can, however, be expected to occur progressively only by a sharing of experiences (the most powerful means of human bonding). Checkland has also noted that discussion of changes is best carried out with "concerned actors." This apparently obvious statement may ultimately hold the key as to whether the many hours of activity actually lead to some useful outcome or not.

6.4.3. Summary

In this section the widely known soft systems methodology of Checkland has been presented as a representative work from the softer thinkers. SSM was developed in order that problematic situations of purposeful human activity might be investigated. The need to develop such a methodology arose for a number of researchers who found a hard means–end approach inappropriate for messy problematic situations typical of organizational studies. An essential output of SSM is that, by taking a variety of perspectives, a set of relevant systems may be identified. This strongly contributes to the success of the methodology as a rigorous learning exercise.

The methodology moves between the real world and the ideal world of pure systems thinking. Thus, the process enables an analyst to compare the actual situation with a "desirable" one. This enables the analyst, in discussion with the problem owners, to discuss the discrepancies and look for culturally feasible and systematically desirable changes to the actual situation. If this is carried out successfully, then the dis-ease felt by actors in the problematic situation will, to some degree, have been reduced.

Readers are directed to Atkinson (1986) for a discussion on how, in application, SSM has been developed into a variety of closely related offshots.

The next section is concerned with how these and other methodological ideas can be taught and learned.

6.5.1. Introduction

In his excellent documentation on Checkland's methodology, Naughton (1977) stated that "we seem to know very little either about how to teach methodology or about how students pick up methodological ideas." Methodology in the natural sciences seems to be well understood from hypothesis to test selection, and then empirical results and confirmation or refutation of the hypothesis. This is the basis of much education from the young teenager upward. However, real-world problems are unlikely to be met until the late teens or after.

Naughton noted that systems scientists, like teachers of other newer disciplines, will have to be more explicit in their presentation of methodology. Methodology needs to be presented overtly to increase accessibility. To this end Naughton, seeking to identify appropriate teaching approaches for methodologies, stated that methodologies are essentially concerned with rules. He referred to Petrie (1968), who proposed that two distinct sets of rules exist, namely, the constitutive and strategic rules. Of these Naughton states that

> the constitutive rules (fundamental principles by which a methodology is governed) are those which must be obeyed to be said to be carrying out a particular kind of inquiry.... Strategic rules (plan of action or policy) on the other hand, are those which facilitate the process of inquiry: they help one select, from amongst the basic moves *permitted* by the constitutive rules, those which are "good" or "better" or "best."

It should be noted, however, that gray areas do exist between the two classes of rules. Nevertheless, a reasonable amount of uncoupling is achievable.

The importance of these rules, in the context of teaching and learning, is that unless the potential users understand the constitutive rules of a methodology they intend to use, they would not be able to claim that they have used that particular method of inquiry. Strategic rules, however, will emerge by effective use of those that are constitutive.

Naughton (1981) proposed a set of constitutive and strategic rules for Checkland's methodology. These are set out below and are followed by a similar analysis we carried out on the Jenkins methodology (representative of the hard systems approach). It is unfortunate that we were not able to consult the late G. W. Jenkins for confirmation of our rule partitioning, as was done extensively by Naughton with Checkland, and hope that our view would fairly represent that of Jenkins.

6.5.2. Rules of Checkland's Methodology

Constitutive rules (a closed set):

1. The complete methodology is a seven-stage process.
2. Each stage from 2 to 6 has a defined output.

3. Outputs of the various stages are as follows:
   Stage 2: Rich picture, relevant systems.
   Stage 3: Root definitions evaluated by CATWOE criteria.
   Stage 4: Conceptual model of the system described in the root definitions built by structuring verbs.
   Stage 5: Agenda of possible changes (derived from comparison of conceptual model with a rich picture expression of the problem situation).
   Stage 6: Changes judged with actors in the situation to be (systemically) desirable and culturally feasible.
4. Conceptual models must be checked against (a) root definitions from which they arise and (b) Checkland's "formal system" model.
5. A conceptual model must be derived logically from its associated root definition *and from nothing else.*
6. A conceptual model is not a description of a system to be engineered (although Stage 6 may yield a decision to engineer a system).

Strategic rules (an open set):

1. Preliminary expression is conducted by searching for elements of **structure** and **process** and examining the relation between the two.
2. Expression is not conducted as a search for systems in the problem situation.
3. Expression may be facilitated by asking "resource allocation" questions:
   (a) What resources are deployed in what operational process under what ... ?
   (b) How is this monitored and controlled?
4. Problem themes, that is, blunt statements of one or two sentences, are used to focus attention on interesting and/or problematic aspects of the problem situation.
5. Iterate, especially around the sequence: relevant system, root definition, conceptual model, relevant system.
6. Set up Stage 5 as a debate with important actors in the problem situation.

And so on.

6.5.3. Rules of Jenkins's Methodology

Constitutive rules (closed set):

1. The complete methodology is a four-phase process.
2. Phases 1 to 3 have defined outputs.
3. Outputs of Phase 1:
   (a) Flow block diagram of the system and its subsystems

(b) Flow block diagram of the system as part of a wider system

(c) Set of objectives of the wider system

(d) Set of ranked objectives of the system

(e) Explicitly defined economic criterion by which system efficiency will be assessed

4. Outputs of Phase 2:

(a) Accurate relevant forecasts (with estimated accuracy)

(b) Optimized quantitative model of the system with known reliability

(c) A control system design

5. Outputs of Phase 3: reports highlighting proposals for action.

6. Use flow diagrams to analyze and formulate objectives of the wider system.

7. Efficiency of the system will be defined in economic terms.

Strategic rule (open set):

1. A set of objectives of the system is collected by questioning, and appreciating the many viewpoints encountered.

2. Conflicting objectives of the system may be resolved by either (a) applying weighting factors on each objective, or (b) imposing constraints on certain variables.

3. Adopt an iterative and adaptive model-building methodology.

4. Discuss the final reports with senior managers before they are issued.

And so on.

6.5.4. Summary

A methodology can be defined by a set of rules. These may be constitutive or strategic; the former must be obeyed and the latter facilitate the process of inquiry. Understanding the constitutive rules of a methodology forms the sound basis by which a potential user may relatively easily access, use, and appreciate the inquiring system.

6.6. WHICH METHODOLOGY WHEN?

6.6.1. Introduction

Our next task is to investigate the feasibility of developing a system of systems methodologies for problematic situations. The aim of the investigation is twofold. First, we wish to identify a means by which methodologies and a range of problematic situations can be coupled. Second, if we have been successful in our first aim, then we hope to enhance the potential user's ability to adopt an appropriate methodological approach for problematic situations which they may have to deal with. The investigation will also introduce the reader to a wider range of methodological approaches.

Substantial efforts have been dedicated to the analysis, development, and refinement of methodologies for problematic situations. A number of these have been documented earlier. Other "reductionist" efforts have investigated specific methodologies (e.g., Rhodes, 1985; Woodburn, 1985). These are a useful aid to substantiating the theory (or not) and to making further adjustments. These knowledge bases for particular methodologies are clearly of great importance. Of equal importance is the consideration of a holistic approach to methodology, whereby various methodological approaches are linked or integrated into a system that reflects the wide variety of situational classes that may exist. The benefit of such an approach is to marry appropriate methodological approaches to types of problematic situations. If feasible, ideally this would give some real directions as to which methodology should be used.

Efforts in this area include "Towards a System of Systems Methodologies" (Jackson and Keys, 1984) and Klir's lengthy research program, which is documented in his recent book *Architecture of Systems Problem Solving* (Klir, 1985a). The former work is conceptually based in social systems theory, whereas the latter has a strong flavor of general systems theory and its associated mathematical foundations. These approaches then represent two very different viewpoints and are reviewed later. Other attempts at holistic classification may be found in Boulding (1956), Checkland (1971), and Jordan (1981).

6.6.2. Architecture of Systems Problem Solving

Architecture of Systems Problem Solving (Klir, 1985a) is essentially concerned with the development and use of a hierarchy of epistemological types of system. The hierarchy evolved by a process of distilling the notions of system from various disciplines, categorizing and then integrating them into a coherent whole. There are five basic levels over which the hierarchical framework is constructed. We will consider each of these in turn. Consult Figure 6.8 for a simplified overview.

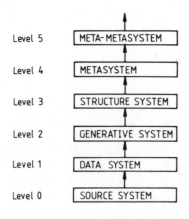

Level 5	META-METASYSTEM
Level 4	METASYSTEM
Level 3	STRUCTURE SYSTEM
Level 2	GENERATIVE SYSTEM
Level 1	DATA SYSTEM
Level 0	SOURCE SYSTEM

FIGURE 6.8. *Architecture of Systems Problem Solving*: "Simple" (Klir, 1985a; reproduced by permission of Pergamon Journals).

Level 0. A system is defined by a set of variables, a set of potential states (values) for each variable, and an operational means of describing the variables and states in terms of their associated real-world attributes. The set of variables is partitioned into two subsets, **basic** and **supporting** variables. The latter, in aggregated form, provides the medium (time, space, population of species) in which the dynamics of the basic variables occur. At this epistemological level a system is at least potentially a source of empirical data and so is termed a **source system**.

Level 1. A system as defined for Level 0, but additionally having a set of data for the basic variables within the support set. This is termed a **data system**.

Level 2. A system as defined for Level 1, but additionally having one overall support-invariant characterization (for example, time-invariance, space-invariance or population-invariance). Invariance means that, no matter how the support set may change, certain features of the "function" which defines the set of data are invariant to those changes. For example, if the parameters (structure) of a dynamic system (support set is time) are constant then the system is termed time-invariant. An overall process by which states of the basic variables are generated within the support set is the nature of these **generative systems**.

Level 3. Each system is defined in terms of a set of generative systems forming subsystems of an overall system. The systems may be coupled, or interact in some other way. They are termed **structure systems**. A good example of a structure system is given by block diagrams, which are introduced in Chapter 3.

Level 4. A system as defined at Level 3; however, at least one generative system displays a support-variant procedure. This is termed a **metasystem**.

Level 5 and Beyond. As with Level 4, except that the system exhibits a support-variant metaprocedure and is labeled **meta-metasystem**. Higher levels are said to exist when support invariance at a lower level is apparent.

Part of the structure of the complete epistemological framework, or the architecture, is shown in Figure 6.9. Klir (1985a) described this as follows:

> Symbols S, D, F denote source, data, and generative systems, respectively. When S is used as a prefix, it stands for structure systems. For example, SF denotes structure systems whose elements are generative systems and SD denotes structure systems whose elements are data systems. Symbol S^2 denotes structure systems whose elements are also structured systems. For example, S^2F denotes structure systems of structure systems whose elements are generative systems (M denotes metasystems).

Two important notes help to clarify the classes of situation that this hierarchy is designed to represent. First, systems on higher epistemological levels are distinguishable by the level of knowledge on the variables of the associated source system. Second, only at the metasystem level is it possible

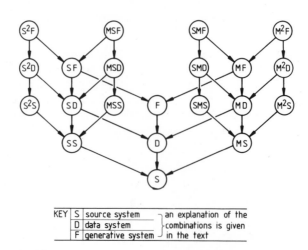

KEY | S | source system | an explanation of the
| D | data system | combinations is given
| F | generative system | in the text

FIGURE 6.9. *Architecture of Systems Problem Solving*: "Complete" (Klir, 1985a; reproduced by permission of Plenum Publishing).

to capture systems phenomena that involve change, such as adaption, self-organization, evolution, and so on.

Some observations on this hierarchy of epistemological types of systems are warranted. The five levels have been developed around a conceptual mathematical approach. In essence, the process passes from qualitative through to quantitative representations; however, the ability to progress is dependent on the nature (or measurability, see Chapter 4) of the situation. By their very nature, social and organizational situations are at best very difficult to measure, but more typically are generally unmeasurable beyond labeling or ranking. We can say that the level of knowledge on these variables is weak. In reality then, social and organizational situations could at best be classified in terms of sets of relevant source systems (relevant to various perspectives) as they may be defined by a set of relevant variables, a set of relevant potential states (usually in a very abstract sense), and by some relevant operational means of defining the variables in terms of (essentially abstract, but sometimes concrete) real-world attributes.

Here lies a fundamental problem. Many social situations display organic behavior in the way their differential growth and evolution (invariance) occur over time, a feature of complexity discussed in Chapter 2, and a feature that is also associated with Klir's metasystems and meta-metasystems. The level of knowledge on the variables, however, does not support the mathematical theory required by Klir's methodological approach to metasystems and beyond.

It appears that Klir's classification is distinct for well-structured situations and indistinct (and inappropriate) for messy unmeasurable (beyond the nominal scale) social situations where the vast majority of problematic issues exist. We therefore need to look for a more appropriate classification that reflects both hard and soft systems theory rather than only (hard) general systems theory.

6.6.3. Toward a System of Systems Methodologies

"Towards a System of Systems Methodologies" (Jackson and Keys, 1984) is concerned with the development of a grid into which system types may be classified. It then considers a range of methodologies and how these fit into the grid.

For the first dimension of the grid a distinction is made between situations that are perceived to be either simple or complex. This does pose some real difficulties, as recognized by Jackson and Keys, particularly in relation to perception. In Chapter 2 we discussed this issue in detail, showing how a situation may be simple in the eyes of one person and at the same time complex in the eyes of another person. Jackson and Keys, however, established some points of distinction, all of which interestingly are on the system (as opposed to the people) wing of the complexity argument proposed in Chapter 2 (as summarized in Figure 2.4). The two distinctions are a small number of elements as opposed to a large number, and few (or regular) interactions between the elements as opposed to many. These, it is suggested, help in the identification of easy and difficult problems. Four additional points are given that enhance the proposed dichotomy.

These four points were taken from Vemuri (1978). Three of these points, we feel, may be considerd as being based on the measurement–data–theory–law sequence (a theme frequently encountered in our text). Our interpretation of these is given as follows:

1. Complex situations are often partly or wholly unobservable, that is, measurements are noisy or unachievable (any attempt may destroy the integrity of the system).
2. It is difficult to establish laws from theory in complex situations as there are often not enough data, or the data are unreliable so that only probabilistic laws may be achievable.
3. Complex situations are often soft and incorporate value systems that are abundant, different, and extremely difficult to observe (measure).

The fourth point raised relates to the criterion that characterizes metasystems in Klir's problem-solving architecture, namely:

4. Complex situations are "open" and thus evolve over time.

Evolution involves a changing internal structure, often differential growth, and environmentally caused adaptation.

These points were consolidated using the work of Ackoff (1974) and his expressions "machine-age" and "systems-age." The concerns of these two different "ages" relate to Vemuri's four points on complexity as shown in Figure 6.10. In the systems-age, it is proposed, concern must be with systems, which are open, have purposeful parts, are partially observable, and for which reductionism is inappropriate (although we did note earlier that M'Pherson,

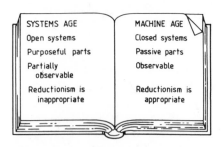

FIGURE 6.10. Machine age and systems age.

1974, suggested that a systems scientist should be both a holist and a reduction-ist). Applying Ackoff's terminology, mechanical problem contexts and systemic problem contexts were adopted by the authors to represent the enhanced simple–complex dimension.

The second dimension of the grid reflects the nature of the decision makers (which is in fact of the people wing of complexity as presented in Chapter 2), in particular considering the degree of consensus among them. If total agree-ment on a common set of goals for the system is achieved, and adhered to during decision making, then the set of decision makers is labeled unitary. If the set is not unitary then it is labeled pluralist.

Therefore, the problem context plane consists of mechanical-unitary, systemic-unitary, mechanical-pluralist, and systemic-pluralist sets (see Table 6.2 and, in due course, compare to Figure 10.1).

To assess the usefulness of the plane-grid it is necessary to consider how well a range of methodologies "fits" in and how meaningful the pigeonholing is to us, both theoretically and in application. To achieve this satisfactorily a representative sample of methodologies (for instance, those presented in this chapter) needs to be considered systematically. This task was duly undertaken in the second part of Jackson and Keys's paper, which is appraised later.

Classical operations research was coupled to mechanical-unitary problem contexts, as, it was stated, this approach can be used only when general agreement about the goals to be achieved and the objectives of the system are attainable. In these cases, deterministic and/or stochastic quantitative model-ing approaches may be adopted. Systems analysis and systems engineering

TABLE 6.2

Problem Context Grid Plane

$M-U$	$S-U$	Unitary		Group consensus
$M-P$	$S-P$	Pluralist		
Mechanical	Systemic			
System complexity				

(the commonalities and differences between these and operations research have been discussed under hard systems methodologies) were also categorized as suitable for mechanical-unitary contexts.

Acceptance of these last two classifications does depend on whether we accept that systems engineers/analysts are dependent upon achieving compromise given multiple (and often conflicting) objectives. The evidence is that they do strongly favor consensus. Approaches that are adopted include individual and group utility functions (see, for example, Keeney and Raiffa, 1976), and Interpretive Structural Modeling, particularly of objectives generated by groups (see, for example, Warfield, 1976). These technique-methodologies certainly show the systems engineer/analyst's affinity for, and convergence toward, consensus (albeit "artificial").

Thus, the reasoning supporting the classification appears to be relatively soundly based. However, considering Figure 6.10, the systems engineer would certainly perceive that he was working in the systems-age in that the systems dealt with are filled with people, are open, have purposeful parts, are partially observable, and cannot be tackled with anything other than a holistic approach.

These last comments also hold with respect to systems analysis. If this were not so then Atthill's Step 4.2 (see under "Systems Analysis"), where the best all-around decision should incorporate contemporary issues such as quality of human working conditions, would certainly not be present.

So, many would find it difficult to see systems engineering/analysis as anything other than of the systems-age. Operations research is nearer to the mechanical-age; however, the clarity required by the grid-plane is too precise and suggests that the boundary is a gray area. To find a mechanical-unitary methodolgy it would be necessary to consider such activities as mechanical engineering.

Cybernetics was considered as a potential means through which systemic-unitary problem contexts could be approached. Stafford Beer's work (considered in detail in Chapter 5) considers the application of a well-tried and tested control system to organizations, namely, the neurocybernetic system of the human body. This cybernetic approach was considered by Jackson and Keys. They concluded that Beer's work was indeed suited to systemic contexts and that its successful use depended on there being full agreement about the goals of the system (unitary). Essentially, the VSM can be used as a diagnostic tool to check for the existence and proper performance of five functions (policy, intelligence, operational control, coordination, and implementation) and the communication channels in any system. As pointed out, however, the Chilean experience (discussed in Chapter 5) highlighted some difficulties of adopting this cybernetic approach. These emerged as a difficulty in attaining "intrinsic control" and "intrinsic motivation." Without these, cybernetic diagnosis would fail. Nevertheless, albeit at a theoretical level, the cybernetic approach exists as systemic-unitary.

Mechanical-pluralist as a single classification appears to be contradictory at first sight. If a system has all the features of the mechanical-age (refer again to Figure 6.10), then it would seem unlikely that consensus on the system's objectives would be difficult to attain and, therefore, a unitary outcome would be expected. Pluralism, then, will have to exist outside the system, that is, in the goals to be served by the system.

For a mechanical-pluralist example, Jackson and Keys referred to the SAST (strategic assumption surfacing and testing) methodology (Mason and Mitroff, 1981; Mitroff and Emshoff, 1979), which is a rigorous application of the approach of Churchman (1979) designed to bring about a synthesis among decision makers so that action can be taken. This has a strong flavor of the consensus-seeking technique-methodologies used by the hard systems school. The approach is claimed by the developers to be useful in systemic problem situations. Jackson and Keys quite rightly accuse the SAST approach of ignoring systemic characteristics, focusing on resolving pluralist issues; however, it is not strictly legitimate to see SAST as primarily an aid to mechanical-pluralist contexts. If SAST does propose that all difficulties stem from pluralism, and the grid-plane is a good one, then SAST has to be criticized for ignoring the mechanical-systemic dimension and cannot, in any circumstances, be assumed to have relevance to one part of that dimension.

So far, using our interpretation, we have for the systemic-unitary problem contexts: systems analysis, systems engineering, and cybernetics. Traditional operations research may be on the boundary with mechanical-unitary. It has also been suggested that some designers (mechanical engineers, for example) would comfortably slot into the mechanical-unitary approach. SAST is unclassified.

Finally, Ackoff and Checkland and the systemic-pluralist problem contexts were considered. Ackoff (1981) discussed "interactive planning" with its three operating principles of participation, continuity, and holism. These are reflected in the five phases of the planning process: formulating the mess, ends planning, means planning, resource planning, and implementation and control. Appropriate use allows full consideration of factors relating to, and between, subsystems, the system itself, and the wider system. An idealized future is "created" or designed into which the current problems "dissolve," and further problems emerge, requiring a continuous planning approach. Systemicity and pluralism are therefore apparent. In Checkland's methodology, relevant viewpoints are encouraged and thus so is pluralism. Equally, the CATWOE mnemonic, among other aspects of the methodology, points to systemicity in the approach.

To the earlier summary, then, drawing upon Jackson and Keys's reasoning, we could categorize the methodologies of Ackoff and Checkland as systemic-pluralist. A fundamental problem, however, does arise here. Throughout their paper, Jackson and Keys discuss the grid-plane as relating to problem contexts. This assumes that situations can be structured to formulate the problem so that it may be related to a problem context. The reasoning of Checkland, one of the authors in question, would seem to reject this idea, suggesting that only problematic situations arise in which a sense of dis-ease is experienced. Using Checkland's reasoning, there can be no assumed structure to the problematic situation. To the soft systems thinker, then, such a grid-plane (in its current form) would have little, if any, value.

Ignoring (temporarily) the difficulties that have been outlined earlier, it is possible to consider the potential practical benefits and difficulties of this system of systems methodologies from the point of view of a hard systems thinker. These include the following points:

1. The problem manager would ideally seek out an appropriate methodology rather than adopting their favorite problem-management approach.
2. This poses some real difficulties by confronting an analyst with the very difficult task of identifying problem contexts correctly in the real world. Perception also will come into play.
3. Some problem contexts will not fit exactly into any one of the four categories. Also, as identified above, some debate is bound to occur as to the actual pigeonholing of methodologies.
4. Some reference points are given that may prove valuable if a problem management task is not perceived to be progressing successfully.

This intriguing work, alongside the less accessible volume of Klir, is suggestive and directive in the way we might think about complementary holistic aspects of methodology. It is continually being built upon both theoretically and through practical usage. An updated version of the grid of problem contexts and appropriate methodology can be found in Jackson (1987). Investigating the idea of a system of systems methodologies has, however, raised some very deep-rooted problems. These are essentially of a philosophical nature and are expanded upon later and in Chapter 10.

6.6.4. Toward a Problem Management Tool Kit for Pragmatists

A useful way of thinking about the appropriateness of methodology is via the concepts of measurement. We have considered the scales of measurement (see Chapter 4) and have found that if a situation is observable and measurable on a ratio scale, theory is likely to become law and hence a situation can be represented with quantitative models. These may be used for quantitative predictions and explanation and hence optimization. (Chapter 9 documents this idea and describes a variety of suitable modeling methodologies.)

One controversy about problematic situations, however, centers around a similar use of numbers for softer situations. Then, observability becomes partial, and the scale of measurement weaker. Measurement becomes problematic. In some cases, without extreme care, measurement may well change situational behavior. The outcome of the Hawthorne studies discussed in Chapter 5 is a classic example of this. There are then some who vehemently oppose the use of numbers for soft situations, accepting only that nominal measurement is achievable.

So, the hard systems approach, which attempts to apply numbers to soft situations, has come under severe attack. However, to optimize, select the best, or chase objectives (deemed as wholly inappropriate by the soft school) does require some comparative method such as system worth (based on normalized utility functions, say). The hard school say that this is the best way to crack a "hard nut," whereas the soft school look for qualitative discrepancies and then set about reducing them.

The case is that both hard and soft systems people believe that their approaches are better suited to the same sort of problematic situations. Clearly, this makes it impossible to design a universally accepted grid-plane such as Jackson and Keys's because there would be no common agreement on what is the correct methodological approach for a given problematic situation.

One empirical solution to the conflict that could be pursued is to look at the validity of each methodological approach. In response, the hard school might again go for validation by numbers that "show" improvements, whereas the soft school would say that (at best) if the dis-ease in a problematic situation has been reduced then the methodology has been effective. Comparative analysis of methodological success would encounter the very same difficulty that it was trying to resolve.

The fact is that the difficulty is deep-rooted. It is a philosophical difference (philosophical in the sense of the search for truth and knowledge of reality). This case can be considered in the light of Burrell and Morgan (1979). They discuss the relationship between ontology, epistemology, methodology, and consequent views of the nature of man. In their analysis, Burrell and Morgan pave the way for philosophical comparisons. Using their approach, Checkland (1981) has recognized the philosophical differences between the approach that he has adopted and that of the hard school. The essence of the difference is that the hard school take an outside objective view of the social world, which, it is believed, exists before, during, and after life. The soft view of Checkland and others is a subjective inside view of the social world, which takes the standpoint that we cannot be confident in the existence of the social world in any other way than via mental constructs. For an expanded discussion on this and other philosophical matters the reader should consider Jackson (1987) and consult Chapter 10 of this volume. Enough has been said, however, to cast real doubt on the universally accepted use of any system of systems methodologies in practice.

For some, there are grounds for optimism if a pragmatic approach is adopted. Complementarity between the hard and soft approaches may be found. A diagram drawn by John Hamwee in 1986 (see Figure 6.11) suggests

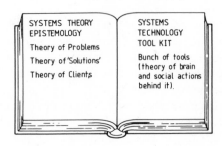

FIGURE 6.11. Systems theory, systems technology (Hamwee, 1986).

an alternative way forward. Here we see two views of systems science. One is systems science as a coherent theory about how to work with people to manage problems. Such a theory would explain what kinds of problem were commendable to what kinds of "solution" with what kinds of client. It would tell you how to work when asked to do a systems study, which amounts to an epistemology. In this chapter, however, we have identified real difficulties in achieving such a general theory. On the other hand, John Hamwee states that there is the view that "systems" is a craft. The practitioners have a bunch of tools that they use, more or less by trial and error, until one works. They have no theory of which would work when or why. Of course, behind the efficacy of the practitioner and the nature of the tools they use, there *is* a theory that can be inferred (about how people relate to each other and how their brains work), but the practitioners do not try to make it coherent or rigorous. This is a bit like the cathedral builders of old. They could do it, but they had no idea why the thing stood up, why a beam fixed one way cracked, but fixed another way did not. They just knew which way to do it. Following this analogy, maybe the left-hand side of Figure 6.11 is systems theory and the right-hand side is a kind of systems technology (Hamwee, 1986).

So a pragmatic approach could be adopted by thinking of a single container in which all methodologies are stored: a tool bag containing a tool kit. Brainstorming, Interpretive Structural Modeling (hierarchy structuring), negative role-playing (playing a role opposite to your actual perspective), and so on could be thrown into this tool bag. Taking some sample tools from the kit, we can consider what their users might say about them as "stand alones":

1. Rich pictures are an extremely effective way of summarizing and aiding understanding of messy situations, particularly useful for thought clarification in everyday life.
2. A utility function is an interesting approach that captures a slice-in-time unitary view of an individual's or group's utility for any given "thing."
3. Root definitions are a concise way of capturing the very essence of a situation from particular perspectives.
4. Interpretive Structural Modeling is a useful way of seeking a unitary position from a pluralist one and as an aid to strategic objective setting.

We could continue exhaustively, but the point is that a mix of tools, as is frequently said, offers a great diversity of ways to deal with problems and problematic situations inside or outside their respective methodological parent.

A stagewise approach would be required; however, this would only need to be in the form of general guidelines. No unidimensional methodological trajectory would have to be adhered to; rather, there is a space in which each individual may plot their own trajectory as the task progresses. The trajectory may well be highly looped, as with the "never-ending" learning cycle of SSM. Each trajectory would reflect current perceptions on the nature of a problem or problematic situation. There would be no one right constitutive trajectory for any problem or problematic situation, although in certain cases it might be appropriate to adopt a methodological constitution (available in the tool bag). For example, the view could be taken that the constitution offered by Checkland may be appropriate if an in-depth learning procedure is required, or, that of Atthill (the constitution is not specified in this book) if evaluation of the economic worth of alternative radar facilities to a military organization, say, is required.

In short, the pragmatist would phase or switch between methodological approaches. The pragmatist would follow a Phased Methodological Approach (PMA) to which only general principles could be attached (unpublished notes, R. L. Flood and K. Ellis).

Systems researchers could continue to contribute to this tool kit. For instance, Jackson (1985) rightly identified the inability of contemporary methodological approaches to deal with political-coercive elements, which abound in organizations, and suggests that some help may be found in the work of Habermas (1971, for example). If this work is fruitful then it too might be added to the tool kit.

There are also some implications of this pragmatic approach from a learning and teaching point of view. Taking the "student" through the soft and hard methodologies, and their constitutive and strategic rules, would remain a necessary first step in the learning and teaching process. Learning the finer tricks of the trade, however, would not only require gaining experience by regular use of the kit (thus ensuring that effective tools are selected for each job), but would also require that the student possesses a *creative flair* and remains open-minded. This approach is almost the antithesis of that proposed by Jackson and Keys, but does reflect the "mood" of many consultants we have encountered outside the academic world. This does highlight a gap between the world of the academic and that of business that, at least potentially, is bridgeable.

This pragmatic approach, however, also has its critics. One strong argument that raises some penetrating questions on this heuristic way of tackling problematic situations asks us to consider the social consequences of trial and error, and the critics say that we cannot afford to get things wrong in this manner.

6.6.5. Summary

Given a set of methodologies, the question "which methodology should be used when?" will inevitably arise. A holistic approach to methodologies, considering either their linkage or integration, has therefore been considered. The aim of this has been to try to identify a way of finding an appropriate methodological approach to any problem context or problematic situation. A number of approaches have been considered. However, despite the authors' good intentions, we are not able to find universal acceptance with either of the approaches reviewed. Our reasoning has identified philosophical differences as the cause of this failure, such that different groups might argue that their approach is the most appropriate to some given problem or problematic situation. This philosophical gap is unbridgeable.

Rather than accept total defeat on this matter, we considered a pragmatic approach and some of the possibilities and consequences of adopting the idea of a systems problem management tool kit. This, however, requires an appropriate learning background and, as with any art, an appropriate creative flair. The approach in no way overcomes the philosophical issues, however, which are effectively ignored. What is also apparent is that the academic and business worlds are a long way apart, the former concentrating their efforts in developing and testing theory, which, in many cases, is not penetrating the rather more pragmatic world of business.

To complete this chapter we will now take a brief look at three studies. Two of these were tackled by the Department of Systems Science at the City University in London, and the third is based on a "real-world problem game."

6.7. THREE CASE STUDIES

6.7.1. Introduction

The aim of presenting case studies is to introduce two "new" methodologies and to give some insight into how methodologies may be operationalized in real-world situations. We do not suggest that the methodologies adopted are right or wrong for the given situations, although the view of the consultants is mostly self-evident.

For further examples on this theme the reader is referred to Checkland (1981) and Wilson (1984). The former, and to a large extent the latter, consider soft systems methodology only. For an alternative perspective, the excellent work of Eden *et al.* (1983) is recommended.

6.7.2. Case Study 1

Introduction

The work presented in this case study is based on that carried out by our colleague Keith Ellis.

The situation under study is an organization engaged in the design and manufacture of electronic control utilities. The problem situation is outlined as follows.

The initial manifestation in the late 1970s came in the form of falling turnover and profits. The company had grown by developing its design and production technologies, enhancing available technology rather than utilizing research and development. In this context the company was a market follower. After some 10–12 years of growth, turnover started falling dramatically with a consequent adverse affect on pretax profits. This occurred while demand for their type of product remained high. Departmental heads attached the blame to domains of authority beyond their own, and, consequently, interdepartmental squabbles broke out. The company directors were unable to define their problems; that is, a consensus view on the problem situation was not achieved. Incredibly, a consensus view of solution via automation had been agreed upon by the board.

The Problem: Structured and Solvable or Messy and Maintainable

Taking the viewpoint of the board, the consultancy would have been a problem of design, selection, and implementation (a systems analysis/engineering approach). This implies a structured and solvable problem, which was contradicted by their inability to define the problem situation.

It was necessary to adopt an approach whereby the directors understood they were faced with a problem situation that contained "unstructured problems, ones in which designation of objectives is itself problematic" (Checkland, 1981). It was explained that automation could not be considered a panacea, although this did not preclude its eventual use.

The essence of this is that a structured and solvable problem might be identified; however, the complexity of the situation posed a messy and somewhat nebulous front. Ascertaining whether an underlying structure could be identified required a method of penetrating that front.

At this stage it was not clear whether the problem could be structured and solved, or whether the results of some ineffective relationships would be identified that would require treatment on a maintenance basis.

This has a pleasing medical analogy. In some cases an illness can clearly be identified and, from a range of alternatives, primary treatment (directed at the root cause) may be exercised as a method of cure. In difficult cases the root cause may not be apparent, so that secondary treatment is exercised as a means of maintaining an equilibrium in the symptoms, allowing the body as a whole to stabilize.

Penetrating the Problem

The first task was to assess how much structure was attainable from the mess. To facilitate this, an interactive participative approach to "intelligence gathering" with the problem owners was chosen; this involved using Nominal Group Technique (NGT) (Delbecq *et al.*, 1975) and Interpretive Structural Modeling (ISM) (Warfield, 1976). During the NGT session, the nominal question which was, What factors are contributing to reduced turnover and profits? produced a list of ranked problem elements (see Table 6.3).

Table 6.3 was assumed to contain the core of a problem. Problem elements were structured using ISM adopting the contextual relationship "strongly contributes to." During further discussions, the problem owners were helped to identify areas of relevant problem structures (see Figure 6.12). The problem element numbers in the figure relate to those in Table 6.3. The initial relevant

TABLE 6.3
Case Study 1: Ranked Problem Elements

Rank	Idea number	Problem element
1	18	Low level of automation in engineering and production.
2	4	Poor product quality, especially in PCBs.
3	1	High product variant content in product mix.
3	22	Losing customers.
5	11	Long delay between acceptance of customer specification and delivery.
6	20	Increasing inventory and work in progress.
7	19	Decreasing production capacity.
7	21	Late delivery to customers.
9	10	No engineering involvement in customer specification negotiations.
10	17	Large number of PCB modifications required to produce product variants.
11	16	Low level of new product development.
12	15	Engineering concentration on design of product variants.
12	6	Increasing warranty costs.
14	24	Poor response to technological change.
15	8	Less competitive products.
15	9	No production involvement in new/variant product development.

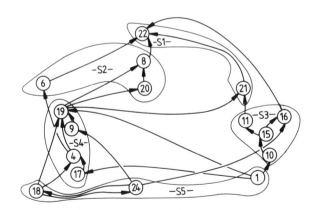

KEY

S1-S5	relevant problem structures
ⓝ	problem element numbers
→	'strongly contributes to'

FIGURE 6.12. Case Study 1: Relevant problem structures.

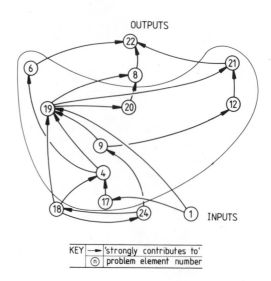

FIGURE 6.13. Case Study 1: Hybrid version of relevant problem structures.

problem structures were defined as follows: S1 output system, S2 cost system, S3 engineering system, S4 production system, and S5 input system. Further assisted discussion gave rise to just two relevant problem structures. These related to functional units of the company; however, a hybrid version was developed as a response to unease with the (unnatural) division of the problem elements into functional units (see Figure 6.13).

This gave a clear structure to the problem elements, and highlighted at which place they could most effectively be tackled. The wider implications of any proposed course of action, however, also required assessment.

Defining the Ideal System

Having identified the problem, the consultancy then moved on to consider an ideal system. This involved:

1. Identifying the desired behavior of the organization
2. Identifying the structure and processes for system representation
3. Identifying the boundary of that system
4. Defining a wider system and an environment

The function of the hybrid engineering/production model was Printed Wired Board (PWB) design and Printed Circuit Board (PCB) assembly. The problem owners helped to identify the structure and processes of this function by answering the lead question which was, What are the required steps to design and fabricate a PWB, and then to assemble the circuit components to the PWB to produce a PCB of acceptable quality? The aim was to generate a set of general verbs that described the basis of what the structure and processes should be. The verbs were expanded to sentences and then structured as shown

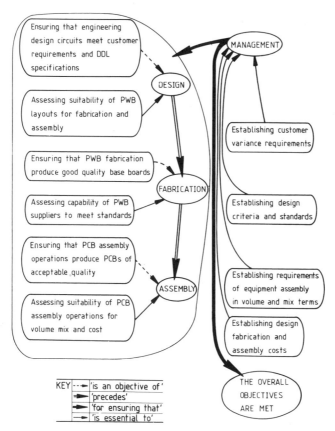

FIGURE 6.14. Case Study 1: Verbs and sentences describing system structure and process.

in Figure 6.14. This produced the basis by which a conceptual model was developed.

Solution Designs

From here on it was possible for the board to compare the ideal system to the problem structure, and consider the following nominal question, aimed at generating "solution" designs: Recognizing the failure of the system, what should be included in an action program to resolve the problem? An agreed "solution" structure was developed, and this is shown in Figure 6.15. Further analysis with the board revealed that two solution elements should be eliminated as they belonged to a higher control level. These were Element 2 and Element 16, which were a matter of engineering management policy.

After examination of the solution structure, four designs emerged as shown in Figure 6.16 (the solution element numbers relate to those in Figure 6.15). The first alternative was then split into manual and computer-controlled automatic component insertion (CCACI). The four resulting designs were as

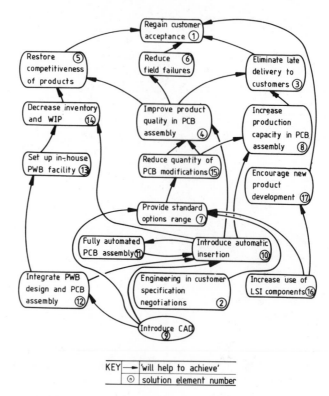

FIGURE 6.15. Case Study 1: "Solution" structure.

follows:

Design 1: Introduce CAD (computer-aided design) and automatic component insertion.
Design 2: Introduce CAD and fully automatic PCB assembly.
Design 3: Introduce CAD and integrate PWB design and PCB assembly.
Design 4: Introduce CAD and integrate PWB design and PCB assembly plus set up in-house PWB factory.

Solution Choice

The reduction in turnover and profit, coupled with the need to plan for the future, presented the directors with a dilemma that served to compound the complexity of the situation. Clearly, the chosen solution design would need to address the immediate aspects of the situation, while not losing sight of the longer term needs.

The directors were, however, no longer confronted by a soft, fuzzy unstructured mess. They were now involved in tangible choices that could be quantified so that objectives could be set. Each solution design could be analyzed for equipment requirements, capital costs, time scales, and benefits/disbenefits. To this end, a set of criteria was established by which the solution designs

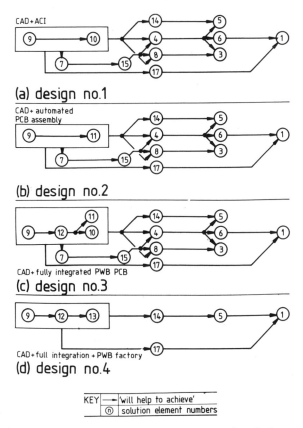

(a) design no.1

(b) design no.2

(c) design no.3

(d) design no.4

| KEY | → | 'will help to achieve' |
| | ⓝ | solution element numbers |

FIGURE 6.16. Case Study 1: Four emerging designs.

could be assessed. Taking into account all relevant factors such as net present value, inflation rate, and so on, the expected monetary values (EMVs) relative to the "worst" (most expensive) case (Design 5, not included in the discussion) were calculated as shown in Table 6.4. A final decision had to be made between Design 1 and Design 2. Even though Design 1 had the best EMV, the directors felt that the design lacked flexibility and would not lend itself to upgrading (longer-term objectives). They were also concerned that the results in terms of quality, improved delivery, and inventory cost reduction might not be sufficient to achieve the superordinate objective of regaining customers' acceptance. Design 2 was therefore selected.

TABLE 6.4
Case Study 1: Comparing EMVs of Four Solution Designs

Design	1	2	3	4
Compared to option (5) (£1,000s)	+4418	+4158	+3447	+2251

Implementation

The directors had recognized the need for change and had agreed on what that change should be. They, as "problem owners" felt they had become "problem solvers." The directors were, however, confronted by the problem of how to implement the agreed changes. Making changes could alter the situation. The originally perceived problems might be eliminated, but new problems could emerge. It was also likely that implementing changes might be problematic in itself (Checkland, 1981). These points proved to be significant in this exercise, as will be discussed later.

The directors were also made aware that responsibility for "who would do what and when" should be arranged, and that translation of the previous activities into a set of assignments and schedules was necessary (Ackoff, 1981). This was successfully achieved.

As described by Besant (1982), the implementation process involved five basic stages: (1) setting objectives, (2) feasibility study, (3) project planning, (4) commissioning, and (5) evaluation.

Stages 1 and 2 had already been achieved. Project planning was restricted by the lack of knowledge of PERT approaches by members of the company; however, a simple implementation plan was achieved. Consultants were then put into a "watching brief." It had unfortunately been decided not to involve consultants in any significant manner during implementation.

Appraisal and Learning

At a later time, the directors requested a renewal of the consultancy in order to review the implementation. Many points arose and the five most pertinent are described below:

1. The implementation activity had been scheduled to be completed at a cost of £k526. The actual cost was £k631.

2. The directors, during the implementation phase, had not taken into account the potential for adverse reaction by employees to the changes, and when hostility and fear had been detected the warning was ignored. They had failed to involve those who would be directly affected by the change. This caused delay and added costs.

3. The concept of a Standard Options Package was available to the Sales Department seven weeks after the start of the implementation activity. The design work, however, was not completed until some three months after the installation of the CAD system. This resulted in the CCACI equipment standing idle, although it was not subsequently made fully operational owing to a dispute with the PCB assembly operators (see point 2).

4. Reject levels for PCBs assembled using CCACI were expected to be below 5%. However, it would be a considerable time before a 5% average was achieved (see point 3).

5. Engineering and Sales had agreed on a progressive reduction in the elapsed time between acceptance of customer specification and the start of design work. The target of six weeks had been achieved. Engineering were

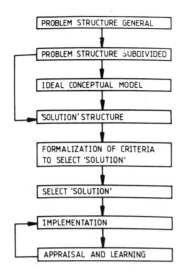

FIGURE 6.17. Case Study 1: Methodological trajectory.

now involved in customer specification. Negotiations and the use of LSI microcircuits would simplify design consideration, lateral integration, and communication.

Although there had been some serious misjudgements during the implementation phase, the consensus of the board was that they had made the right decision. They were encouraged by the fact that PCBs assembled using CCACI equipment were showing significant improvements in quality with substantially reduced assembly times. The directors were of the opinion that the most significant achievement was the improvement in their working relationships. It was recognized that the implementation of the chosen solution design had resulted in additional problems to be resolved (work force being disgruntled), as well as the need to solve those initial problem elements not yet fully dealt with.

Progress had been made and was reflected in the optimism, or reduction in the dis-ease, of the board. A summary of the actual methodological trajectory that was adopted is shown in Figure 6.17.

6.7.3. Case Study 2

Introduction

The work presented in this case study is based on that of Steven Edmunton.

The situation under study is a large and historically successful manufacturer of predominantly data processing equipment. The domain of interest is an engineering department within Ferranti Computers Ltd. and the particular concern was the effectiveness and efficiency of the information management system.

The problem situation was perceived to have arisen in the aftermath of the oil price rises in the 1970s, which had some significant impact on UK Ltd. (that is, UK as a manufacturing unit). This manifested itself in high unemployment, a decline in traditional manufacturing industries and (consequently) the overall manufacturing output, and loss to foreign competition. In addition to this background, there were expectations that much of the future economic activity and international trade would be in the area of robotics, microelectronics, and information technology. Members of the company perceived that a significant portion of British industry had become leaner and fitter, and capable of taking on foreign competitors in both the domestic and export markets. They were concerned as to whether they too had achieved leanness and fitness, particularly in the light of issues such as their decline in overseas contracts, loss of contracts to competitors, the move away from cost plus contracts to fixed price contracts, and responses to changing government attitudes.

One vital area that contributes substantially to the efficient and effective running of an organization, such as that being considered here, is its information management system (IMS). This aspect of the company provided one problematic area where a pilot investigation was commissioned. The question to be answered was whether the IMS required improvement. The task was clearly defined and the consultants were asked to work specifically to this brief.

The Problem under Consideration

In the early stages of the investigation informed discussions were held in order to gauge the extent of the perceived problem. Thought was then given as to how to investigate the problem. Some early inquiries were made using a questionnaire approach on managers in the system. However, this pilot study yielded a poor response and the instrument of measurement tended to prestructure the answers and omit some important details (a sort of censorship). Because it was realized that this approach was neither systemic nor systematic, time was taken to develop a prototype methodological approach (with the knowledge that this might evolve during the course of the study). The methodology that was drawn up is shown in Figure 6.18. It can be seen that Stages 1–3 constitute the main learning process, and it is this that we shall concentrate on. A few notes on the methodology are given below in order to enhance the reader's understanding of our report on the inquiry.

The framework features two models of information:

1. Model 1 examines each department's information requirements to perform its task or service. This model is based on control theory and considers the department's task or service as a transformation process, initiated by "source" information, acted upon by "base" and "control" information, and producing "output" information (see Figure 6.19 and note the resemblance to Figure 3.18). These information types are defined below.

SOURCE INFORMATION.   That which constitutes a starting point for subsequent development or transformation of that information into another form.

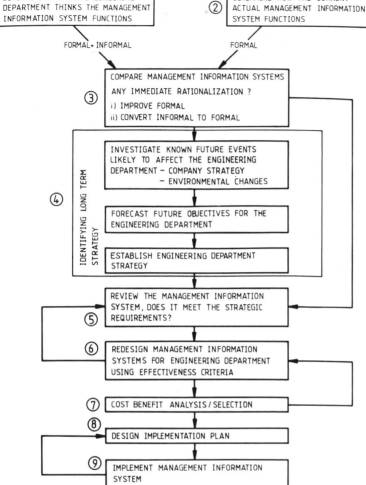

FIGURE 6.18.   Case Study 2: Methodological trajectory.

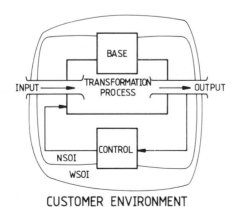

FIGURE 6.19.   Case Study 2: Basis of model information flows.

CONTROL INFORMATION.   That which exercises a restraining or directing influence over the task/service (giving direction, regulation, and coordination).

BASE INFORMATION.   That which provides the background or reference knowledge necessary in order to carry out the task/service.

OUTPUT INFORMATION.   The transformed source, base, and/or control information that leads to an output.

2. Model 2 examines each department's role and position within the overall organization. This model considers "the principal decision-making areas" of a manufacturing organization (these are principally ones of strategy, business, manufacturing, and design), to determine in which area each department predominantly resides.

The Learning Phase

These are Stages 1–3 of the methodology. During Stage 1, the managers of a department or subdepartment of the engineering department were asked to draw their picture (literally) of the direct system's processes within a structured (functional) map of the organization (developed by the consultants from the organizational family tree), as they perceived it, for each model of information. These perceived system pictures must, by definition, contain both formal and informal information flows.

During Stage 2, heads of each section within the engineering department were asked to supply sample copies of all formal means of communication used to convey information both internally and externally. Interviews were held in which each manager was asked questions on each document that was supplied. From this information the consultants were able to draw the *actual* systems map of each department and subdepartment, for each model of information. These actual system pictures must, by definition, contain only the formal information flows. Data relating to the quality, efficiency, and effectiveness of each document was held on a data base. A sample of one department with perceived information flows is given in Figure 6.20.

During Stage 3, the actual and perceived system pictures were compared using matrix techniques, that is, technique interpretation rather than human interpretation. A matrix structure was chosen as a vehicle for storing, coordinating, and manipulating data for two reasons: the ease of manipulating data and the ease of computerization. Manipulation was performed using a standard spreadsheet package; however, computerization is a possibility for such activities.

Analysis of the matrices and data base revealed such information as the percentage of yearly time spent filling in and handling each category or type of document. Short-term observations were categorized as follows: (1) that there was duplication, (2) that there were routine problems, and (3) that there was redundancy. Thus, recommendations for elimination of nonproductive

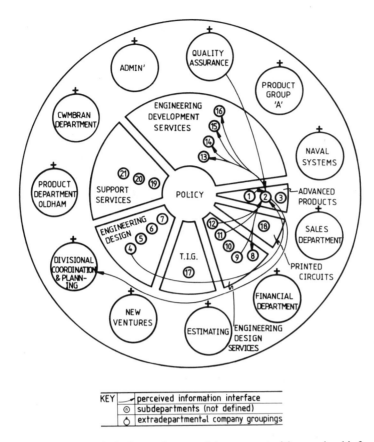

KEY

⌐	perceived information interface
⊙	subdepartments (not defined)
○	extradepartmental company groupings

FIGURE 6.20. Case Study 2: Example map of department with perceived information flows.

and counterproductive documents were made, offering some real short-term benefits.

Furthermore, the volume of information traffic between the subdepartments of the engineering department and the rest of the division, and in particular the satellite sites, was drawn together. This information, alongside the available information from Model 1 results, provided the basis by which a data networking system for the company, expansion of the company telephone system, and the movement or marriage of departments onto new sites could be designed. In essence, the longer-term benefits were of the form:

1. Identification of features of the system that were worth retaining
2. Identification of features of the system that required scrapping
3. Identification of new features that would enhance the overall efficiency and effectiveness of the department

Thanks are extended to Ferranti Computers Ltd. for allowing us to document parts of this case study.

6.7.4. Case Study 3

Introduction

The work reported in this case study is based on the outcome of one group's efforts in a "problem management game." The approach adopted is that of the soft system methodology (see Figure 6.4) so that the constitution described in Section 6.5.2 was adhered to.

The system under study is an organization with three subsidiaries. The first subsidiary is concerned with manufacturing a variety of grades of steel from raw material shipped in from abroad. These are then transported to the second subsidiary, where the steel is shaped and cut for various end uses. Finally, there is a storage subsidiary consisting of a number of warehouses on one site. The problem emerged when the head of the subsidiary dealing with stocks requested an expansion to the existing warehouse, this being his solution to counteracting a small drop in sales during a period of rising demand for his product. The managing director requested a group of consultants to consider whether he should invest what amounted to quite a sizable sum of money in warehouse expansion.

The Methodology in Action

Following the soft systems methodology, a rich picture was drawn up to represent the problem situation. This is shown in Figure 6.21. Note how the whole situation has been considered, rather than merely the warehouse. From the rich picture the following relevant systems were drawn out:

1. A customer satisfaction system
2. An ore transformation system
3. A manufacturing system
4. A transportation system
5. An employment system

Ws of the purposeful activities were identified, being either primary task (functional and typically defined as departments in the organization) or issue-based factors (such as balancing demands on resources and a number of company policies).

In anticipation of drawing up appropriate root definitions of the system, a number of possible transformations were considered (each transformation being a T in a potential CATWOE definition). Three of these are given below:

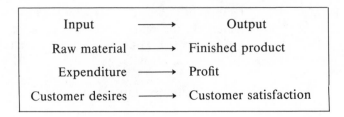

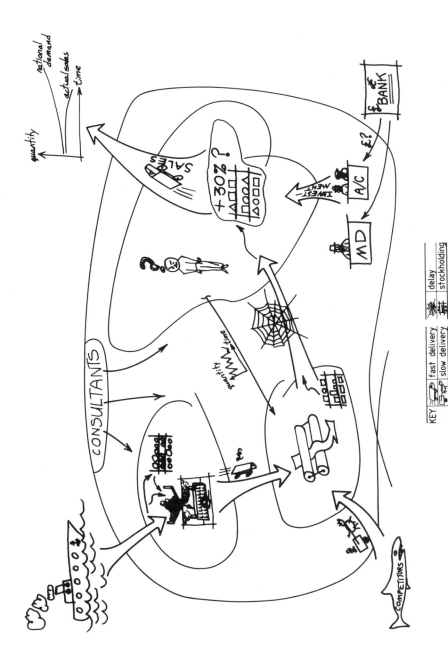

FIGURE 6.21. Case Study 3: Rich picture of problematic situation.

A number of transformation systems had therefore been defined. Two were recorded more explicitly:

TRANSFORMATION SYSTEM 1.   A system to transform a customer with needs into a satisfied customer.

TRANSFORMATION SYSTEM 2.   A system that transforms raw ore into graded steel.

Although the second system appeared to be the more obvious, the group perceived that the first option was more promising at this stage. So they progressed with the notion that the situation might be usefully thought of as a customer satisfaction system. Having identified both T and W, the group proceeded to write out a full root definition of the system:

> A multiownership (bank, customers, share holders) system developed in order to satisfy customers by employing workers and by being aware of the relevant market trends.

A CATWOE analysis of this revealed the following:

C: The actual customers who purchase the steel products being manufactured
A: The workers
T: Conversion of customers with desires into satisfied customers
W: Customers should be satisfied as a priority
O: Bank, customers, and shareholders
E: Relevant market and its trends

Moving forward to constructing a conceptual model, the group identified the following verbs and made an attempt at structuring them logically (recorded in the numbers in the parentheses next to the verbs):

to develop (?)
to satisfy (7)
to employ (4)
to be aware (1?)
to supply (6)
to produce (5)
to compete (?)

Progress was halted for a long period until one member "realized" that there were two interacting processes involved. The group then quickly drew up the conceptual model shown in Figure 6.22 (which would normally be developed further).

The actual situation shown in the rich picture of Figure 6.21 was compared to the conceptual model of Figure 6.22. From this comparison, and by using

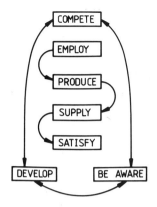

FIGURE 6.22. Case Study 3: Conceptual model.

the idea of agenda setting, Table 6.5 was drawn up. Note that each verb
(activity) was considered systematically.

The reader should note from the table that the analysis was truly systemic
in that the whole system has been considered, including the structure and
processes therein. An important observation that arose from this learning
process (which might not have been achieved without such an approach) is
that a competitor was currently in the process of developing new techniques
of production (improved technology), which, despite the possibility of warehouse investment and so on, would have seriously endangered the organization's survival as a whole. At a local level, the following matters were

TABLE 6.5

Case Study 3: Agenda for Discussion

Activity in conceptual model	Present in real-world situation?	Comments	Include on agenda?
Employ	Yes	Staff level OK? Quality of staff OK? Wages sufficient?	No
Produce	Yes	Are production systems efficient? Steel mill doubts!	Yes
Supply	Yes	Is there enough production? Ordering policy of warehouse in doubt	Yes
Satisfy	No	Demand exceeds "our" supply	Yes
Compete	?	—	Yes
Be aware	Yes	Market research and consultancy used	No
Develop	No	Competitors developing new techniques	Yes

identified; that production may be inefficient, the effectiveness of ordering policies were in doubt, delivery was not good, and that possibly getting those "right" would remove the perceived need for warehouse expansion.

6.7.5. Summary

This section has been included to provide a means of throwing some light on the methodological ideas presented earlier in the chapter. Through this operationalization, it is also possible for the reader to make some initial assessment of the systems technology approach, which is exemplified by Case Study 1. Case Study 2 is different from Case Study 1 in many ways. The most important difference is the tighly defined brief given to the consultants. The approach adopted was one of learning and design. Both Case Studies 1 and 2 would be classed as HSMs in the sense that they seek a defined end point. Case Study 3 uses the systemic SSM in order to consider a problematic situation, which is presented to fellows and students at our university, with restricted information.

6.8. CONCLUSION

In this chapter we have considered, in detail, the systems view of problem management and problematic issues. It has been shown that there are in fact several viewpoints within the systems movement. These are well reflected in the three hard methodologies and the soft systems methodology which have been presented within the chapter. The difficult task of knowing which methodology to use and when has been discussed. The possibility of linking the methodologies via a "systems classification" has been shown to fall foul of philosophical differences that, in many instances, would result in differences of opinion in situation and methodology classification. Instead of accepting total defeat, however, we considered a pragmatic approach, or a systems technology, whereby all the systems problem management tools are integrated and used in a fashion according to the problem manager(s)' perception of the nature of the "problem." Many practitioners adopt this approach (implicitly). Being aware of all that is available in the tool bag, it has been proposed, allows those with a creative flair to draw their own trajectory through a problematic situation. General principles (a systems problem management philosophy) are of course a necessary base from which to work. This approach also has its critics.

The implications of these issues for teaching and learning methodologies have been considered. The rules of following predefined methodologies provide a good first step in this process. Practice and creative flair are necessary in order that consultants can operate to good effect.

This chapter has concentrated on the use of systems methodologies in application. The following chapter is concerned with the use of systems in theory development in the area of the social sciences, specifically in the discipline of international relations.

PROBLEMS

6.1. List some distinguishing features of hard systems methodologies.

6.2. Hard systems methodologies can be conveniently considered under the headings: systems analysis, systems engineering, and operations research. What are the main commonalities and differences between these three strands?

6.3. Describe a systems analysis approach.

6.4. Describe a systems engineering approach.

6.5. Describe an operations research approach.

6.6. What reasons led Checkland (1972, 1975, 1981) to develop soft systems methodology?

6.7. Describe Checkland's (1981) soft systems methodology (it may be useful here to make reference to examples such as those in Section 6.4.2).

6.8. Naughton (1977) stated that methodologies are essentially concerned with rules. What are the two types of rule he outlined? Define each type.

6.9. What are the rules of the systems analysis approach described in Section 6.3.2?

6.10. Discuss the opinion that Klir's (1985a) architecture for systems problem solving is distinct for well-structured situations and indistinct (inappropriate) for messy "social situations."

6.11. How successful is Jackson and Keys's (1984) system of systems methodologies in answering the question, "which methodology when?"

6.12. Is the idea of a problem management tool kit for pragmatists a desirable one?

Chapter Seven

SYSTEMS THEORY IN INTERNATIONAL RELATIONS

7.1. INTRODUCTION

The aim of this chapter is to highlight the potential of systems science in theory building and qualitative explanation in International Relations (IR), a discipline that has "traditionally" assumed structure in advance of identifying processes.

This chapter offers a systemic interpretation of "traditional" IR before describing an alternative contemporary behavioral approach. This is particularly useful in displaying the Development Cycle 2 of Figure 1.1, showing how systems thinking has strongly influenced IR, one area of social theory, and vice versa. The following is based on an article by Ellison and Flood (1986). As this chapter is primarily a review, the terminology adopted in the reviewed articles has necessarily been used.

7.2. SYSTEMS AND INTERNATIONAL RELATIONS

7.2.1. The Current Position

As with systems science, IR may be regarded as a new field of inquiry with a history not longer than 40 to 50 years. Further similarities exist between systems science and IR in that both the substantive content and the methodo-logical approaches of each discipline have changed significantly over recent years. Indeed, this process of change is continuous, and in neither case has research yet led to the crystallizing of a universally accepted view of what constitutes the substantive area of study or which particular methodologies should be adopted. In fact there are some researchers who believe that it would be inappropriate for such a process of crystallization yet to have occurred. Given this state of affairs, our aim for this section is to discuss and assess the input, and the value of the input, that systems science has made to IR. A review of this kind is hardly unique in its goal (many papers exist that provide a body of criticism of research efforts, and an evaluation of these is offered below); however, the review is novel in its approach and findings.

7.2.2. The International System

One of the first writers to use systems concepts in IR was Morton Kaplan. Kaplan's international system consisted of states interacting in six possible patterns or structures (Kaplan, 1957). These six are described below.

1. Multipolar: a balance of power type of arrangement; a literal billiard ball model
2. Loose bipolar: two main opposing spheres with satellites of varying degrees of adherence to either side
3. Tight bipolar: like 2, but with no wavering in the middle
4. Universal: a confederation; everybody under one government
5. Hierarchical: significant groupings that are functional rather than territorial; a federation
6. Unit veto: each can destroy all others, everyone has to give consent and there is mutually assured destruction (MAD)

Kaplan's concerns were with the intrinsic or relative stability of each of the different types of system (historical examples exist for only two structures, the balance of power of the eighteenth and nineteenth centuries, and the post–World War II loose bipolar system), and how, and under what conditions, systems transformation would occur. Kaplan used the systems concept of homeostasis and *homeorhesis* (transition from one state to another) to examine the change brought about by the number of elements within the international system. He postulated that some structures are more stable than others. For instance, the balance of power system has stability owing to its relatively large number of elements. His reasoning suggests that in structures with fewer elements, there is a tendency for such elements to be continually "firing" at each other, thus causing instability.

Kaplan's work is difficult to follow, in part because of some apparent contradictions and in part because of the jargon used. However, it has been recognized by Mitchell (1978) as "by far the most intellectually rigorous of the earlier works on international systems analysis."

> few of Kaplan's "essential rules" for his six international systems have turned out on examination to flow in a logically necessary fashion from his regulatory hypotheses. Those that do tend to be tautological or incapable of operational verification and falsification, or both. . . . Given the nonoperational or tautological nature of the bulk of the "essential rules" of his systems, it follows that Kaplan's conclusions concerning systemic stability and transformation are not compelling.

In a similar vein, and calling on the cybernetics terms that Kaplan uses, Rosencrance (1963) presented nine periods of international politics, historically from 1740 to the present day. He discussed regulation and disturbance, and "major determinants which promote or inhibit stability/instability internationally." Rosencrance's approach is essentially a historical study where systems concepts (stability and feedback) are used as organizing tools and as means of expressing generalizations that are arrived at through historical analysis. It is for this sort of reason that some have argued that no new insight has been gained by the use of systems concepts and approaches.

Both Kaplan and Rosencrance considered an international system to consist of interacting nation states. In a similar vein, other studies have applied systems ideas to specific geographic regions. Examples of these are Bowman (1968): The Subordinate State System of Southern Africa; Zartman (1967): Africa as a Subordinate State System; a general work by Banks (1969): Systems Analysis and the Study of Regions; Modelski (1961): IR and Area Studies: The Case of South-East Asia; Brecher (1963): IR and Asian Studies: The Subordinate State System of Southern Asia; and Binder (1958): The Middle East as a Subordinate International System.

In Modelski's study, he too addresses stability and the conditions necessary for the continued survival of a subsystem, but he also examines the foreign policies of the states as elements of the system and superpower influence as an input into the subsystem. Michael Brecher divides up the "international system" into the dominant system consisting of superpower relationships and subordinate systems (those parts of the system that do not constitute the dominant system). Again, the superpower input to the system is dealt with under the "linkage between the subordinate and dominant systems."

Brecher also discussed factors including interaction and communication between the system's elements, the level of material development, and the "common and conflicting ideologies and values (and) diversity of political systems" (meaning governmental expression of ideologies and values). He also considered stability and conditions necessary for a system to survive. However, the system's source of stability or instability does not follow from the effects stemming from the number of elements in the system (as with Kaplan's reasoning) and changes to this structure, but from an individual country's internal stability and its spillover into relations among the states. The works of Kaplan, Rosencrance, Modelski, and Brecher are all dealt with in some depth by Weltman (1973), who does a thorough job in reviewing the way each author uses systems ideas, and whether the use of such ideas has facilitated new insight into IR or enables analysis of a kind that would not otherwise have been afforded. Weltman's conclusions were somewhat negative and do not reflect the conclusions of the current chapter for reasons argued below.

Another work, known as WEIS (World-Event/Interaction Survey; see McClelland, 1966), again took nation-states as the elements in the international system and looked at the interactions between them. This was based on the "empirical" evidence of significant interactions presented in a number of reputable newspapers and reports. McClelland uses the system concepts of cybernetics and black box models to view the decision-making process of the state. He depicts a two-level state control system where "transactions," or routine movements, between states are dealt with by the state administration (bureaucracy) and the nonroutine event-orientated interactions are dealt with by the higher level of the decision-making process (upper officialdom). Explained under the guise of the "hierarchy of information action over a ten-year period," he found that 10% of the nations account for 60% to 85% of the activities. This implies that some countries are insignificant on the international scene (if the data source is assumed to be accurate). Results show a core group of states forming the dominant system (to use Brecher's language). The major powers fall into this category, as do the states of regions in which conflict appears to be the norm.

The results of the WEIS project provide further fuel to the fire of the debate in Weltman's book on the effect of the number of elements on overall stability. For instance, does the amount of attention an actor is able to devote to each response produce distortion, or produce uncertainty, and therefore reduce or exacerbate stability (implying a contribution to reasoned response)? As Weltman points out, no definitive position can be concluded from so much contradictory evidence/theory. He appears to find this a depressing situation; not only does the systems approach fail on this account for Weltman, but he also feels that it should have provided us with a means of choosing the "correct" or "best" theory, which, he says, it does not.

It would be a brave person indeed who would argue that attempts to use systems ideas in IR have resulted in unqualified success, and indeed many reviews (in the same vein as Weltman's) have come to similar conclusions (see, for instance, Stephens, 1972, and Banks, 1969). However, there are some problems with regards to Weltman's analysis and his major assumptions. The impression that he has made up his mind about the nonvalue of systems ideas arises when he uses references such as "coreligionists" when meaning fellow functional sociologists in political science. Furthermore, systems approaches *ipso facto* make fewer *a priori* assumptions than most other investigative endeavors, which is one of their strengths, and is the very point on which Weltman is hoist by his own petard. Weltman's selection of studies all reflect one particular assumption, namely, that IR consists of states as elements in the "international system" and is primarily concerned with relations and interactions between the state elements. Naturally, a review of this kind must reflect the mainstream of work carried out, and it is true that much of the application of systems ideas to IR at the time of Weltman's writing was in this mold. However, the "failure" of this and other studies is due to the limitation of the conceptualization of IR as consisting of interacting states as discrete units. A system is a "system of interest," with the observer deciding what is, and what is not, of interest, but there are no intrinsic systemic reasons why in IR the system of interest should be restricted to states as interacting elements. So why did Handleman *et al.* (1973), in their paper "Color It Morganthau" discover that the Morganthau paradigm (the traditional power-state-centric approach; Morganthau, 1967) is represented almost exclusively in the supposedly new approach outlined above?

Is the problem perhaps one of the level of analysis? The answer in systems terms is an unequivocal no. Merely looking at individuals, groups, and so on would lead only to the denial of their importance in shaping events because of the nature of the state-centric approach (the state-centric theory or paradigm is structured to discount these factors). The problem can be viewed in the light of a point presented in Chapter 3, where system identification was discussed as being either structurally based (the state structure is the basis of the assumptions of Weltman and others) or based on behavior, or process, through which a structure is identified (which ignores state boundaries, often identifying transnational systems). This point will be discussed later in the chapter.

Kaplan and Rosencrance represent one type (the traditional school) of international system studies. The works of the Stanford School (1914 Project; Holsti, 1965), the Simulation-Northwestern School (Inter Nation Simulation [INS]; Coplin, 1966), and the work of Singer and Small (Correlance of War, [COW], 1966) represent a move from the traditional school toward a more quantitative approach. These latter three claim, at least in part, to use systems approaches in their studies.

The 1914 Project (a short name for the Stanford Studies in International Conflict and Integration) uses the systems concepts of cybernetics to study the decision-making process in a crisis situation (one where war is a likely outcome) and uses the concept of nested systems and subsystems to examine conflict (the long-term structural antecedent of war) within and between states. The authors, adopting an overtly systemic approach, certainly seem to embody in their work all the "hard system" assumptions in vogue at the time, adhering to epistemological positivism, being methodologically nomothetic, and taking a deterministic view of human nature (see Chapter 10 for a full insight into these philosophical issues).

INS, another serious attempt at quantifying IR, is built around interacting states as units within a region that is taken to be a closed global system. INS is a simulation model of the international relations, and while its substantive paradigm can be questioned (and it is in "Color It Morganthau"; INS here is referred to as a caricature of the Morganthau paradigm), later generations of this model (Internation Process Simulation, IPS and others) have, however, addressed the state-centric bias.

The exercise of simulation and modeling in general can be regarded as one of the successes of the use of systems approaches in IR. Simulation research, while felt not to have provided a theory of IR, has an excellent track record as a learning device for students, and as an explicit way of dealing with theory thus enabling operationalization of theory. Simulation has also contributed to identifying weaknesses in theory where operationalization has proved to be impossible.

As with the studies discussed earlier in the chapter, if these quantitative studies are to be criticized it is just as valid to do so on their embodiment of a substantive paradigm as it is on their use of systems concepts. The main point is that the paucity of results from many of the studies does not denote a failure of systems ideas in IR, and although the systems paradigm is a powerful tool it cannot make an inappropriate or outdated theory or substantive paradigm relevant. This is true for methodologically traditional or scientific studies alike.

Another point that Weltman has made is that in the 16 years from 1957 (when Kaplan wrote) to 1973 when he published his critique, adequate time had passed for more fruit to have been borne from the application of systems ideas in IR. At the 1973 juncture he felt that the future of systems approaches in IR held little hope and that researchers should not pursue such a line of study. Fortunately, this advice was not heeded.

Two points are of interest here. Sixteen years can be regarded as a very short span of time. More important though is the development of system theory itself and the general shift of emphasis that has taken place in the systems movement since the early 1970s (notably Checkland's methodological and philosophical statements discussed in Chapters 6 and 10, respectively). Weltman made a very curious remark about the philosophical base of systems science, which is interesting in this respect. He noted three possible philosophical standpoints:

1. That "bodies are minds"—which we interpret to mean ontologically a nominalist position and, in systems terms, to mean that hard situations are a special case of soft situations
2. That "minds are bodies"—which we interpret as ontologically realist, and in systems terms to mean that soft situations are a special case of hard situations
3. That minds and bodies are distinct—which we interpret as meaning, in scientific terms, that social and natural phenomena are governed by separate rules such that social matter cannot be studied scientifically, and within systems terms to mean that separate methodologies apply to the study of hard and soft situations

Of the three positions, he criticized IR theorists for basing their approach on standpoint 2 and for failing to comprehend standpoint 3. Although there certainly has been a move toward 3 (from 2) by part of the systems movement, this more recent systems thinking is also favorably disposed toward 1. This is expounded by Checkland in his soft system methodology, which is a corollary to the doubt in part of the systems movement that social subject matter could be dealt with using the same methodological approaches developed in the natural sciences. Weltman suggested that natural and social sciences should be seen as distinct, which was a reaction against position 1, but particularly position 2, outlined above. Weltman's remark was farsighted since, as noted above, the shift in systems thinking (by the soft systems protagonists) moved systems methodologically closer to his preferred approach.

Weltman might have presented a more balanced view of both IR and systems science if he had made mention of the work of Karl Deutsch, whose book *The Nerves of Government* (1963) is an example of the direct application of cybernetic concepts to political behavior. Deutsch's works stand out both for their genuinely original attempt to discuss IR from a non-state-centric power perspective, and for the insight they bring to IR from the application of systems concepts in this way. In Deutsch's work, the long-time (accepted as fact) divide between politics within states and international relations between states is discarded in favor of a truly systemic approach where actual intensities and discontinuities of interactions and exchanges between social groupings are examined.

If one discards the state as the basic unit of analysis, politics and IR cannot be seen as being separate. With this approach, the same processes are observable within and across state boundaries, which suggests the viewpoint of a global society. In this context, Burton's work constitutes the most uncompromising rejection of the billiard ball model (Burton, 1965, 1968). Burton's international system assumes no system of interest at the state level. He even goes so far as to say that complexity of ties between social and interest groupings bears no relation to, and cuts across, state boundaries. This would render state-level analysis at best an irrelevance, and at worst an obscuring, of the real substance of IR (or world society as Burton calls it).

Burton's expressing of a world society in systems terms is illuminating. What we see in Burton's work is an innovative paradigm in IR taking its lead from, and expressed in, systems terms. It is at this level of analysis that Burton expounds the theory that conventional politics can be explained, and that any denial of interaction at this level leads to conflicting or nonsystemic behavior. Burton's work further develops in the direction of human needs, their existence, of the drive to fulfill them, and their shaping of world society. This latest development has proved to be more controversal than his other ideas and is strongly contested.

Following Burton are writers with a less functionalist (sociological sense) emphasis, ignoring needs theory altogether. While accepting the essence of politics (politics and international relations) to be systemic interaction in the Burtonian way, they also introduce new dimensions.

While not overtly systemic in their approach writers such as Keohane and Nye (1977) in their book *Power and Interdependence* present a continuation of the wholehearted rejection of the Morganthau paradigm.

The work of Keohane and Nye is particularly interesting in that it represents power politics and global politics as two extremes on a continuum of types of global political situations. They recognize that in some political issues, power relations between states may be crucial, but that in others economic and ideological power may become potent and have a significant effect on outcomes. In the latter case, a situation of complex interdependence exists such that traditional power (a superior physical force) is moribund or impotent. Keohane and Nye suggested that even if power politics adequately described international relations in the past, since the World War II complex interdependence most accurately describes the international dimension of politics.

Keohane and Nye's work has been criticized by Willetts (1982), for instance, for not completely rejecting the concept of power politics in the way that Burton did. Both sets of writers, however, have moved away from the functionalist (sociological sense) strain of Burton's work and expand on the concept of issue areas and issue salience to replace a fixed hierarchy of high versus low politics (traditional power versus economic and social matters). They have expanded the definition of power to include economic and social resources as well as physical force.

Systems concepts, as discussed in the earlier parts of this book, distinguish between structure and process, elements and their attributes, and interactions and exchanges. The dominant wisdom in the discipline has been that of hard systems thinking, and of structured approaches to perceived structurable situations. Within politics this has resulted in a search for the structure of politics, or the actors, and then an observation of the processes, or exchanges between actors. Witness Kaplan and others assuming the state structure and looking at interactions between states. The behavioral approach discussed in Chapter 3 suggests that we take as our starting point the process, or processes, and from them find the structure. Working this way a variety of relevant structures will eventually be established (if the situation is structurable) and we can be more certain that these are representative.

It is very important that a structure is not taken as given, and with respect to IR that counts for a global politics paradigmatic structure as well as for a power politics one. This distinction is discussed by Reynolds (1980), who delineates microinternational relations (which focuses upon actors on the international stage) from macrointernational relations (which is concerned with interactions), their nature and interrelationships, and changing patterns therein. The formalism of macrointernational relations is holistic and tends toward soft systems reasoning. By viewing IR in this way, the salient, relevant, or realistic structure of actors in IR may be identified.

7.3. CONCLUSION

International Relations (IR) is a very young discipline, and has developed in parallel with systems science. Both have benefited from the cross-fertilization of ideas, although it is impossible to quantify the mutual contributions.

Early research and theory building in IR was based on the structural assumption that states existed as the distinct units of analysis, and that politics clearly existed within each state but not between states. The early theoretical models were based on the anarchic billiard ball concept, where state action-reaction was between governments. Stability was a particular concern here. This structural assumption opened systems science and IR to wide criticism. The role of systems approaches in theory building and explanation was at one time perceived as having failed completely.

However, new theories based on process have developed. These range from total rejection of the state-centric approach, to the acceptance of that concept integrated into other types of cross-national interactions. Current systems thinking appears to favor the latter as it is difficult to deny that governments do participate in significant interaction. New IR theories, and consequently alternative explanations, have been achieved with the use of evolving system theories.

Interestingly, the methodological change in systems (from hard systems thinking to incorporate a softer approach) is reflected in IR. This has stimulated researchers to consider behavior rather than structure, and consequently has led to the acceptance by some of transnational politics and global systems. The paradigm shift discussed by Kuhn (1975), which in his view is typical of scientific revolutions, does appear to be present in systems science. This point has also been raised by Jackson (1987). The implications of this for IR are difficult to assess however. Certainly at a microsocial level Checkland's action research has proven to be most effective. Quite how the basic tenets of the interpretive paradigm can methodologically be incorporated at a macrosocial level is a question which, on the one hand suggests that a potentially explosive area has yet to be investigated, while on the other hand warns of a difficult, as yet unpenetrated, front which demands our attention.

Our conclusion, therefore, is strongly in support of the idea that systems science has contributed significantly to IR for good or bad. Stepping out of the functionalist paradigm (philosophical sense), however, may well be the necessary revolution that will shape and integrate systems science, IR and social theory building in general.

PROBLEMS

7.1. Discuss the main concerns of the theorists whose conceptualization of the international situation is restricted to states as interacting elements.

7.2. "The exercise of simulation and modeling in general can be regarded as one of the successes of the use of systems approaches in international relations." Discuss this statement, taken from text, in relation to the problems associated with modeling large-scale social situations.

7.3. What differences might occur when conceptualizing aspects of the international situations with behavior, rather than structure, being the main determinant in system identification?

7.4. Is it possible to use an interpretive approach, such as that developed by Checkland, to help to conceptualize a large-scale international social situation?

SYSTEMS QUANTIFICATION

From Stone Age to Space Age

8.1. INTRODUCTION

The preceding chapters have considered a variety of aspects of systems science, and have discussed many of the complex issues that arise in worldly affairs. We have shown how systems science has contributed, and continues to contribute, theoretically and in application. The discussion to date has covered issues of a qualitative nature; however, quantitative issues have not been neglected. At appropriate points we have noted that quantification can usefully, and indeed should, be employed. It was also noted that studies of structured complexity may require mathematical and statistical approaches. There are many other instances where quantification is appropriate. Chapter 9 will discuss these in a comprehensive manner.

Recently, in the Department of Systems Science at City University in London, the role of quantitative methods in the Management and Systems degree has been examined. Two objectives were identified that have relevance for any person considering the benefits of developing quantitative skills. These were (1) to increase understanding of a wider range of situations, for instance by using quantitative models as tools for analysis (including operations research techniques); and (2) to produce potential managers who are both literate and numerate, thus enhancing their competence. We feel that managers who are either literate or numerate, but not both, are unlikely to exhibit the competence of a manager who enjoys skills in both areas, particularly in contemporary society.

The purpose of this chapter, then, is to bridge the gap between the qualitative systems investigations of the previous chapters and the quantitative systems studies considered in Chapter 9. This will be achieved by presenting a selection of useful approaches. The first four sections are designed particularly for those who may consider themselves nonnumerate. We then move into areas that progressively increase in quantitative sophistication. The latter part of this chapter, unfortunately, will be accessible only to those who have developed quantitative skills. All readers should at least attempt to reach and understand Section 8.6.

For the nonnumerate person we feel that being realistic at the outset will be beneficial in the long run. So we do not pretend that the trip through this chapter will be easy for everybody. It will require some determination. If, however, you feel despondent at any stage, then reflect on Einstein's mood when he stated that "whatever problems you have with mathematics, mine are greater." Perseverance may be greatly advantageous, as even a little mathematics (and so on) will go a long way.

8.2. USING LETTERS INSTEAD OF NUMBERS

Let us first consider a simple description of an economic situation that could be encountered in some elementary text. The description is in fact taken from Brewer (1973) and is a slight adaptation of that presented in Chapter 2.

> In a national economy one of the fundamental observations that can be made is that the gross national product can be derived from the addition of consumption, investment, and government expenditures. Consumption expenditure itself is a fraction of last year's gross national product, as a rise in wealth will lead to increased purchasing power, and is also proportional to the current population level. Investment expenditure will rise/fall as money available for consumption increases/decreases. This can be related to the increase/decrease in consumption expenditure over the last year, and then added to the actual investment last year. Population size also has some augmenting relationship here. Government expenditure has also been observed to rise/fall, in response to the previous year's rise/fall in gross national product, and has been found to increase as the population rises. Population size will vary according to the net rate of population change (if this is zero then population size will not change), the latter being determined from births less deaths as a percentage of the current population.

We can see from the above paragraph that, as we would expect with verbal-sentential models, a small amount of complexity imposes excessive demands on the ability of words to give a precise meaning. This was well expressed by Gowers (1954), as pointed out by Hussey (1971) when he wrote "words are an imperfect instrument for expressing complicated concepts with certainty; only mathematics can do that." The role of mathematics or quantification as a whole, however, is subject to our ability to measure the situation as discussed in Chapter 4. Nevertheless, we can attempt to represent words symbolically and we shall do precisely this for the description of the national economy given above. The symbolic representation will take the form of the algebraic equation, which is indeed a mathematical representation that uses letters to represent quantities that we may wish to investigate.

Our first task is to assign a letter to each numerical variable that has so far been described using words. This will give us a symbolic representation. The variables are relatively easy to identify from the verbal description. Gross national product will be labeled Y; consumption expenditure C; investment expenditure I; Government expenditure G; population N; net rate of population change PRN; and birth and death rates BR and DR, respectively. Let us draw up the first equation.

It is stated that Y can be calculated from the addition of C, I and G. We can now make the final conversion from a symbolic representation into an algebraic one. We shall represent the word "add" with "+" so that:

$$Y_t = C_t + I_t + G_t \qquad \text{(8.1)}$$

Note here that we have included the subscript, t, in order to tell us that we are considering a dynamic system that changes over time, t. The paragraph describing the national economy does so in terms of years, so we will take the units as \$ per year. To find the value for Y_t as t changes we require a means by which we may calculate C_t, I_t, and G_t, as these are not constant values; they too vary as time progresses. Referring back to the description of the national economy we find that C_t is a fraction of Y_t. We are unsure what the fraction is at this stage, so let us call the fraction α_1 (alpha is a Greek symbol commonly used to represent constant values); α_2 is similarly used to represent the effects of N on C. We may now write the relationship out as follows:

$$C_t = \alpha_1 Y_{t-1} + \alpha_2 N_t \qquad \text{(8.2)}$$

Note here that the time subscript $t - 1$ has been used to refer to last year's gross national product. Now it was also stated that I is related to the change in C over the last year ($C_t - C_{t-1}$), which will increase/decrease I from its last year's value. The current population is also an important factor:

$$I_t = \beta_1(C_t - C_{t-1}) + I_{t-1} + I_{t-1} + \beta_2 N_t \qquad \text{(8.3)}$$

β_1 (beta, another Greek symbol which represents a constant) represents some fraction of the change in C and β_2 is similarly used to represent the effect of N on I. G, it was stated, will vary as a proportion of last year's Y and this year's N:

$$G_t = \gamma_1 Y_{t-1} + \gamma_2 N_t \qquad \text{(8.4)}$$

γ_1 (gamma, yet another Greek symbol representing a constant value) defines the proportional change in G according to changes in the previous year's Y. γ_2 is similarly used to represent the effects of N on G. Finally, we wish to draw up algebraic equations to represent the population dynamics. We shall

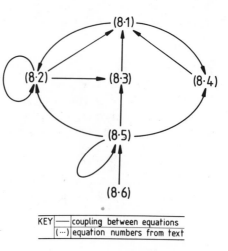

FIGURE 8.1. Equation map of a simple economic model of the national economy.

represent N as a function of its previous value and PRN:

$$N_t = N_{t-1} + \text{PRN}_{t-1} \qquad (8.5)$$

If PRN has a zero net value then $N_t = N_{t-1}$. PRN is equal to the difference in BR and DR:

$$\text{PRN}_t = \text{BR}_{t-1} - \text{DR}_{t-1} \qquad (8.6)$$

We have now developed a set of coupled equations (the coupling is shown in Figure 8.1). In order to solve this set of equations it is necessary to have starting values for the variables C, I, G, N, and PRN (the last via the inputs BR and DR) at $t - 1$. The values of Y, C, I, G, N, and PRN at t can then be derived directly. In advance of solution, however, the parameters (constants) α_1, α_2, β_1, β_2, γ_1, and γ_2 will have to be identified. It can be seen from Figure 8.1 that, assuming the system is in a steady state, there are only two ways of introducing a perturbation. This can be done by altering the values of BR and/or DR (inputs), or changing the values of any of the parameters (as parts of the structure). The latter change actually alters the structure of the system representation (the model).

8.3. RATE OF CHANGE

An example of the rate of change, which is familiar to everyone, relates to a vehicle traveling a known distance over a given time. Take, for instance, a car that travels 60 miles in 1 hour. We can say that the average rate of change is 1 mile (distance) per minute (time). If the car were traveling along a highway at a steady 60 miles per hour, and we had followed it for 1 hour, then the

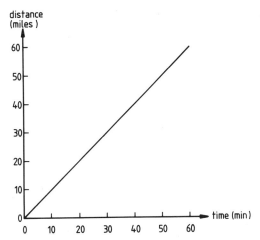

FIGURE 8.2. Average rate of change of distance against time for a car traveling at a steady speed.

graph of its distance versus time would be linear (see Figure 8.2). Now consider the car starting from a stationary position, accelerating, cruising, and then slowing down at a destination. A possible graph for this is shown in Figure 8.3. This is nonlinear and contains information about the precise rate of change at any particular point on the graph.

In the linear example (Figure 8.2) we have said that the average rate of change is 1 mile per minute. This may be discovered easily because the graph forms a right-angled triangle with the time axis (see Figure 8.4, which shows such a right-angled triangle). This means that the rate of change is constant and is measurable by the slope of the graph (change in distance divided by the change in time). For any interval of time, on the linear graph, this value is 1. So there is a positive rate of change (the slope is rising) of 1.

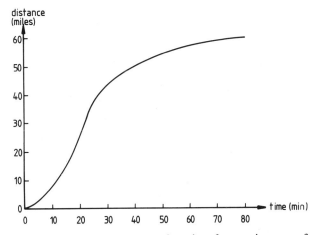

FIGURE 8.3. Graph of distance against time for one journey of a car.

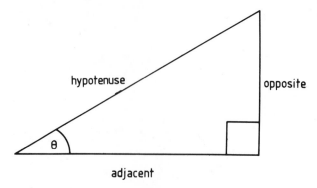

FIGURE 8.4. A right-angled triangle with each side labeled and the angle between the adjacent and the hypotenuse being defined by θ.

For the nonlinear graph (Figure 8.3), we can gain the same sort of information for any one point on the graph by drawing a line at a tangent to the exact point of interest. A tangent is a straight line that meets a curve at a point but if extended does not intersect it at that point. A tangent thus touches the curve at an exact point. Now consider the tangent drawn on Figure 8.5, which is completed as a right-angled triangle. The hypotenuse has been drawn sufficiently long to cover an easily identifiable time interval of 20 minutes. From the tangent, 20 minutes is associated with 35 miles, so that the slope of the tangent is 35/(20/60), which gives a positive slope of 105 miles per hour. The slope is the measure of rate of change at the point at which the tangent touches the curve.

Note here that the rate of change of distance by time is speed (velocity). After 1 hour the vehicle is motionless and so the rate of change is zero. In a similar way, we can say that the rate of change of speed is acceleration.

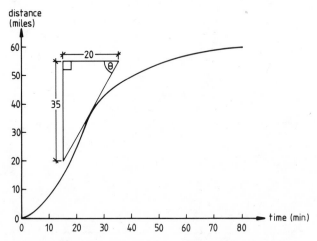

FIGURE 8.5. Deriving the rate of change using a tangent at one distinct point on the graph shown in Figure 8.3.

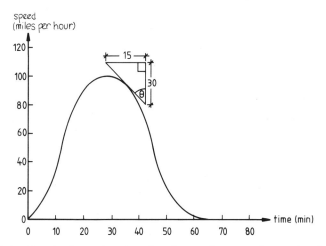

FIGURE 8.6. Graph of speed against time for one journey of a car showing a tangent to the curve.

Consider Figure 8.6 which represents a similar journey to that above, but now we are considering speed against time. After approximately 45 minutes the speed is about 100 mph; however, the rate of change of speed is $30/(15/60)$, which gives a deceleration (negative slope) of 120 miles per hour per hour, or 120 miles per hour^2 (where the superscript 2 means the square of hour, that is, hour multiplied by itself).

A rate of change, then, may be positive, zero, or negative. We have now described a method of determining the rate of change at any specific point; however, this method is time consuming and cumbersome. There is a need for a method by which the rate of change at any specific point can be determined quickly, and without the messiness of graphical work. This can be achieved with differential calculus as shown later.

8.4. DRAWING UP DIFFERENTIAL EQUATIONS

Consider the size of a bacterial population, which, in the first phase of the population's existence, is found to correspond to the equation

$$P = t^2 + t \qquad (8.7)$$

where P is population and t is time. This relationship could be plotted graphically and tangents drawn at any one point in order that the rate of change might be derived. Let us now, however, develop the ideas associated with tangents. For the above example, we can say that at any point the rate of change is $\Delta P/\Delta t$, where Δ (delta) means "an increment of." This relationship verbally reads "the rate of change of the population with respect to time." As $\Delta t \to 0$ (delta t approaches zero), the slope of the hypotenuse becomes nearer and nearer to the precise slope of the tangent under consideration. Now suppose that we are at the tangent point precisely and that we add a small increment of t, Δt, so that P also becomes slightly larger by ΔP. As $\Delta t \to 0$ it becomes very small and we shall call that dt; similarly $\Delta P \to 0$ and we shall call that dP so that the rate of change at any one point is dP/dt.

Now consider that we are at a precise point on the slope described by Equation 8.7 and, in a similar way to that described above, we add a very small increment of t, dt. This has to be reflected throughout the equation as shown below:

$$P + dP = (t + dt)^2 + (t + dt) \tag{8.8}$$

What we really want to know is dP/dt, which we can find by algebraic manipulation. Initially, we will multiply out the brackets:

$$P + dP = (t + dt)(t + dt) + (t + dt) = t^2 + 2t \cdot dt + dt^2 + t + dt \tag{8.9}$$

Now let us subtract $P = t^2 + t$ from this equation as we are only interested in specific points on the curve and not the ranges $0 \to t$ and $0 \to P$. So subtracting

$$
\begin{array}{l}
P + dP = t^2 + 2t \cdot dt + dt^2 + t + dt \\[4pt]
\underline{-P \qquad\;\; = -t^2 \qquad\qquad\quad - t} \\[4pt]
dP = \qquad 2t \cdot dt + dt^2 \quad + dt
\end{array}
\tag{8.10}
$$

We now divide the resultant equation through by dt to achieve dP/dt:

$$\frac{dP}{dt} = 2t + dt + 1 \tag{8.11}$$

As we have previously stated, we wish to consider a point on the graph that would be arrived at when $dt \to 0$, so we will carry out this action on the above equation:

$$\frac{dP}{dt} = 2t + dt + 1 = 2t + 1 \tag{8.12}$$

In effect we have differentiated P with respect to t and have found that performing this process on $(t^2 + t)$ gives the result $(2t + 1)$. A general rule of differentiation can be taken from this example:

$$\frac{dP}{dt} = nP^{n-1} \tag{8.13}$$

so that t^2 leads to $2t$ and t leads to $1t^0 = 1$. In a similar way a set of rules can be derived for a variety of functions so that, given an equation, the derivative can be found by rule of thumb. A few examples are shown below:

$$e^x \rightarrow e^x$$

$$\log_e x \rightarrow 1/x$$

$$\sin x \rightarrow \cos x$$

where e is the exponential function, $\log_e$ is the logarithm to the base e, and sin and cos are trigonometric functions, in all cases of x. Although the above discussion has given us a good understanding of the differential form of equations, and how the graphical method can be replaced by differential calculus, in most cases when we develop a mathematical model we shall develop the differential form and thus need to "work backwards" in order to find the actual value of (in the case of the above example) population. We have seen that where $dP/dt = t + 1$ the actual value of P could be calculated from $P = t^2 + t$. So, for our purposes, we require a means of reversing the process of differentiation. This is called integration. The fundamental theory of calculus is that differentiation and integration are reverse processes. In symbols:

$$\int \frac{dP}{dt} = P + c \qquad (8.14)$$

where $\int$ refers to integration and c is a constant that appears in the integration process but would then disappear on subsequent differentiation (the rate of change of a constant is zero). Integration of differential equations is described in the following section, with particular reference being made to solution by computer.

Before describing how we typically formulate differential equations in modeling, a brief note on the order and type of differential equations is required. Consider again the example of a traveling car. The rate of change of distance with respect to time was identified as speed (velocity), and the rate of change of speed with respect to time was identified as acceleration. In symbols:

$$\frac{dx}{dt} = s \qquad (8.15)$$

where x is distance and s is speed (velocity). Additionally:

$$\frac{ds}{dt} = \frac{d(dx/dt)}{dt} = \frac{d^2x}{dt^2} = a \qquad (8.16)$$

where d^2/dt^2 is a second derivative and a is acceleration. So, d/dt is a first order and d^2/dt^2 is a second-order differential form. Note that d/dt can be written as D, which is termed the D operator.

We may also want to consider the dynamics of a system with respect to time and, say, distance. This may be necessary when considering the mixing of a substance in a river, for example, where localized effects exist in the river's dynamics. For instance, water flows much faster in the centre of a channel than at the edge. In this case we use partial derivatives. Here d (referring to ordinary differential equations) is replaced by ∂ (referring to partial differential equations), so that if y is concentration, x is distance, and t is time, we may represent the rate of change of concentration with respect to distance and time by $\partial y/\partial(x, t)$. Second-order partial derivatives can also be formed. Furthermore, if a variable exists at all values of time, it is said to be continuous, for example, the continuous measurement of body temperature. If the variable only exists at a finite countable number of values, t is said to be a discrete time variable, t_k (with $k = 0, 1, 2, 3, \ldots$), and the system variable is said to be a discrete time variable, for example, the rate of arrival of customers at a bank. These equations are written in the form

$$y_k = y_{k-1} + \tau \cdot x_{k-1} \tag{8.17}$$

where y_k is the integral, y_{k-1} is the immediate past sampled value of y, x_{k-1} is the immediate past value of the variable being integrated, and τ is the time interval over which integration is taking place. The Equation 8.17 is known as a difference form.

To summarize, differential equations may be of first, second, or higher order; differential equations may be classed as ordinary or partial; and differential equations represent continuous systems, whereas difference equations represent discrete systems. For the great majority of systems that we may wish to model, first-order ordinary differential equations will be all that are required. These, then, will be our focus of attention.

Many systems in which we have a quantitative interest will contain matter that will exist as a spatially distributed content. So we may wish to follow the movement of mass into, around, and out of the system. This requires conservation of matter (matter cannot be created out of, or disappear into, nothing) so that mass balance equations are required. These are of the form

$$\frac{dx}{dt} = I - O \tag{8.18}$$

where x is the content, I the input rate, and O the output rate of matter. There may be several inputs, for example, from the environment and/or to another space in the system. There may also be several outputs to the environment and/or other spaces in the system.

8.5.1. Introduction

A large proportion of structured situations can be modeled with sets of first-order ordinary differential equations that are amenable to analytical solution. There are, however, two types of difficulty that encourage us to look for an alternative approach. The first difficulty is the particular problem of obtaining solutions for equations of a nonlinear form. The second difficulty relates to the tedious task of solving large sets of equations. Both of these factors may substantially hinder progress. In these instances it is desirable to use computer simulation methods. Simulation may be carried out using analog, digital, or hybrid computers. It is this simulation aspect of computing that we shall consider first.

8.5.2. Simulation by Analog, Hybrid, and Digital Methods

An **analog computer** typically consists of a number of independent electronic units that can perform mathematical operations on voltages that represent the variables within the mathematical model. The basic operational units include integrators, summers, multipliers, and others (see Figure 3.6 for a description of these). The units are interconnected such that the variables obey the differential equations of the model. The independent variable is time and variations in voltage levels in the computer correspond to variations of the model variables as functions of the independent variable of the model.

A feature of the modern analog computer is the speed at which it solves a model. Sets of differential equations may be solved hundreds of times per second. This is due to the parallel arrangement of the computing elements. Solution speed is not affected by model size, but increasing complexity does require a greater number of units.

The principal limitation is that, relative to digital computers, the accuracy is often significantly lower. This is a problem only in circumstances where there is little inherent uncertainty associated with the structure (including the parameters) of the model. Here, accuracy is of prime importance. Where there is inherent uncertainty, however, the loss of accuracy tends to be offset by speed of simulation and the facilities for user interaction.

The major problems with analog computers arise from the need to make unsatisfactory approximations in models of nonlinear functions and (pure) time delays. This latter requirement is achieved using high-order differential equations, which are demanding in terms of the number of computing elements used. In some instances, it may be appropriate to use **hybrid** techniques, utilizing digital and analog methods together. Care needs to be taken to divide the model efficiently, for instance, to ensure digital methods are used to generate time delays and for the representation of other nonlinear functions. Another problem associated with both hybrid and analog methods is that scaling is required, that is, the variables are normalized within the model equations to ensure optimal use of the limited accuracy of the analog computer. This requires *a priori* knowledge of the maximum values of the variables. In addition, a suitable scale factor relating units of time in the simulation to time in the "real" situation is also required.

Digital simulation methods are widely available, given the advent of microcomputers and their relatively low costs. They are also relatively accurate although rather slow. The majority of readers will be concerned only with the use of digital methods, and the comparative advantages and limitations with analog methods will be of largely academic interest. For this reason we shall now concentrate our efforts on digital methods.

8.5.3. Solving Differential Equations Using Digital Computers

Earlier in this chapter we saw that systems could be represented by either discrete or continuous equations. Discrete equations are of a difference form, which, unlike the differential form, which we have shown to be capable of analytical solution, may be solved using numerical integration. If, however, we wish to solve differential equations on a digital computer, then it is necessary to draw upon numerical techniques and consequently we need to find a means by which a differential form can be converted into a difference form. This technique is illustrated below with a simple differential model of population.

Let us assume that the following observation is true. For the next five days the rate of change of a bacterial population is expected to rise according to the following equation:

$$DP = kP \qquad (8.19)$$

where P is population level (millions), t is time (days), D is the D operator, and k is a constant, say 0.5. The difference form of Equation 8.19 is

$$P_{t+1} = P_t + DP \cdot h \qquad (8.20)$$

where the change in population over the time $(t + 1) - t$ is the product of the rate of change DP, and that time interval $(t + 1) - t$ which we shall denote as h. By substituting Equation 8.19 into Equation 8.20 we have

$$P_{t+1} = P_t + (kP_t)h \qquad (8.21)$$

In order to solve this equation it is necessary at any one time step to carry out the solution using a number of integration steps. The number of integration steps is derived from h using this simple formula:

$$m = (t_1 - t_0)/h \qquad (8.22)$$

where m is the number of integration steps.

Given that the population is, say for simplicity sake, 1 million at the start of the current day, then we may wish to calculate the population level for 12 hours ahead. That is, $P(0) = 1$, and we wish to calculate $P(\frac{1}{2})$. Let us select $h = 0.1$ so that $m = (t_1 - t_0)/h = (0.5 - 0.0)/0.1 = 5$. We shall therefore have to iterate five times. Now consider the simple set of integration steps shown below, which is, in fact, what is known as a Euler integration method:

$$P_{0.1} = P_0 + h(\text{DP}_0) = 1 + 0.1[0.5(1)] = 1.05$$

$$P_{0.2} = P_{0.1} + h(\text{DP}_{0.1}) = 1.05 + 0.1[0.5(1.05)] = 1.1025$$

$$P_{0.3} = P_{0.2} + h(\text{DP}_{0.2}) = 1.1025 + 0.1[0.5(1.1025)] = 1.1576 \qquad \textbf{(8.23)}$$
$$\vdots$$
$$P_{0.5} \approx 1.276$$

It was noted above that the value of h is crucial in determining the accuracy of the solution. This can be seen from the following:

if $h = 0.5$ then $P \approx 1.25$ using just one step
if $h = 0.25$ then $P \approx 1.265$ in two steps
if $h = 0.1$ then $P \approx 1.276$ in five steps

The "exact" answer (by analytic methods) is $P \approx 1.284$ (to three decimal places). If, however, h becomes very small, then m would become very large and the real time required to solve the equation would become excessive (even by computer). In addition, as small errors creep in on each calculation, there comes a point when the increased accuracy enjoyed when reducing h is exceeded by the accumulating errors introduced via the many calculations. Consequently, the model solution becomes highly inaccurate and "blows up," that is, it becomes unstable.

Implementing numerical integration on a digital computer is an easy task. To illustrate this an integration routine in BASIC is given below:

```
  5  REM EULER ROUTINE
 10  INPUT X0, T0, T1, H
 20  PRINT
 30  LET X = X0
 40  LET M = (T1 − T0)/H
 50  FOR N = 0 TO M − 1
 60  LET X = X + H*DX
 70  NEXT N
 80  PRINT X
 90  STOP
100  END
```

where X is the state variable, DX is the rate of change of X (in the population example above DX = kX, where X = P), X0 is the initial condition of X, T0 is the start and T1 the end of the time step, M is the number of integration steps, and H is the integration constant. This program can easily be typed into a personal computer and the accuracy and time difficulties associated with the integration constant assessed.

8.5.4. Constructing a Program

By the time the model is ready for computer implementation, a set of differential equations and a set of supporting algebraic equations will be available. A simulation program can be developed from these. A typical structure is shown in Figure 8.7. There are a number of points to be noted from this figure. In this program it can be seen that the difference equations are solved in advance of the algebraic equations. Also, the output sent to a file to store could equally be replaced by a simulation time graphics routine. In a similar way to T0 (the point at which entries to a file are made) another time point could be selected, so that when it is reached either model inputs or parameters could be changed in order to assess the model's response.

When constructing such a program it is vital that the author puts in comment statements at each distinct program "event" in order to allow themselves, and others, to follow the logic inherent in the code. An important decision that has to be made is whether each constant and variable should be represented by a mnemonic, or whether the variables and constants should be accumulated in vectors. The set of vectors could be **X** for the state variables, **DX** for the rates of change, **P** for the computed variables, and **A** for the constants. The advantage of the vector approach is the tidiness in the program

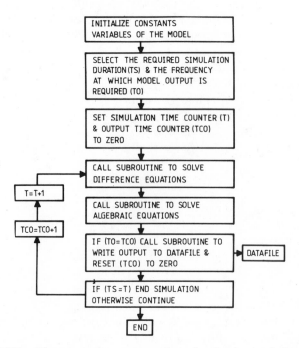

FIGURE 8.7. Diagrammatic representation of a simple simulation program.

and enhanced testability, although the readability of the code is severely restricted, requiring a supporting list of definitions made available as a hard copy. With the mnemonic approach the program may be cluttered, particularly at the beginning where each mnemonic "word" and its value would have to be declared individually (rather than simply reading in values for the five vectors from the data file). It is, however, much easier to read and understand each line of code with the mnemonic approach.

Once the model is "up and running" it has to be tested and debugged. For our type of representation we know that, without any parametric or input changes (time invariance and the input equaling the output), the model will run in the steady state. Therefore, the values in the **DX** vector should all equal zero after the first time iteration. If this is not the case, then one (or more) of the variables of the difference form(s) does not equal zero and so is incorrect. This is usually because the function describing that variable has been incorrectly formulated (or incorrectly typed in). Additionally, some of the parameters may need to be defined to a larger number of decimal places as they may produce small errors that accumulate over successive time periods. Once the model has been shown to run indefinitely in the steady state over time (there is a good representation at this level, and no numeric aberrations) then a full validation program of the model itself is undertaken. This is discussed in the following chapter.

8.5.5. Simulation Languages

Constructing a computer program for each new model that is developed can be tedious, particularly with such general-purpose high-level languages as FORTRAN where adherence to formating is required. Of benefit to the user, who may not be an expert in computing topics such as FORTRAN programming or numerical techniques, are the widely available special-purpose high-level languages such as DYNAMO (and its microversion), ACSL, and MIMIC. These have been written specifically for the digital simulation of continuous systems. Such continuous system simulation languages allow programs to be written quickly and efficiently. They enable speedy implementation of mathematical models and a high rate of first-run success. The following reasons for this have been summarized by Finkelstein and Carson (1985):

1. A variable-step-length integration routine is usually incorporated that automatically solves the differential equations to a specified accuracy
2. Such languages are often block or equation orientated so that the source program retains the structure or format of the original mathematical model
3. Some continuous system simulation languages (micro-DYNAMO, for example) have an equation sorting routine that enables the program statements to be placed in any order, thus providing great flexibility

This convenience and flexibility, however, is offset by the additional time required for execution (although, for instance, professional-DYNAMO is vastly improved on this account) by a lack of flexibility in designing the particular user interface and, in some cases, by the lack of facilities for user interaction at run-time. The interested reader is referred to the book on computer simulation by Roberts *et al.* (1983), which provides an excellent introduction to, and examples of, DYNAMO programs.

8.5.6. Summary

Computer simulation is necessary when there are large sets of equations to be solved, or when the equations are of a nonlinear form. Simulation may be carried out with analog, digital, or hybrid methods. Digital methods, being widely available, have provided the basis for much of the discussion. Solving differential equations, after converting them to a difference form, using numerical methods has been described. Structuring, testing, and debugging programs have also been discussed.

8.6. QUANTITATIVE CYBERNETICS

8.6.1. Introduction

In this section we propose to take forward the cybernetic ideas from Chapter 1 (which have been developed elsewhere in a qualitative manner, for example, in Chapter 5 in the context of management) and discuss some of the fundamental principles of quantitative cybernetics by developing the mathematical ideas described earlier in this chapter.

8.6.2. Dynamics and Feedback

The example that we shall describe in this section is a typical water supply system. This is a simple but effective way of showing the importance of feedback and control for structured and quantifiable systems.

A simplified water supply unit without feedback is shown in Figure 8.8. Let us suppose that a water authority wishes to meet the demand (d_0) of a populated area, but also wishes to maintain water pressure by keeping the actual level (L_a) reasonably constant. Assuming that a linear relationship exists between d_0 and L_a, then we can describe the demand for water by incorporating a constant k_a:

$$F_0 = k_a L_a \qquad (8.24)$$

Now, if the demand for water rises by 20% (as is likely in peak periods such

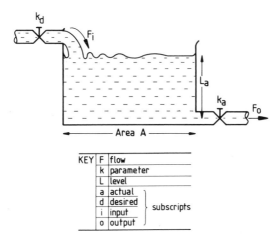

KEY

F	flow	
k	parameter	
L	level	
a	actual	
d	desired	subscripts
i	input	
o	output	

FIGURE 8.8. A simplified diagram of a water supply system without feedback.

as early morning), then effectively k_a increases by 20% for a given level (say L_{a1}). Therefore

$$F_0 = k_a L_{a1} \tag{8.25}$$

so that

$$(1.2F_0) = (1.2k_a)L_{a1} \tag{8.26}$$

Now let us consider the fluid balance equation for the reservoir:

$$F_i = A \cdot D(L_a) + F_0 \tag{8.27}$$

where A is the area, F_i is the input, and $A \cdot D(L_a)$ is the rate of change of the volume (volume is height multiplied by surface area). Substituting Equation 8.24 into Equation 8.27 we have

$$F_i = A \cdot D(L_a) + k_a L_a \tag{8.28}$$

which is a first-order linear differential equation. A supply valve in the reservoir could be calibrated so that the setting would represent "desired level." We will again assume a linear relationship between the desired level (L_d) and the supply rate (F_i):

$$F_i = k_d L_d \tag{8.29}$$

and by substituting Equation 8.29 into Equation 8.28 we arrive at

$$k_d L_d = A \cdot D(L_a) + k_a L_a \tag{8.30}$$

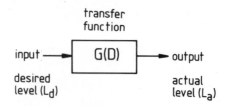

FIGURE 8.9. Black-box transfer function diagram without feedback.

which relates actual level to desired level. This may be rewritten as

$$k_d L_d = (A \cdot D + k_a) L_a \tag{8.31}$$

or

$$L_a = [k_d/(A \cdot D + k_a)] L_d \tag{8.32}$$

From the black-box form of Figure 8.9 we can see that the transfer function may be identified:

$$G(D) = k_d/(A \cdot D + k_a) \tag{8.33}$$

where $G(D)$ is the transfer function. Let us assume a particular desired level setting is L_{d1} and that the initial level is L_{a1}; then the general solution of the differential Equation 8.32 using analytical methods is

$$L_a = \underbrace{(k_d/k_a) L_{d1}}_{\substack{\text{Particular} \\ \text{integral}}} + \underbrace{[L_{a1} - (k_d/k_a) L_{d1}] e^{-(k_a/A)t}}_{\text{Complementary function}} \tag{8.34}$$

The particular integral represents the steady state, whereas the complementary

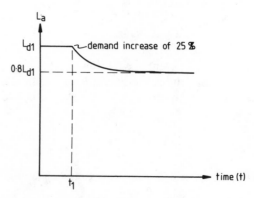

FIGURE 8.10. Effect of an increased demand of 25% on the water supply system without feedback.

function represents the transient or dynamic component of the response. Concentrating on the steady-state solution:

$$L_a = (k_d/k_a)L_{d1} \qquad (8.35)$$

we find that if $k_d = k_a$ then $L_a = L_{d1}$, that is, the actual level precisely equals the desired level, a satisfactory state of affairs. If, however, the demand for water rises by 25% such that $k_a = 1.25k_d$, then $L_a = (k_d/1.25k_d)L_{d1} = 0.8L_{d1}$. The physical observation of interest is that the pressure would drop. The result of this change in demand is represented in Figure 8.10. According to our initial brief, this is unsatisfactory.

We now propose to show how the ideas of feedback and control can usefully be employed in a quantitative fashion so that level and pressure fluctuations are minimized. This will be achieved by including a monitoring device on the level of the reservoir, which will act as an information system to a control unit, which then brings about a change to the flow into the reservoir via an activating unit. This idea is well represented in Figure 3.11 and is fundamental to cybernetics.

Now consider Figure 8.11, which shows the simple reservoir system with feedback, and Figure 8.12, which is represented as a transfer function, black-box, feedback diagram. From this latter representation we can see how the variables are related:

$$G_1 = L_a/(L_{d1} - L_a) \qquad (8.36)$$

which can be written as

$$G_1 = o/e \qquad (8.37)$$

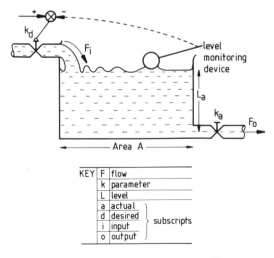

KEY	F	flow
	k	parameter
	L	level
	a	actual
	d	desired
	i	input
	o	output

subscripts (a, d, i, o)

FIGURE 8.11. A simplified diagram of a water supply system with feedback.

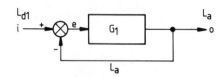

KEY

G_1	forward function
L	level
a	actual
d1	demand 1
e	error
i	input
o	output

subscripts

FIGURE 8.12. Black-box transfer function diagram with feedback.

where G_1 is the "forward" function which relates o, the output, and e, the error. Additionally,

$$e = i - o \qquad (8.38)$$

where i is the input. Manipulating Equation 8.37 we get

$$o = e \cdot G_1 \qquad (8.39)$$

and manipulating Equation 8.38 we have

$$i = e + o \qquad (8.40)$$

so that we can say

$$G_T = o/i = e \cdot G_1/(e + o) = e \cdot G_1/(e + e \cdot G_1) \qquad (8.41)$$

where G_T is the transfer function. Removing the term e we obtain

$$G_T = G_1/(1 + G_1) \qquad (8.42)$$

which in terms of Figure 8.12 is

$$L_a = \frac{G_1}{1 + G_1} \cdot L_{d1} \qquad (8.43)$$

or

$$L_a = \frac{k_d/(A \cdot D + k_a)}{1 + k_d/(A \cdot D + k_a)} \cdot L_{d1} \qquad (8.44)$$

Multiplying through by $(A \cdot D + k_a)$ we get

$$L_a = \frac{k_d}{A \cdot D + k_a + k_d} \cdot L_{d1} \qquad (8.45)$$

The analytical solution to this is

$$La = \underbrace{[k_d/(k_a + k_d)]L_{d1}}_{\text{Steady-state solution}} + \underbrace{B e^{-[(k_a + k_d)/A] \cdot t}}_{\text{Dynamic solution}}$$

(8.46)

Looking at the steady-state solution we may note that if $k_d \gg k_a$ ($\gg$ means much greater than) then $L_a \approx L_{d1}$, that is, L_a is independent of k_a (which reflects demand).

Now let us assess the actual benefits of this during periods of changing demand. Suppose that $k_d = 100k_a$ (k_d is the control parameter); then $L_a = (100/101)L_{d1}$ so that $L_a = 0.99L_{d1}$. Here, a very small error has been introduced at this one point; however, the benefits are made clear below. Now let us again consider $k_a = k_d$ and suppose that demand increases by 25%, that is, k_a increases by 25% so that $1.25k_d = k_a$. We can say that without feedback $k_d = (1.0/1.25)k_a = 0.8k_a$. If feedback and the factor of 100 are reintroduced such that $k_d = 80k_a$ then $L_a = (80/81)L_{d1} \approx 0.99L_{d1}$. The error, then, has been reduced by an order of magnitude, from 2×10^{-1}, which resulted from Equation 8.35 without feedback, to approximately 1×10^{-2} by adjusting the ratio of k_a to k_d in Equation 8.46 with feedback.

If we now look at Equation (8.46) again, and consider the dynamic solution, we can see that as k_d rises the negative exponential (system response) becomes much "faster" so that the model moves more rapidly toward its steady-state value (see Figure 8.13). This is also the case for k_a; however, the steady-state value would become less desirable. Although we are not concerning the reader with second- and third-order linear or nonlinear models, it should be noted that although control parameters (such as k_d) may improve the steady-state response (that is, the final error is reduced), they may also cause oscillations where none existed previously, may increase the frequency of

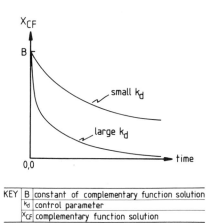

KEY	B	constant of complementary function solution
	k_d	control parameter
	X_{CF}	complementary function solution

FIGURE 8.13. Effect of speed of response on water supply system by varying the value of the control parameter k_d.

existing oscillations, or result in oscillations that increase in amplitude (an unstable model).

8.6.3. Summary

The dynamic characteristics of first-order linear models have been presented in quantitative terms. The aim was to introduce some quantitative ideas of cybernetic thinking and to highlight the benefits of their use. These ideas present only the very basics of the subject matter, purposely neglecting areas such as high-order and nonlinear models.

8.7. AUTOREGRESSION AND MOVING AVERAGES

8.7.1. Introduction

The previous sections have covered the essential background required to support the mathematical modeling that is contained in the following chapter. These next two sections provide the support material for the statistical component of Chapter 9. Other introductory texts on ARIMA and statistical transfer models (the latter is covered in the next section) include Chatfield (1980) and Nelson (1973); however, the comprehensive work of Box and Jenkins (1976) is the most accessible. The reader may find that the material in the remaining sections is of a higher degree of difficulty than that presented so far. This is in part due to the fact that we are considering series of data rather than representing structure and processes in the models. Remember though, symbols represent numbers or operations on numbers.

8.7.2. Variance and Covariance

If n samples (a time series, data readings, or measurements) are taken on an attribute of two variables of interest at n discrete points in time, say X_i and Y_i (the attributes), $i = 1, \ldots, n$, then the mean (average) values of each are

$$\bar{X} = \sum_{i}^{n} X_i / n, \qquad \bar{Y} = \sum_{i}^{n} Y_i / n \qquad (8.47)$$

where $\bar{X}$ and $\bar{Y}$ refer to the mean values of each, and $\sum_{i}^{n}$ means the sum from $i = 1$ to n. The variances of the series are calculated by finding the difference between each data point and the mean value of that particular series. This is then squared (multiplied by itself, for instance, $2 \times 2 = 2^2 = 4$) and added to the values calculated in an identical way for all other points in the series. Finally, the single value output using this technique is divided by the number of data points. The variance then is a measure of how far, in general, the time series is distant from the mean value. Squaring in this technique clears away negative values $[(-2)^2 = 4$, for example] so that we are considering only distance from the mean values and not worrying which side of the mean any particular point is on. This can be written for the X and Y series as follows:

$$\sigma_x^2 = \sum_i^n (X_i - \bar{X})^2 / n, \qquad \sigma_y^2 = \sum_i^n (Y_i - \bar{Y})^2 / n \qquad \text{(8.48)}$$

where σ_x^2 and σ_y^2 are the variances of X and Y, respectively. The covariance relates the two variables in the following manner:

$$\sigma_{xy}^2 = \sum_i^n (X_i - \bar{X})(Y_i - \bar{Y}) / n \qquad \text{(8.49)}$$

where σ_{xy}^2 is the covariance of X and Y. The covariance is a measure similar to the variance; however, we operate the technique between the two sets of data (hence the prefix "co-") and allow negative values to enter into the calculations, which enables us to derive a measure of how the two series vary in relation to each other.

8.7.3. Stationarity and Differences

Now consider a time series plotted on a graph. If the series displays an affinity for its mean value (that is, it remains in the space in the neighborhood of the mean value) then the series is termed stationary. If the series does not display stationarity (which can be assessed from a correlogram as discussed later), then stationarity may be achieved by taking the differences along the time series. Differences are calculated by the following operation: $X_{i+1} - X_i$ (the difference between adjacent pairs of the series), and then sequentially incrementing i by 1 until $i = n - 1$. The length of this first set of differences will be $n - 1$. If the first differences do not display stationarity, then the second differences may be found by carrying out the same procedure on the set of $n - 1$ values of the first differences. This procedure may continue until stationarity is achieved. This technique is central to the development of autoregressive and moving average models.

8.7.4. Autocorrelation

Autocovariance (the prefix "auto-" is used because it is the covariance between different observations in the same series) is defined by the equation:

$$v_j = C(X_t, X_{t+j}) \qquad \text{(8.50)}$$

where v_j is the autocorrelation and C relates to covariance. This is equivalent

$$v_j = E[X_t - EX_t)(X_{t+j} - EX_{t+j})], \qquad J = 1, 2, 3, \ldots n \qquad \text{(8.51)}$$

where E relates to the expected or the mean value. This will be positive if a higher/lower than average observation is followed by a higher/lower than average observation j periods later. Alternatively, it will be negative if a higher/lower than average observation is followed by a lower/higher than average observation j periods later. Therefore, a series of negative values implies a regular passage over the mean, whereas a series of positive values implies lengthy excursions away from the mean. The autocorrelation function is calculated by taking v_0 as the standard and then sequentially comparing all other autocorrelations to that standard:

$$p_0 = v_0/v_0 = 1$$

$$p_1 = v_1/v_0 \qquad \text{(8.52)}$$

$$p_2 = v_2/v_0$$

and so on, where the p_i, $i = 1, 2, 3, \ldots, n$ constitute the autocorrelation function.

8.7.5. Correlogram

A correlogram is a graph of the autocorrelation function (see, for example, Figure 9.21). If C_j is the *estimate* of v_j, that is,

$$C_j = 1/n \sum_{t=1}^{n-1} [(X_t - \bar{X})(X_{t+j} - \bar{X})], \qquad j = 1, 2, 3, \ldots, n \qquad \text{(8.53)}$$

then we can define an estimated or sample correlogram, which may be written as

$$r_j = C_j/C_0, \qquad j = 1, 2, 3, \ldots, n \qquad \text{(8.54)}$$

where r_j is the estimated autocorrelation function. If the correlogram tails off, then stationarity of the time series can be assumed. This also provides the basis for selection of an appropriate moving average model as discussed below. Distinguishing what is important from what is not important in a sample correlogram can be achieved by carrying out a test for statistical significance. This can be achieved using Bartlett's formula, so that a standard error (SE) for r_j is

$$\text{SE}(r_j) = 1 \bigg/ \sqrt{n} \left(1 + 2 \sum_{n=1}^{q} r_1^2 \right)^{0.5}, \qquad j > q \qquad \text{(8.55)}$$

If $r_j < \mathrm{SE}(r_j)$, then it is deemed to be insignificant. It should be noted, however, that about 5% of autocorrelation coefficients will show spurious significance.

8.7.6. Partial Autocorrelation

With the estimates of r_j we can write the following equations (which are known as the Yule–Walker equations):

$$
\begin{aligned}
r_1 &= \phi_1 + \phi_2 r_1 + \cdots & + \phi_p r_{p-1} \\
&\vdots & \vdots \\
r_p &= \phi_1 r_{p-1} + \phi_2 r_{p-2} + \cdots + \phi_p
\end{aligned}
\tag{8.56}
$$

so that estimates of the ϕ_j can be made resulting in the set of $\hat{\phi}_j$. The $\hat{\phi}_{jj}$ denote the values of $\hat{\phi}_j$ implied for the solution of the system for $p = j$ and are referred to as the estimated partial autocorrelations. This is central to the identification of an appropriate autoregressive model. If the time order of the autoregression is p^*, then

$$
\hat{\phi}_{jj} = 0 \qquad \text{for} \quad j > p^* \tag{8.57}
$$

(there are a finite number of ϕs).

8.7.7. Moving Average Process

A moving average process occurs when $\theta_1 = 0$ for $i > q$ (there are a finite number of θs) in the following equation:

$$
X_t = \mu + U_t - \theta U_{t-1} - \cdots - \theta_q U_{t-q} \tag{8.58}
$$

where μ and θ are fixed parameters and the time series, $(\ldots, U_{t-1}, U_t, \ldots)$ is a sequence of disturbances with zero mean and variance σ_u^2, often referred to as "white noise" because the observations are a moving average in the disturbances reaching back q periods. In essence, this process is one where μ is the average value and a random component is added/subtracted to/from μ according to a moving average of the disturbances of X from the mean. A moving average is one where the average tails back over q time periods and is updated with every new data point. This process is therefore defined in terms of the current disturbance and all past disturbances.

8.7.8. Autoregressive Process

An autoregressive process is defined in terms of the current disturbance (U_t) and all past observations on the attribute of interest:

$$
X_t = \phi_1 X_{t-1} + \phi_2 X_{t-2} + \cdots + \phi_p X_{t-p} + \delta + U_t \tag{8.59}
$$

where ϕ and δ are fixed parameters and $\phi_i = 0$ for $i > p$ (this series is finite). The term "autoregressive" is derived from the fact that the above equation is essentially a regression equation in which X_t is related to its own past values instead of to a set of independent (external) attributes of variables.

8.7.9. ARIMA Process

An autoregressive integrated moving average (ARIMA) process is a natural extension to the above two processes, where the two types of process are integrated into one form. A given observation in a time series generated by an ARIMA(p, d, q) process may be expressed in terms of past observations of order p, and current and past disturbances of order q, where the series has been filtered by differencing d times to give stationarity:

$$x_t = (1 + \phi_1)x_{t-1} + (\phi_2 - \phi_1)x_{t-2} + \cdots + (\phi_p - \phi_{p-1})$$

$$- \phi_p x_{t-p-1} + \mu + U_t - \theta_1 U_{t-1} - \cdots - \theta_q U_{t-q} \tag{8.60}$$

8.7.10. Requirements and Tests on ARIMA Processes

Invertibility (stability) for this process is essential. This requires that the parameters on past disturbances become small as i becomes large and do so rapidly enough so that $\sum_{i=1}^{n} \pi_i$ converges (π relates to parameters in general), that is, the parameters sum to a value less than unity.

We may also draw upon the theory of estimation to make inferences about the parameters based on information contained in the time series data. We may use two approaches:

1. Define an estimator, which "predicts" the value of the parameter.
2. Make decisions concerning the value of the parameters by hypothesis testing.

We will consider each in turn.

Initially, we will consider an estimate of the model, a "parameter" formed by two numbers that determine an interval within which we expect the model parameter to fall. This is called an interval estimate. We may assume that a parameter value has an associated probability defined by Figure 8.14, such that there is a 100% probability that the parameter value is in the range defined by the X axis (the whole of the area under the graph), 95% probability that the parameter value is in the range defined by the shaded area (95% of the area under the graph is shaded), and so on. Then, if we can find a means of identifying distances away from the central value in both directions, we can define the two numbers that determine the (probability) interval. This can be achieved by using the time series data to calculate standard deviations away

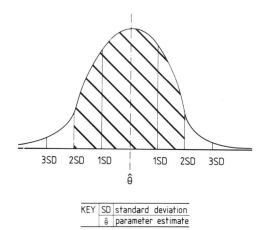

KEY | SD | standard deviation
| $\hat{\theta}$ | parameter estimate

FIGURE 8.14. Probability distribution of a parameter value showing intervals from the central point of a normal distribution curve.

from the average value of the data. This is calculated from

$$\text{SD} = 1/(n-1) \sum_{i=1}^{n} (X_i - \bar{X})^2 \qquad \textbf{(8.61)}$$

We can draw upon the following empirical rule for mound-shaped distributions (as in Figure 8.14), namely, that we have the following intervals and probabilities/certainties:

1. $\bar{X} - \text{SD}$ to $\bar{X} + \text{SD}$—approximately 68% certainty
2. $\bar{X} - 2(\text{SD})$ to $\bar{X} + 2(\text{SD})$—approximately 95% certainty
3. $\bar{X} - 3(\text{SD})$ to $\bar{X} + 3(\text{SD})$—approximately 99.7% certainty

and so on, where $\bar{X}$ is the central value. Using the notation from the ARIMA examples, we can say:

$$[\hat{\theta}_i - 1.96\text{SD}(\hat{\theta}_i)] < \theta_i < [\hat{\theta}_i + 1.96\text{SD}(\hat{\theta}_i)] \qquad \textbf{(8.62)}$$

which means that we are 95% confident that the parameter θ_i lies within the defined interval.

We can develop this idea further and define an appropriate test on the model parameters, using standard deviations, to help assess the significance of a parameter. To do this we begin by stating a hypothesis about one or more parameters of the model, say $\theta_i = 0$. The decision to accept or reject this null hypothesis will be based on the value of some quantity observed or computed from the time series data. This value functions as a decision maker and is known as the "test statistic." The stages of our statistical test are as follows:

1. Set a null hypothesis that a parameter, say θ_i, equals zero and is insignificant to the model.

2. Set an alternative hypothesis that if θ_i is not insignificant to the model then the parameter is significant to the model.
3. Select a test statistic that can be computed from the data; in our case we have selected the t-ratio (see below).
4. Define a rejection region that gives a set of values of the decision maker that are contradictory to the null hypothesis and hence imply its rejection (see below.)

The t-ratio is the null hypothesis (the proposition) that $\theta_i = 0$, that is

$$\text{Prob}[-1.96 < (\hat{\theta}_i - \theta_i)/\text{SD}(\theta_i) < 1.96] \tag{8.63}$$

for a 95% confidence, where SD is the standard deviation and $\hat{\theta}_i$ is the parameter estimate. If the t-ratio $\geq \|1\|$ (the modulus of 1, that is, $\|1\|$), $\hat{\theta}_i$ is said to be significantly different from zero.

8.7.11. Summary

In this section we have introduced and defined the main concepts of the ARIMA process. This has included the basic manipulations on a time series of data which help us to identify (p, d, q), the actual model itself, and the means by which we can test the identified model process.

8.8. STATISTICAL TRANSFER FUNCTIONS

8.8.1. Introduction

In this section we extend the idea of transfer functions, which have been introduced under the umbrella of cybernetics, to incorporate the idea of statistical transfer function modeling of time series sets of data. The necessary requirement is that at least two pairs of data are available, one set representing inputs to the unit and another representing outputs. The unit itself is assumed to be a black box. These sets of data are initially investigated using the ARIMA methodology (see Chapter 9). We will be considering the bivariate case of one input and one output (see also Box and Jenkins, 1976).

8.8.2. Cross-Correlation

The two data series can be cross-correlated in a similar way to Equation 8.49 for the covariance and Equation 8.51 for the autocorrelation function. The cross-correlation function for a bivariate process is defined by

$$v_{xy}(j) = E[(X_t - \mu_x)(Y_{t+j} - \mu_y)] \tag{8.64}$$

and hence the cross-correlation coefficient at lag j is

$$P_{xy}(j) = v_{xy}(j)/(\sigma_x\sigma_y) \qquad (8.65)$$

Identifying the lagged response of the output to changes in the input is an important aspect of transfer function modeling.

8.8.3. Transfer Function Models

The idea of statistical transfer function modeling is to produce a combined transfer-function and noise model (remember that error or noise on measurements of structured situations is the major difficulty to contend with and leads to the necessity for a filter, as discussed in Chapter 4) of the form:

$$Y_t = \delta^{-1}(B)w(B)X_{t-b} + N_t \qquad (8.66)$$

where X_t and Y_t are the input and output series, respectively, $\delta(B) = 1 - \delta_1 B - \delta_2 B^2 - \cdots - \delta_r B^r$ and $w(B) = w_0 - w_1 B - \cdots - w_s B^s$ are polynomials (algebraic expressions consisting of three or more terms) of orders r and s, δ and w relate to parameters of the model, s is the right-hand operator (relating to input), and r is the left-hand operator (relating to the output), b is the delay (lag, or "dead time") parameter, N_t is the noise component, and B is the backward shift operator (that takes the series back r and s time periods for the output and input, respectively). This is based on the general linear model for representing continuous dynamic systems:

$$(1 + G_1 D + \cdots + G_R D^R) Y(t) = g(1 + H_1 D + \cdots + H_s D^s) X(t - r) \qquad (8.67)$$

which in the case of discrete dynamic representations has the general linear difference equation:

$$(1 + z_1 \nabla + \cdots + z_r \nabla^r) y_t = g(1 + n_1 \nabla + \cdots + n_s \nabla^s) x_{t-b} \qquad (8.68)$$

which is a transfer function of order r, s. This equation can be written as

$$\delta(B)y_t = w(B)x_{t-b} \qquad (8.69)$$

which is of the form shown in Equation 8.66 without the noise component and with δ on the left-hand side of the equation. If the input is known to vary, then X_t and Y_t are deviations at t from equilibrium, thus the inertia of the system can be represented by the general linear filter:

$$Y_t = v_0 X_t + v_1 X_{t-1} + v_2 X_{t-2} + \cdots$$

$$= (v_0 + v_1 B + v_2 B^2 + \cdots)X_t \qquad (8.70)$$

$$= v(B)X_t$$

so that the transfer function of the model may be written as:

$$v(B) = \delta^{-1}(B)w(B) \qquad \textbf{(8.71)}$$

which is the ratio of two polynomials. It is important to assess the stability of the resultant model. The techniques involved in making such an assessment constitute a significant area of systems analysis in their own right. As such they lie outside the scope of the current chapter, but the interested reader will find full details in texts such as Box and Jenkins (1976).

8.8.4. Summary

In this section we have shown how the basic idea of transfer functions can be extended to include the statistical bivariate time series case, so that input and output data may usefully be transformed into a model that will predict output from input data. Multivariate transfer function models can be developed using the same principle.

8.9. RECURSIVE ESTIMATION

8.9.1. Introduction

The aim of this section is to introduce the idea that a quantitative representation can simulate dynamic structure (as defined by parameters that change over time) as well as dynamic processes. Previously we have seen how models can be used to represent dynamics, but in all cases the parameters have been held constant. They do not vary with time. They are time invariant. If we wish to represent changes in structure itself, then we must let the parameters vary with time in such a way that they reflect the dynamics of the structured situation. These parameters are termed time-varying. An example of this is the pathophysiological case where the parameters that define the patient's structure are changing according to some disease process. This section is designed to show how the parameters of statistical transfer function models and state-space models can be updated in a recursive manner with an algorithm that acts upon fresh data points.

8.9.2. Transfer Function Models

The aim is to set a "cost" function J that may be used to minimize the loss with respect to **a**, the vector of model parameters. The cost function (see Figure 8.15) is assumed to be a parabola such that if the gradient is positive, a value to correct the parameters must be deducted ($-\alpha\varepsilon$), and if the gradient

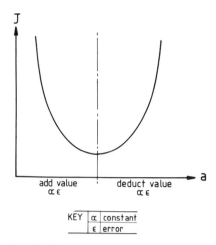

FIGURE 8.15. Cost function for recursive estimation assuming a parabola shape.

is negative a value to correct the parameters must be added ($\alpha\varepsilon$). The following theory is in part based on the work of Young (1974).

The cost function described by Figure 8.15 can be drawn up in equation form:

$$J \overset{\Delta}{=} \sum_{i=1}^{k} (\mathbf{x}_i^T \hat{\mathbf{a}} - y_i)^2 \tag{8.72}$$

where $\mathbf{x}_i$ is a vector of past observations and past inputs, and y_i is the actual observation at times i, $i = 1, 2, 3, \ldots$ which is of the form:

$$y_i = \mathbf{x}_i^T \mathbf{a} + \varepsilon_{yi} \tag{8.73}$$

where ε_{yi} is the noise, or error, term. Equation 8.72 can be minimized by differentiating with respect to $\mathbf{a}$, which can be written as

$$\nabla_{\hat{a}}(J_i) = \left(\sum_{i=1}^{k} \mathbf{x}_i \mathbf{x}_i^T \right) \hat{\mathbf{a}} - \sum_{i=1}^{k} \mathbf{x}_i y_i = 0 \tag{8.74}$$

The right-hand side of the equation may be better understood if written in the form:

$$\begin{bmatrix} \sum x_1 x_1 & \sum x_1 x_2 & \cdots & \sum x_1 x_k \\ \vdots & \sum x_2 x_2 & & \vdots \\ \vdots & & \vdots & \\ \sum x_k x_1 & \sum x_k x_2 & & \sum x_k x_k \end{bmatrix} \cdot \begin{bmatrix} a_1 \\ \vdots \\ \vdots \\ a_k \end{bmatrix} - \begin{bmatrix} \sum x_1 y \\ \vdots \\ \vdots \\ \sum x_k y \end{bmatrix} = 0 \tag{8.75}$$

Here y is a scalar; it is a single value that alters the $\mathbf{x}_i$ magnitudes. This can be represented by

$$\mathbf{M}\hat{\mathbf{a}} = b \tag{8.76}$$

so that by algebraic manipulation:

$$\hat{\mathbf{a}} = \mathbf{M}^{-1}b \tag{8.77}$$

where $\mathbf{M}^{-1}$ is an inverted matrix, so to achieve $\hat{\mathbf{a}}$, a matrix inversion at every k is necessary. To find a recursive form without inversion it can be noted that

$$\mathbf{M}_k = \sum_{i=1}^{k-1} \mathbf{x}(i)\mathbf{x}(i)^T + \mathbf{x}(k)\mathbf{x}(k)^T \tag{8.78}$$

which can be written in the difference form:

$$\mathbf{M}_k = \mathbf{M}_{k-1} + \mathbf{x}(k)\mathbf{x}(k)^T \tag{8.79}$$

and similarly in difference form:

$$b_k = b_{k-1} + \mathbf{x}_k y_k \tag{8.80}$$

Carrying out matrix manipulation as discussed in Eykhoff (1974) leads to the following expression:

$$\mathbf{M} = \mathbf{M}^{-1} - \mathbf{M}^{-1}\mathbf{x}(\mathbf{I} + \mathbf{x}^T\mathbf{M}^{-1}\mathbf{x})^{-1}\mathbf{x}^T\mathbf{M}^{-1} \tag{8.81}$$

which can be rewritten as

$$\mathbf{M} = \mathbf{M}^{-1} - \mathbf{M}^{-1}\mathbf{x}(1 + \mathbf{x}^T\mathbf{M}^{-1}\mathbf{x})^{-1}\mathbf{x}^T\mathbf{M}^{-1} \tag{8.82}$$

that is,

$$\mathbf{M}_k = \mathbf{M}_{k-1} - \mathbf{M}_{k-1}\mathbf{x}_k(1 + \mathbf{x}_k^T\mathbf{M}_{k-1}\mathbf{x}_k)^{-1}\mathbf{x}_k^T\mathbf{M}_{k-1} \tag{8.83}$$

therefore, using the error covariance matrix defined by

$$\mathbf{M}_k^* = \sigma^2\mathbf{M}_k \tag{8.84}$$

where σ^2 is the variance of the sequence of errors, two equations can be drawn up for recursive estimation. From Equation 8.84 we can derive the form:

$$\hat{\mathbf{a}}_k = \hat{\mathbf{a}}_{k-1} - \mathbf{M}_k^*/\sigma^2(\mathbf{x}_k\mathbf{x}_k^T\hat{\mathbf{a}}_{k-1} - \mathbf{x}_k y_k) \tag{8.85}$$

and from Equation 8.84, substituting in Equation 8.83 for $\mathbf{M}_k$ we get

$$\mathbf{M}_k^* = \mathbf{M}_{k-1}^* - \mathbf{M}_{k-1}^*\mathbf{x}_k(\sigma^2 + \mathbf{x}_k^T\mathbf{M}_{k-1}\mathbf{x}_k)^{-1}\mathbf{x}_k^T\mathbf{M}_{k-1}^* \tag{8.86}$$

where $(\sigma^2 + \mathbf{x}_k^T\mathbf{M}_{k-1}\mathbf{x}_k)$ is simply a scalar quantity so that there is no need for direct matrix inversion.

8.9.3. State-Space Models

Consider a continuous time stochastic model described by the following state-space differential equation:

$$\dot{\mathbf{x}} = \mathbf{A}\mathbf{x} + \mathbf{B}\mathbf{u} + \mathbf{D}\mathbf{z} \qquad (8.87)$$

where the dot notation $\dot{\mathbf{x}}$ denotes differentiation of $\mathbf{x}$ with respect to time, $\mathbf{x}$ is an n-dimensional state vector, $\mathbf{u}$ is a one-dimensional vector of inputs, $\mathbf{z}$ is an m-dimensional vector of zero mean white noise disturbances representing model uncertainty and situational variability. $\mathbf{A}$, $\mathbf{B}$, and $\mathbf{D}$ are $n \times n$, $n \times q$, and $n \times m$ matrices, respectively. Model outputs may be represented by

$$\mathbf{y}_k = \mathbf{C}\mathbf{x}_k + \mathbf{n}_k \qquad (8.88)$$

where $\mathbf{y}$ is an n-dimensional observation vector, $\mathbf{n}$ is an n-dimensional vector of white measurement noise, and $\mathbf{C}$ is a $p \times n$ observation matrix.

An occasion may arise where some of the parameters of $\mathbf{A}$ and/or $\mathbf{B}$ are unknown, but where both the model states and the unknown parameters require estimation. The solution to the problem lies in the knowledge of the vector $\mathbf{u}$ and discrete observations of the model behavior taken from Equation 8.88.

One approach is the Extended Kalman Filter (EKF), where the state vector is augmented with the unknown parameter vector $\mathbf{a}$. The augmented state vector thus becomes

$$\mathbf{x} = \left[\frac{\mathbf{x}}{\mathbf{a}}\right] \qquad (8.89)$$

The initial prediction is of the form:

$$\hat{\mathbf{x}}_{k/k-1} = \hat{\mathbf{x}}_{k-1} + \int_{t_{k-1}}^{t_k} \mathbf{f}(\hat{\mathbf{x}}_{k-1}, \mathbf{U})\, dt \qquad (8.90)$$

with the covariance $\mathbf{P}$ defined by

$$\mathbf{P}_{k/k-1} = \mathbf{\Phi}_k\mathbf{P}_{k-1}\mathbf{\Phi}_k^T + \mathbf{Q} \qquad (8.91)$$

where $\mathbf{\Phi}_k$ is the linear state transition matrix from t_{k-1} to t_k defined by

$$\mathbf{\Phi}_k \overset{\Delta}{=} \mathbf{e}^{F\Delta t} = \mathbf{I} + \mathbf{F}_k\mathbf{\Delta} + \mathbf{F}_k^2\frac{\Delta t^2}{2} + \cdots + \mathbf{F}_k^n\frac{\Delta t^n}{n!} \qquad (8.92)$$

$\mathbf{\Delta t}$ is the sampling interval, e is exponential, ! means factorial (product of the numbers and all numbers below it, for example $3! = 3 \cdot 2 \cdot 1 = 6$), and $\mathbf{F}_k$ is the Jacobian matrix with elements $\delta f_i / \delta x_j$ (evaluated at $\hat{\mathbf{x}}_{k-1}$); n is chosen to ensure satisfactory convergence and $\mathbf{Q}$ is the discrete time covariance matrix of $\mathbf{z}$. The second stage of correction is of the form:

$$\hat{\mathbf{x}}_k = \mathbf{x}_{k/k-1} + \mathbf{K}_k[\mathbf{y}_k - g(\hat{\mathbf{x}}_{k/k-1})] \tag{8.93}$$

where $\mathbf{K}_k$ is the Kalman gain matrix described by

$$\mathbf{K}_k = \mathbf{P}_{k/k-1}\mathbf{C}_k^T(\mathbf{C}_k\mathbf{P}_{k/k-1}\mathbf{C}_k^T + \mathbf{R})^{-1} \tag{8.94}$$

where $\mathbf{R}$ is the covariance matrix of the output noise $\mathbf{n}_k$. The linearized output matrix $\mathbf{C}_k$ has elements $\delta y_i / \delta x_j$ (evaluated at $\hat{\mathbf{x}}_{k-1}$).

8.9.4. Summary

In this section we have shown how structure that changes over time can be represented by using recursive estimation techniques on model parameters. We have shown that this is possible for models of data, for instance the statistical transfer function representation, and for models that represent structure and process such as the state-space representation.

8.10. CONCLUSION

The aim of this chapter was to build a bridge between the qualitative investigations presented in the previous chapters and the quantitative investigations of Chapter 9. This we have achieved by presenting a selection of useful quantitative approaches which also support the quantitative modeling exercises in Chapter 9. We have also shown that both process and structure may be represented dynamically. We now have all the tools necessary to proceed into the theory and application of quantitative modeling.

PROBLEMS

8.1. Find a verbal description of any situation (from a textbook or magazine) and rewrite it using letters (symbols) to represent the main variables.

8.2. Explain what is meant by "rate of change."

8.3. By adding an interval, Δ, of P and t to the equation below, and by following the example in Section 8.4, differentiate P with respect to t:

$$P = t^3 + t$$

How does this comply with one of the general rules of differentiation outlined in the same section?

8.4. What is the fundamental theory of claculus?

8.5. Convert the following differential equation to difference form:

$$DP = k_1 P + k_2 P$$

8.6. Given that

$$DP = kP$$

and that at time $t = 0$, $P(0) = 2$,

1. What is $P(1)$?
2. Show how the accuracy of your solution varies according to h (use a programmable calculator, or computer if possible).

8.7. Draw a black-box representation without and with feedback. Show how the steady-state solution of a system of equations without feedback differs from that of a system of equations with feedback (refer to Equations 8.35 and 8.46, respectively, and your two black-box representations).

8.8. Describe the following operations and functions that support ARIMA modeling:

1. Variance and covariance
2. Stationarity and differencing
3. Autocorrelation and correlogram
4. Partial autocorrelation

8.9. Show in symbols how the following processes are formed:

1. A moving average process
2. An autoregressive process
3. An autoregressive integrated moving average process

8.10. What is the symbolic representation used for a statistical transfer function model? Briefly explain the equation you have written out.

8.11. Describe the important systemic phenomena that can be simulated by use of recursive estimators.

Systems and Modeling II
PROCESS, PURPOSES, AND APPROACHES

9.1. INTRODUCTION

In Chapter 2 it was shown that systems are objects as perceived by people (see Figure 2.1). A system was also defined as an abstraction from the world, which is in fact a model. Miller (1967) talked about formulation of chunks of information when a threshold of complexity was passed, and it was also noted in Chapter 2 that these are recursively updated as more information is received. This is conceptual/mental modeling. Much of our everyday life is concerned with this sort of activity. Despite the gross simplification, however, the process is one of reduction to a level of usefulness. It does help us to progress through everyday life; it is parsimonious.

During specific and in-depth studies conceptual/mental models are often not sufficient to cope with the type of complexity involved. The level of simplification employed is too great for these purposes. Man has, therefore, necessarily sought more formal structured approaches to modeling, including sentential, diagrammatic, statistical, mathematical, and logical types of representation.

In this context, the objective of Chapter 9 is to consider in some detail the modeling process by investigating modeling philosophy, methodology, and techniques for the modeling of structured systems. The points raised are further elucidated with a set of case studies on the theme "models for patient management in a hospital environment."

For many readers, the quantitative investigation in these studies may prove to be the most demanding part of the book. Chapter 8 has provided, in as simple terms as possible, a clear explanation of the quantitative concepts used in the case studies. We have increased the accessibility of this chapter by presenting only modeling theory in the main text, leaving all quantitative analyses for the case studies. This will enable all readers to gain at least a good conceptual understanding of quantitative modeling for structured systems.

9.2. THE MODELING PROCESS

9.2.1. Introduction

The aim of this section is to familiarize the reader with the modeling process. To achieve this, philosophical and methodological issues and the use of techniques will be discussed. The reader is advised to refer back to Chapter 6 for operational definitions of philosophy, methodology, and technique, which are also valid in the context of this chapter.

9.2.2. Modeling Purposes

The modeling methodology of Carson *et al.* (1983) is a generally accepted view of the mathematical modeling process. This is illustrated in Figure 9.1.

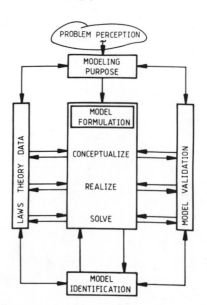

FIGURE 9.1. Mathematical modeling methodology (Carson *et al.*, 1983; reproduced by permission of John Wiley & Sons).

Finkelstein and Carson (1985) considered modeling methodology in the context of modeling purpose. They discussed three general types of purpose for mathematical modeling: description, prediction, and explanation. As outputs from models, description is the weakest, explanation the strongest, with prediction somewhere in between. Chatfield (1980) shared a similar view for statistical time series models. The essences of both the mathematical and statistical considerations are contained in Table 9.1.

Figure 9.2 shows the relative success of such mathematical and statistical approaches in achieving the purposes identified above. Here, Q refers to qualitative and Q^* to quantitative forms. Additionally, heavy shading means almost always successful, light shading means sometimes successful, and no shading means rarely if ever successful at achieving modeling purposes in relation to modeling approach. The figure additionally considers sentential/diagrammatic (conceptual) and logical modeling approaches. This patterned matrix provides some guidance to the appropriate modeling approach for a given modeling purpose. It should be stressed, however, that it is general within approaches and relative between approaches. There are, however, other factors that determine which approach should be taken. These include the nature of the situation being modeled, resource availability, and the time scale of interest.

TABLE 9.1

The Modeling Purposes for Mathematical and Statistical Time Series Models:
Description, Prediction, and Explanation

Purpose	Mathematical models (Finkelstein and Carson, 1985)	Statistical time series models (Chatfield, 1980)
Description	For the sake of conciseness and economy of description and the resultant ease of analysis and handling data.	Obtaining simple descriptive measures of the main properties of the series.
Prediction	To determine how a system would respond to a stimulus (typically feedforward control, in order to produce a predicted desired state, or to prevent a predicted undesired state; Flood *et al.*, 1985).	Given an observed time series, the modeler may want to predict the future of the series. This may be closely associated to control, in that, if a movement away from a desired level is predicted, then corrective action can be taken.
Explanation	Explanatory power lies in the ways in which different features of system behavior and structure are shown to depend upon each other.	When observations are taken on two or more variables, it may be possible to use one time series to explain the variation in another series, therefore leading to a deeper understanding of the mechanisms that generate a given time series.

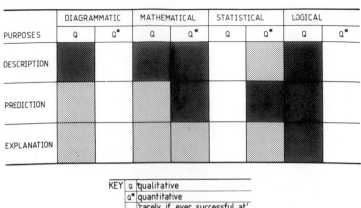

PURPOSES	DIAGRAMMATIC		MATHEMATICAL		STATISTICAL		LOGICAL	
	Q	Q*	Q	Q*	Q	Q*	Q	Q*
DESCRIPTION								
PREDICTION								
EXPLANATION								

KEY		
Q	qualitative	
Q*	quantitative	
	'rarely if ever successful at'	
	'sometimes successful at'	
	'almost always successful at'	

FIGURE 9.2.   Relative success of modeling approaches in achieving qualitatively and quantitatively modeling purposes (Flood, 1987a).

The nature of the situation determines its measurability (see Chapter 4) and hence the quality and manipulability of the data. Additionally, it determines whether theory or laws are available or attainable (very much a function of whether a situation is hard or soft). Resources determine how readily we can deal with measurements, how easily models can be solved, and so on. Time scale is closely related to resources. In systemic scientific research time may not be a problem, but if acting on a contract, for example, it will be finite.

The reader is offered further insight into modeling purposes and the modeling process in Figure 9.3 (developed from Flood, 1985, 1987a). This should be considered alongside the following explanation:

1. Block 1 represents the acquisition of data.
2. Block 2 can be reached by using data and observations and/or theory and/or known laws.
3. Block 3 can be reached by using data and statistical theory.
4. Block 4 can be reached by further structuring of Block 2, or directly from Block 1.
5. Block 7 can be reached by logical structuring of Block 2, which may have been achieved from Block 4.
6. If Blocks 2, 4, or 7 have been achieved to a reasonable degree of satisfaction, then it would be meaningful to progress to Block 5 and/or 6.
7. Validation of Blocks 2, 3, 4, and 7 will be qualitative in nature.
8. Block 3 is merely informative and factual.
9. Block 8 may be reached via Block 3 with estimated parameters, or from Block 4, although in the latter case it is not necessary for the parameters to be identified/estimated.
10. Blocks 9 and 10 can be meaningfully achieved from Block 8 only if parameters have been estimated/identified and the model validated.

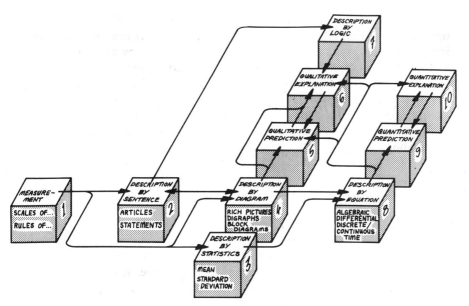

FIGURE 9.3. The modeling purposes and process (adapted from Flood, 1985).

11. Validation of Block 8 will be both qualitative and quantitative in nature.

Figure 9.3, together with the explanation given above, provides a concise summary of the modeling methodologies that will be discussed in Section 9.3. The reader is advised to return to this figure when reading the methodological descriptions presented a little later.

9.2.3. Summary

From modeling purposes and other considerations, such as the nature of a situation, an appropriate modeling approach may be selected. These approaches, and their associated methodologies and uses, are considered in detail in the following section.

9.3. MODELING APPROACHES

9.3.1. Introduction

Having acquired a feel for modeling purposes and the modeling process, it is now appropriate for us to look more closely at modeling approaches. The early part of this chapter clearly defined a mathematical modeling methodology. This section concentrates on methodologies associated with mathematical and various other approaches. Each approach (whether senten-tial, diagrammatic, mathematical, statistical, or logical) can be broken down into types, and each type has an associated methodology as well as a range of uses. Mathematical, statistical, and logical models are therefore considered in the context of type, methodology, and then use. More general comments are sufficient for sentential and diagrammatic approaches. Let us initially consider the importance of reviewing the efforts of other researchers at the outset of any modeling exercise, and the need to declare explicitly all the assumptions that are made while developing models.

9.3.2. Critical Reviews

At the outset of many modeling exercises, particularly those in difficult areas, it is generally useful, and often very important, to critically review relevant extant models. This provides an insight into the approaches that have been adopted, and the success arising from their use. It also sharpens our attention to how controversial aspects of the situation have been dealt with in a practical rather than a theoretical way. This step is also an important aid in the selection of an appropriate modeling approach and type.

9.3.3. Declaring Assumptions

As modeling by its very nature involves simplification, it is vital that the assumptions made during the simplification process are detailed. This documentation adds a degree of transparency for others who may wish to consider the representation. This is particularly the case for structured systems which are represented by quantitative models. Now let us consider five model-ing approaches.

9.3.4. Verbal-Sentential

Sentential methods are the commonest types of model (other than mental/conceptual models), either in verbal or written form. Everyday con-versation allows us to pass on loosely structured models, for instance, during a telephone conversation where other modeling approaches would be difficult (mathematical) or well nigh impossible (diagrammatic) without some multiple translator (computer and some coded language). By adding a degree of structure (grammatical and syntactic), verbal models can be recorded in written form, for instance, poetry, essays, or a book.

9.3.5. Diagrammatic

The types and vocabulary of diagrammatic models of well-structured and poorly structured situations have been presented in Chapter 3. It is worth reiterating here, however, that diagrams are several orders more powerful than verbal/sentential models owing to our mental ability to process the information contained in them in a parallel rather than in a sequential fashion.

9.3.6. Mathematical

Types

Compartmental models are a commonly used class of lumped parameter deterministic model. These models assume that distributed effects can be lumped together and the compartmental contents are assumed to be homogeneous throughout. The principle of conservation of mass must be upheld. This type of representation is ideal for flows of matter/material and typically uses first-order ordinary differential equations; see Figure 9.4. Here, R_{ij} is the flow of matter from compartment j to compartment i. Where i or j is 0, this refers to the environment and not a compartment. Q_i is a compartmental quantity and Y_i is an observation.

Lumped deterministic models may be linear or nonlinear. Linear representations are not appropriate when the intrinsic dynamics of a situation are essentially nonlinear, unless only small perturbation or steady-state studies are sufficient see Figure 9.5. In the illustration we have a linear function defined by $x = f(y)$ and a nonlinear function defined by $x = F(y)$. Between a and b on the x axis, $x = F(y)$, which approximates to $x = f(y)$. However, if gross perturbation is applied, so that, say, $y = e$, then for the nonlinear case $x = c$ and for the linear case $x = d$. This would give a significant error equal in magnitude to $d - c$ if the linear function was used to represent the nonlinear function.

Compartmental models may be strictly compartmental. Such models represent processes in which flux of materials from one compartment to another

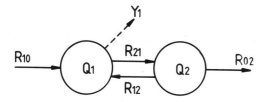

$$\dot{Q}_1 = R_{10} + R_{12} - R_{21}$$
$$\dot{Q}_2 = R_{21} - R_{12} - R_{02}$$
two first order ordinary differential equations
$$Y_1 = f(Q_1)$$

KEY		
R_{ij}	flow of matter	
Y_i	observation (measurement)	
Q_i	compartment (state variable)	
f	is a function of	

FIGURE 9.4. General representation of a two-compartmental model with equations.

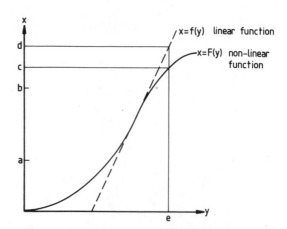

FIGURE 9.5. Inappropriateness of a linear approximation for a nonlinear function.

can be assumed to depend , linearly or nonlinearly, on the mass (or a direct derivation from the mass—concentration, for example) in the source compartment only. The class of models that includes active control (hormonal control in the body, say) is termed a control system model.

System dynamics is concerned with a similar control system representation and is used for simulating structured socioeconomic situations (Roberts *et al.,* 1983), although it is more suitable for harder situations, for instance, representing a technological system like coal excavation as developed by Wolstenholme (1983b). To complement the systems dynamics approach, a software simulation package DYNAMO (and micro-DYNAMO versions, designed in parallel with the textbook of Roberts and co-workers) has been developed. Many examples of system dynamics exercises can be found in Roberts (1978).

If a lumped parameter compartmental model is not appropriate, that is, the heterogeneity of compartmental contents cannot effectively be assumed to be homogeneous, then a distributed representation must be adopted using partial differential equations. These can be employed to include further spatial dimensions. Another consideration is that deterministic models can take no account of random effects. Probabilistic representations are often necessary when modeling stochastic processes. The reader is advised to consult Carson *et al.* (1983) for further details.

Methodological Considerations

Experience of dynamic mathematical modeling (the block sequence 1-2-4-8, Figure 9.3) has shown that the transition from Block 2 to Block 4 is probably the single most important step of the sequence. It is at this conceptual stage that both the structure and complexity of a model are largely determined. Assumptions may include aggregation (the extent to which different components are lumped into a single entity), abstraction (the degree to which certain aspects of a situation are considered in a model), and idealization (the approximation of structure and behavior that is difficult to describe). This further highlights the importance of developing diagrammatic skills and the need for Chapter 3 which is dedicated to this craft.

The specific task of selecting variables (achieving parsimony, that is, simplification to a level of usefulness but not beyond) for inclusion in a mathematical model (assuming an appropriate level of resolution has been decided upon during aggregation, abstraction, and idealization) may be considered in the light of Figure 9.6. This is an adapted version of a diagram first conceived by Onno Raddemaker and developed by Flood (1985). As the number of variables included rises, the predictive ability rises to a peak value beyond which the continuing decrease in manipulability and increase in errors (numerical errors during computer simulation) tends to force the predictive ability downward. Furthermore, by increasing model complexity it is easy to fit short-term output from the mathematical model to empirical data (unlike statistical models where the degrees of freedom are reduced). However, this is at the expense of medium- and longer term accuracy brought about by increased model uncertainty. On the other hand, by increasing complexity the explanatory power, albeit qualitative in nature, rises as the way in which different features of behavior and structure depend on each other are increasingly developed.

An optimality curve can be drawn by lumping these concepts together. This relates the model to the modeling objectives, or purposes. The optimal number of variables may be at the point x on the abscissa. This axis should be thought of in the context of an ordinal scale (variables are included from left to right in order of importance or relevance to the modeling purposes). The point y shows failure to achieve optimality. The result of this on the various curves can be read off the achievement axis.

An effective data filtration approach, diagrammatic representation, and eventual selection of variables is therefore crucial, although after the model has been fomulated there are further ways of testing for redundant variables (for instance, using sensitivity analysis) or redundant subsystems (for instance, using perturbation theory). Sensitivity analysis will highlight variables that do

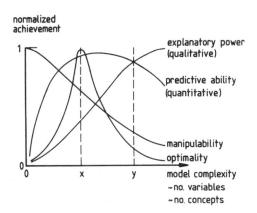

FIGURE 9.6. Conceptual means of considering parsimonious modeling (adapted from an original idea by O. Raddemaker).

not change significantly during a wide range of parameter changes, suggesting that the removal of such variables will have no effect on model performance if replaced by a parameter. For instance, if a representation contains the function $X = aY \cdot bZ$ and the variable Y in fact remains constant over a series of sensitivity tests, then aY may be replaced by a constant such that $X = cZ$. Perturbation analysis may be used to identify weak links in a model's structure. It is therefore useful for model decomposition (breaking the model down into subsystems) by locating sets of variables that interact richly among each other, but are at best loosely coupled to the rest of the model. If the coupling of any subsystem is found to be very weak, and remains so as t becomes large, then that subsystem (assuming it does not contain observables of importance) may be discarded (see Figure 9.7). Here, if the weak link σ remains weak as t becomes large, then the system S may be decomposed into two separate subsystems S_1 and S_2. If, say, S_2 contained no observation of interest, then it could be discarded. An important point to note is that models that have been decomposed do not necessarily segment into functional units as we perceive them (Flood *et al.*, 1987a).

Following conceptualization (data transformation, sentential and diagrammatic modeling), the structure and processes have to be translated into algebraic and differential equations. This is termed mathematical realization.

Algebraic functions are formed that represent the relationship between a dependent variable and appropriate independent variables. This is easy for linear relations between two or more variables where data are freely accessible by use of linear and multiple-linear regression (a statistical technique with measures of confidence in the correlation coefficient). If the relationship is nonlinear, a nonlinear function (for example, exponential, logarithm, or square) that closely approximates the relationship has to be found. Alternatively, a nonlinear function can be broken down into a piecewise continuous linear function (see Figure 9.8). Referring to the figure we can see that the nonlinear function $y = i(x)$ can be approximated by a piecewise continuous

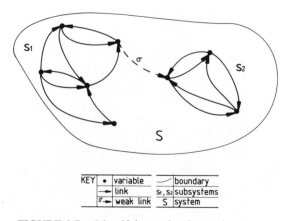

KEY	•	variable	⌒	boundary
	•→	link	S_1, S_2	subsystems
	σ•→	weak link	S	system

FIGURE 9.7. Identifying redundant subsystems.

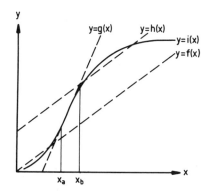

FIGURE 9.8. General representation of a piecewise continuous linear function.

linear function such that

$$\text{if } x \le x_a \qquad \text{then } y = f(x)$$

$$\text{if } x_b \ge x > x_a \qquad \text{then } y = g(x)$$

$$\text{if } x > x_b \qquad \text{then } y = h(x)$$

Differential equations for homogeneous strictly compartmental models are of the form given in Figure 9.4. For control system models, a number of approaches can be adopted so that a model will respond to deviations from the steady state, the commonest being the set point approach as shown in Figure 9.9. Refer to Figure 3.6 for the conventions of this block diagram. From Figure 9.9 we can note the following. The state variable A will change if the actual value of one or more variables (X_a, Y_a, Z_a) deviates from the normal

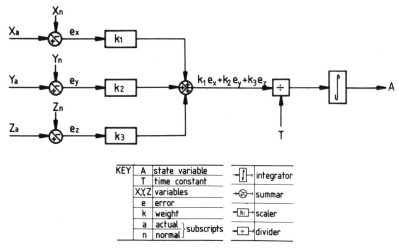

FIGURE 9.9. The set point approach for control system modeling.

values (X_n, Y_n, Z_n) such that at least one of the following hold: $e_x <>0$, $e_y <>0$, $e_z <>0$. The expression for the differential equation for A is an additive weighted sum (k's are the weights) of the deviation of the stimuli from their set points. This is also subject to the time constant (delay) T.

Usually, the model (now a set of equations) is solved by computer simulation, therefore the differential equations are written for discrete time simulation and solved numerically using an Euler or a more complex integration routine (for example Runge–Kutta).

Mathematical simulation can only take place after the parameters of the model have been identified. In a complex model this is intensely iterative, whereby nonunique parameters are crudely estimated and then tuned by comparing simulated output to empirical data, and adjusting parameters to improve the fit. For compact models, unique parameter estimation is often possible with the use of the least-squares estimation (LSE) or maximum likelihood estimation (MLE) (Godfrey, 1983). Increasing confidence in the representational capabilities of a complex model is of prime concern, thus a full validation program is required.

A number of criteria are used for the validation of complex models. A methodology for model validation relates to modeling purpose, current theories, and experimental data pertaining to the system of interest. These have to be assessed for conditions within the model (internal criteria) and to aspects external to the model (external criteria). Leaning (1980) defined these criteria more specifically:

Internal Criteria. Consistency validity criteria: The model should contain or entail no logical contradictions. In mathematical models this can be checked by examining algebraic loops. For computer programs with multiconditional branching points it may be difficult to determine consistency completely.

Algorithmic validity criteria: These are a number of tests for checking that the algorithm for solution (analytical), or simulation of the model, are correct and lead to accurate solutions. Algorithms for numerical approximation may be checked for stability and asymptotic convergence (for example, Euler, Runge–Kutta, or Gear's methods for integrating differential equations). Rounding off errors should also be tested.

External Criteria. Empirical validity criteria: This requires that the model should correspond to data available. This may be done at all levels in strict validation, although a "level of validation" may be chosen at an appropriate level of resolution. Validation may be carried out via qualitative and quantitative feature analysis and by sensitivity tests.

Theoretical validity criteria: This entails model comparison with currently accepted theories and models. This is important in examining assumptions, structure, elementary submodels, and so on.

Pragmatic validity criteria: These are tests of the model in satisfying general and specific utilitarian objectives. This should involve a definition of the measure of effectiveness in the NSOI and then determining whether the objective has been achieved. As some models will modify the WSOI once in use, a model may have to be assessed in terms of the potential benefit it offers or the understanding that it gives to people involved in the practical situation.

Heuristic validity criteria: These tests are concerned with the assessment of the potential of the model for scientific understanding and discovery, that is, its role as a heuristic device. They are mostly concerned with whether a model will be fruitful or promising for future developments. Specific criteria may include the resolution of an outstanding anomaly or giving better understanding.

Uses

Mathematical models are essentially used for simulation and prediction. There are a variety of reasons for wanting to pursue such activities. In systems engineering, for example, the design of technological processes can be thoroughly investigated. Additionally, mathematical models are becoming of greater importance to a number of drug firms in response to the activities of antivivisectionists concerning animal rights. Consequently, the effects of drugs are now increasingly simulated with models, and, incidentally, these companies should be able to cut their spending by so doing.

The application domain is extensive. Patient care, water management, weather forecasting, pilot training in in-flight simulators, and systemic research in general, are just a handful of other examples.

9.3.7. Statistical

Types

There are many types of statistical modeling technique available. In this subsection, statistical modeling will be considered under the broad headings of data driven and probabilistic state transition techniques.

Observable data available for statistical analysis are typically sequential, consisting of measurements of the processes, inputs, and outputs of a perceived system. In general, these sequences are generated in two modes. The first is monitoring where the acquisition of data is often subject to a significant time lag, a low data rate, and a low sample size. For these situations we will assume $5 \leq n \leq 50$ is a typical range (where n is the number of measurements). The second arises where rapid and instant measurement details are available, for instance during on-line monitoring; this is rarely subject to time delays, having a fast data rate and a large sample size. For these situations we shall assume $n > 100$ would be expected. The model-based techniques for estimation and prediction from data generated in both modes come under the heading of time series analysis (TSA). The multivariate nature of much available data permits the use of both univariate and multivariate techniques. The work of Box and Jenkins (1976) will be presented as an example of both univariate (autoregressive integrated moving average, ARIMA) models and bivariate (transfer function, TF) models.

Probabilistic state transition models are of a different nature. Given that a situation can be represented as a system in a particular state, that there are a finite number of discrete states that the system may move into, and that each transition has a known time-invariant probability (time-varying probabilities are possible, but require vastly increased quantitative sophistication), and given the current state and probable inputs, it may be meaningful to represent dynamic change using a probabilistic state transition model. This approach, as presented below, is based on the principles of Markov chains. A Markov chain is a finite-state stochastic process where future probabilistic behavior depends on the present state of the SOI.

Three modeling approaches will therefore be considered in this subsection, the data-driven ARIMA and TF approaches, and the probabilistic-based Markov chain approach.

Methodological Considerations

ARIMA **Models.** The objective of an ARIMA modeling exercise is to build a model of a univariate time series, expressed in terms of past observations, and errors between current and past observations, in order to make predictions about a particular variable of interest.

An ARIMA process is conventionally written ARIMA (p, d, q) with p referring to the autoregressive and q the moving average part of the process, while d relates to the number of differences that are necessary to achieve stationarity of a time series set of data.

MINITAB is a statistical software package (developed at Pond Laboratory, University Park, Pennsylvania 16802, USA) useful for the ARIMA modeling methodology and supports the numerical manipulations required. Figure 9.10 shows a summary of the ARIMA methodology, which is expanded upon below.

It is useful in the first instance to plot the time series. This enables outliers to be quickly located. Outliers often arise from errors in measurement. However, large changes in some processes may occur naturally, and the possibility of such changes should not be discounted. If errors are suspected, then the outliers may be removed by replacing the actual values concerned with their expected values. The same approach can be adopted for missing values.

The correlogram of the raw data is then inspected and assessed for stationarity. If the series displays nonstationarity, then the first differences of the series are taken and these are inspected and assessed. If stationarity has not been achieved, then the second differences are calculated and so on. The value d in ARIMA (p, d, q) has thus been identified. When stationarity is achieved, and after the partial autocorrelation function has been calculated, the standard errors of the autocorrelation and partial autocorrelation functions are taken, that is, the standard error values of these function plots are assessed for significance. The results of these standard error tests are then considered in the light of the information presented in Table 9.2. This shows the characteristic behavior of autocorrelations and partial autocorrelations for three classes

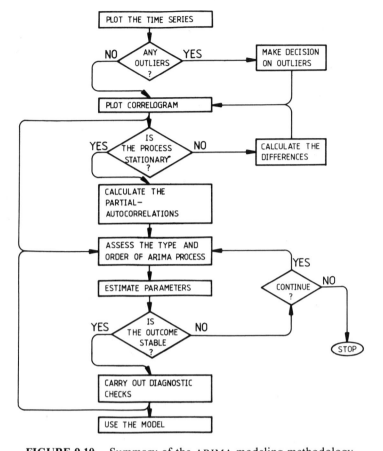

FIGURE 9.10. Summary of the ARIMA modeling methodology.

of process. An ARIMA process is then selected by identifying the time lags p and q (either may be zero). Interpretation is clearly highly subjective and experience in using the methodology is therefore of great value.

The next step is maximum likelihood estimation, where the parameters of the autoregressive and moving average parts are identified. Initial crude parameter estimates can be calculated as described by Box and Jenkins (1976). However, MINITAB works from initial parameter estimates of 0.1 (although the user is permitted to enter the initial crude estimates if desired). The output of MINITAB provides final parameter estimates, standard deviations, t-ratios and sums of squares. Thus, both the significance and the confidence intervals of each parameter are available. The model also has to be tested for invertibility (stability).

If there had been some doubt over the p, d, or q values of the ARIMA (p, d, q) process, then an alternative model could be identified and the MINITAB outputs compared.

The final stage of the methodology requires some diagnostic checks (validation). The method used either confirms or refutes the proposed model.

TABLE 9.2

Characteristic Behavior of Autocorrelations and Partial
Autocorrelations for Three Classes of Process[a]

Class of processes	Autocorrelations	Partial autocorrelations
Moving average	Spikes at lags 1 through q, then cut off	Tail off
Autoregressive	Tail off according to: $r_j = \phi_1 r_{j-1} + \cdots + \phi_p r_{j-p}$	Spikes at lags 1 through r, then cut off
Mixed autoregressive-moving average	Irregular pattern at lags 1 through q, then tail off according to: $r_j = \phi_1 r_{j-1} + \cdots + \phi_p r_{j-p}$	Tail off

[a] Nelson (1973). Reproduced by permission of Holden Day.

Initially, the hypothesis is that the proposed model has one extra parameter on p, and hence the t-ratio of the final estimate for that parameter is considered for significance. The result of the hypothesis $p = p^* + 1$ (where p^* is the initial identification of p) is then either accepted (it is significant and reduces the sums of the squares) or otherwise rejected in favor of p^*. This is carried out for $p \pm 1$ or $q \pm 1$.

Further diagnostic checks involve investigating the residuals of the model for serial correlation; that is, if the modeling exercise has succeeded in transforming the observed data to random noise, then the residuals would have the properties of random numbers.

TF Models. The TF modeling methodology was developed along the lines of the ARIMA methodology. As with ARIMA models, Box and Jenkins defined three stages in TF model building: identification, estimation, and diagnostic checking (validation) (see Figure 9.11 for a summary of the methodology). The approach is based on black box type input–output data. MINITAB also supports many of the quantitative manipulations used in the TF methodology.

Initially, the type and order of the input time series is assessed as an ARIMA process. Using this process, the input series is transformed to an uncorrelated white noise series. Using the same process, the output series is also transformed to an uncorrelated white noise series.

Calculation of the cross-correlations between the transformed input and output series is the next step. From the cross-correlations the lag between the two series can be identified. The impulse response function is then calculated and may be compared to the examples given by Box and Jenkins in order to identify the appropriate (r, s, b) model (where r refers to the output and s the input series, while b represents the lag between the two series). This part of the methodology requires further subjective assessment, where one of a number of possible alternatives is selected. Experience in using the methodology is therefore of great value.

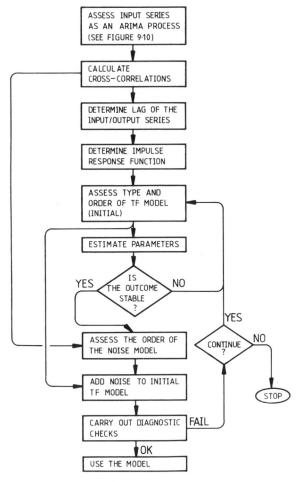

FIGURE 9.11. Summary of the TF modeling methodology.

Parameter estimates are then made and the model assessed for stability. If the stability criteria are not satisfied, then an alternative (r, s, b) model, which may have been tentatively identified in the previous step, may be considered. This step is iterated until a model, satisfying stability criteria, is identified.

In Chapter 4 (on measurement), the problem of noise on empirical data was discussed. In order to cater to this in TF model building, a noise model is also constructed. Noise can be identified by using the correlation functions on the transformed input and output series and by using an equation derived by Box and Jenkins (presented in the case studies which follow). The order of the noise model can thus be ascertained. The process also has to be identified as an ARIMA (p, d, q). The full noise model can then be written and added to the TF part of the model derived in the earlier part of the methodology. Diagnostic testing must also be carried out.

Markov Chains. The objective of building a Markov chain is to construct a model that facilitates the prediction of future states of the situation, given knowledge of the current state, all other possible states, and the transition probability between these states. Probabilities are considered here as being time-invariant, although the Markov concept can be extended to include time-varying probabilities, in which case it is known as a semi-Markov chain.

The methodology requires that the inputs and outputs that affect state transition are identified and a set of discrete states are named. In addition (using either laws, theory, or data) the probability of the one-step transitions (the probability of moving from one state to another over one time period) is made explicit. From this a transition matrix is formulated, which provides the core model for a variety of state transition studies. Producing a manageable model where the transition probabilities can be estimated requires that the discrete number of states should be kept relatively small. States that are rarely encountered can be lumped together with others without introducing too much error. If estimates of the probability of moving from one state to another differ significantly, say for two different subclasses of values of the state occupied at the previous time period, it may be necessary to split the "donor" state into two substates reflecting the subclasses. The incremental lumping and splitting process, although statistically crude, is the way that many chains are fitted in practice. The state space is thus contracted or expanded until an acceptable trade-off is attained between manageability and detail (Daellenbach *et al.*, 1983).

Uses

The uses of the data-driven and state transition models are essentially for prediction. They are particularly appropriate where the generative mechanisms of a situation are unknown (in the case of weak knowledge or controversial theory, for example) or where the underlying structure of a situation is changing (during a disease process, for example). The TF approach is particularly useful when control of a variable(s) of interest is required. This may be strictly regulated by controlling an input(s) which helps to produce the desired output. Box and Jenkins (1976) showed the latter used to good effect with their gas furnace model (although this has caused some controversy among experts). The application domain in technological control is extensive. Other areas have recently been investigated, for example, in medical decision support tools, as described in the case studies at the end of this chapter.

Stochastic state transition investigations allow us to consider the probabilities of finding the model in each state at the beginning or end of a transition. It is also possible to consider how long it will take for the model to reach a particular state of interest for the first time. The long-term steady state of the model may also be calculated.

The application domain is vast but includes: reservoirs given the probability of rainfall (input) and demand (output); market analysis on the share of the market for a number of brands; modeling of a disease process and the effect of drugs (which may alter state transition probabilities) on the disease progress in a patient; and reliability or failure analysis.

223
Process, Purposes, and Approaches

9.3.8. Logical

Types

In some senses it is slightly unreal to separate out "logical models" as a distinct class within the spectrum of modeling approaches that is being considered in this chapter. Any model should represent the logical structure and connectivity of the processes under investigation. Equally, assessment of logical consistency is an important ingredient of model validation.

Nevertheless, there are types of model in which representation of the logical structure is the dominant feature. Many of these are particularly associated with decision problems and the logical rules that underpin such decision processes. One such is the decision tree, which, although also a form of graphical model, portrays the branching logic of alternative choices emanating from decision nodes.

Many of the other forms of logical model are based on the constructs of Boolean logic. In this way a richer range of logical relationships can be modeled than is possible with the simpler branching tree logic. For example, the full range of sentential logic can be used, enabling connectivity of the form of AND, OR, EXCLUSIVE OR, IMPLICATION, and NEGATION to be expressed, a richness of logical relationship such as is to be found in structured complexity.

In essence these logical models are symbolic knowledge based, and constitute artificial intelligence type representation, in contrast to the mathematical models considered earlier, which are essentially cybernetic representations. A further form of symbolic representation is the conceptual graph. This type of model, like the decision tree, spans the graphical and the logical forms, providing a vehicle for highlighting the structure and connectivity within suitable complex situations.

Methodological Considerations

The approach to developing decision trees is essentially relatively simple, but does take several forms. One form, which is of particular interest to us, is to start off with an initial finding and then to seek out the likely cause. The initial finding then constitutes the superordinate point on a hierarchy. The aim is to systematically work down levels in the hierarchy toward a set of causes that are known (expert knowledge is required here) to be related to such a finding. This may be achieved by defining a set of empirical tests that connect the top and bottom of the hierarchy. Each test will give a number of outcomes, which then form new branches in the tree. Each branch may also identify further tests, which again give another set of outcomes, and consequently provide other branching points. In this way the tree expands until the "leaves" (the causes) are arrived at. Thus, given an initial finding, it is possible to work down the tree by carrying out the predefined tests until the likely cause is found.

The development of symbolic knowledge representation is entirely different from the decision tree approach, resembling the general approach that is suitable for developing mathematical models. The methodology passes through stages of conceptualization. Initially a conceptual graph is developed, and then from this a list of statements is drawn up. Using the metalanguage of, say, a software language suited to logical representation, the statements are converted into code for computer implementation.

Uses

Logical models find application both in explanation and in decision making. They can provide a clear picture of logical connections and, as such, aid in the understanding of complexity. Equally they have a role in diagnosis, in decision making, and in management where rule-based models can provide advice and, where appropriate, propose a particular course of management action that could be implemented. An indication of the way in which logical expressions can be encoded in one of the logic programming languages such as PROLOG is given in the case studies at the end of this section.

9.3.9. A Methodology for Modeling Structured Situations

This and the previous section document, in a rational conceptual format, both fundamental and novel lessons that have emerged in our experience over a number of years of modeling. We now offer a comprehensive consolidation of these ideas in the shape of a methodology for the use of modeling approaches applied to structured situations. The methodology is summarized in Figure 9.12. A brief verbal summary is given below.

Initially there is some task that focuses the attention of some investigator(s), hence, making the following activities purposeful. There is a need for task formulation. Structured approaches must not be considered a panacea for all task situations, and task formulation will help initially in deciding the appropriate route forward. An exit route from this methodology (to a nonstructured approach) is therefore essential. Nevertheless, for an investigator to have entered this methodology there will have been a strong sense (one usually arising out of experience) that the task is one for structured modeling.

In this case it is important to set the modeling purposes in order to identify an appropriate approach. This can be substantially aided by undertaking a critical review of extant models. The investigator will then be able to incorporate a pragmatic element according to previous findings. The pragmatic review may suggest that structured approaches are not appropriate, hence exit may be required.

In many instances, the model will be incorporated into an existing situation and hence the modeling purposes will be utilitarian in nature. The proposed

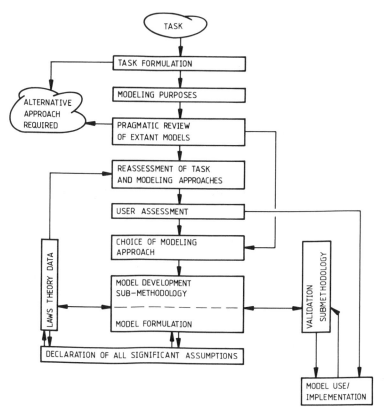

FIGURE 9.12. A methodology for modeling structured systems (adapted from Carson *et al.*, 1983).

use has to be reflected in the model development and may influence the choice of modeling approach. A choice is then made. However, this can be altered at a later stage.

At this point, model construction begins by use of a model development submethodology. Incorporated into the thinking must be the availability of data (the problems of measurement), theories, and law. A set of assumptions concerning the model must be declared, adding a higher degree of transparency and falsifiability. These will be related to the quality of the data and the availability of laws.

Validation (which is in fact an explicit part of the model development submethodology) then has to be considered more formally. This will be achieved via a distinct validation submethodology. When some satisfactory correspondence between the situation, the model, and the modeling purposes has been attained, then model use and implementation are appropriate. This should reflect the needs of the user; however, validation will continue throughout this stage, particularly as the model may change the situation in which it is used.

9.3.10. Summary

A variety of modeling approaches, including methodological considerations as well as their uses, have been reviewed in this section. Attention has also been given to methodological issues and to the uses of models. The approach adopted has been essentially conceptual so that all readers have been able to progress this far with relative ease. In the following section a number of case studies are presented, each of which draws upon the relevant conceptual framework.

9.4. CASE STUDIES

9.4.1. Introduction

A representative set of modeling approaches and types has been introduced in this chapter. The discussion up to now has centered around modeling theory, although aspects of application have not been totally excluded. The aim of this section, however, is to switch the emphasis from theory to application, thus providing a complete modeling story. The reader is advised to make reference to the relevant methodologies described in Section 9.3 in order to consolidate the lessons of the case studies.

We have chosen patient management in a hospital as our theme. In particular, we shall be considering fluid volume maintenance in the adult patient. This constitutes an area of real difficulty in measurement and hence rigorously tests the approaches in application. By focusing upon one particular area, we anticipate that the readers will be able to concentrate their efforts on gaining an understanding of the modeling types. Nevertheless, it is necessary in the first instance to provide the reader with a working knowledge of fluid-balance in man as well as a clear statement of our modeling purpose. This is briefly set out below and is followed by a variety of statistical, mathematical, and logical modeling approaches, which all share the utilitarian objective of clinical application. At appropriate points during the presentation, the approaches are discussed and compared in relation to the modeling purpose.

9.4.2. Background and Purposes

In contemporary society the management of scarce resources is one of man's cardinal activities. Medicine is an essential service of society, is widespread (the National Health Service is the largest single employer in Britain), and consequently is a voracious user of society's resources. As a result, there is great pressure to find ways of using scarce resources efficiently and, hence, improving the quality of health care available for patients.

One of the most valuable resources is time (it can be considered as a resource since it is available for disposal). Time is closely related to cost, for example, the cost of a bed per day, cost of nursing hours, and cost of internal services for patient care such as the clinical laboratory. Methods of improving cost efficiency are therefore greatly sought after by central government and health service administrators alike, while at the same time these groups as well as the clinical, nursing, and paramedical staff are concerned with maintaining and improving the quality of patient care.

It is therefore surprising to find that clinical laboratories are involved in what does not always appear to be the most efficient of hospital activities. Patients in the critical care unit, for instance, are subject to continual monitoring and biochemical surveillance. Samples of blood and urine are sent to chemical pathology laboratories for measurement and documentation. This has led to a growing bank of data from which only a limited amount of information is extracted. Static data profiles displaying slices of information at discrete times are presented to the clinician as a decision aid. At best (although only occasionally) these profiles are accompanied by some simple statistical analysis, for example, descriptive statistics or more rarely by linear regression.

The first problem for consideration arises here. Man has limited information-processing capabilities (as discussed in Chapter 2) so that no matter how sophisticated the presentation of static data profiles may be, clinicians will inevitably pass over much of the information contained in the data and many of its implications. The onus is thus on the laboratory to provide more effective support.

This gives rise to the second problem for consideration. Up to the present time, patient management and quantitative decision support have been treated as separate disciplines. This has tended to lead to autonomous development and consequent mismatch between these areas of medicine. Working toward an interface between these separated areas requires that many of the gaps that have evolved must be bridged. Thus, the onus is on the laboratory to provide more effective decision support, but the objectives must have an emphasis on practical requirements.

The way forward with these problems, and the purpose of the research reported in the following case studies, can be considered in the objectives tree of Figure 9.13. In essence this shows the role of clinical chemistry (chemical pathology) in the data transformation process.

Five hierarchically organized objectives can be seen explicitly. Implicit in the figure, and expressed by the dotted "feedback," is the identification of essential as opposed to redundant data, which may suggest areas where more efficient data production might be achieved.

The research documented here considers these objectives in the context of fluid therapy. We carried out this program of work in collaboration with Professor Derek Cramp of the Department of Chemical Pathology and Human Metabolism at the Royal Free Hospital School of Medicine, London.

Fluid–electrolyte, acid–base balance (FAB) was selected as the area of interest as it is important to many clinical problems and subsequent clinical decision making. However, as FAB is such a large domain, it would not be productive or desirable to dilute research efforts over the entire range of problems that could be encountered. It was therefore decided to investigate

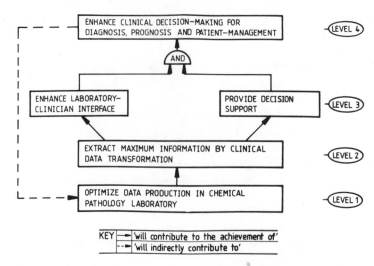

FIGURE 9.13. Objectives tree associated with the case studies.

specifically the problem of maintaining fluid volume in acutely ill patients. Before presenting details of the modeling exercises, however, a brief introduction to fluid dynamics is presented.

9.4.3. Fluid–Electrolyte Acid–Base Balance

Rather than give a sentential description of the structure and processes, we intend to present the material in diagrammatic form where possible. The structure can be considered (abstracted) as having three general compartments where all analytes (substances of interest) may be contained. These are the

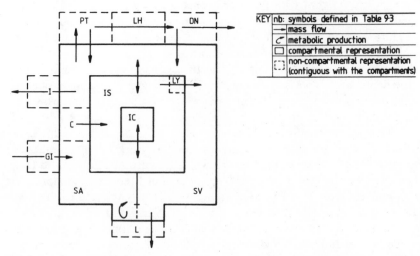

FIGURE 9.14. Basis structure and processes of the fluid-electrolyte, acid–base balance.

TABLE 9.3

Symbols Used in Figure 9.14

Symbol	Explanation
C	Capillaries
DN	Distal nephron
GI	Gastrointestinal
I	Insensible routes
IC	Intracellular
IS	Interstitial
L	Lung
LH	Loops of Henle
LY	Lymphatics
PT	Proximal tubule
SA	Systemic arteries
SV	Systemic veins

intracellular (cells), interstitial (space between the cells), and plasma compartments. In the first of these the representation of body cells is lumped together as "one large cell." The organs associated with fluid balance and the routes by which analytes may move are shown in Figure 9.14. The symbols used in Figure 9.14 are defined in Table 9.3. Movement by these routes may be by diffusion, hydrostatic pressure, or active pumping (of various forms). The dynamics and control of FAB are summarized in the signed digraphs of Figures 9.15–9.18. Studying these diagrams for ten minutes or so is the alternative we offer the reader to volumes of text. These diagrams also show how we identified

TABLE 9.4

Symbols Used in Figures 9.15–9.18

Symbol	Explanation
ADH	Antidiuretic hormone
ANG1	Angiotensin 1
ANG2	Angiotensin 2
HCO_3^-	Bicarbonate
HPO_4^-	Phosphate
IC	Intracellular
IS	Interstitial
K^+	Potassium
NA^+	Sodium
NH_3^-	Ammonia
pH	Acidity
PL	Plasma
Pr^-	Protein
U	Urine
IC-IS	Net flow intracellular to interstitial
IS-IC	Net flow interstitial to intracellular
IS-PL	Net flow interstitial to plasma
PL-IS	Net flow plasma to interstitial
[ ]	Concentration

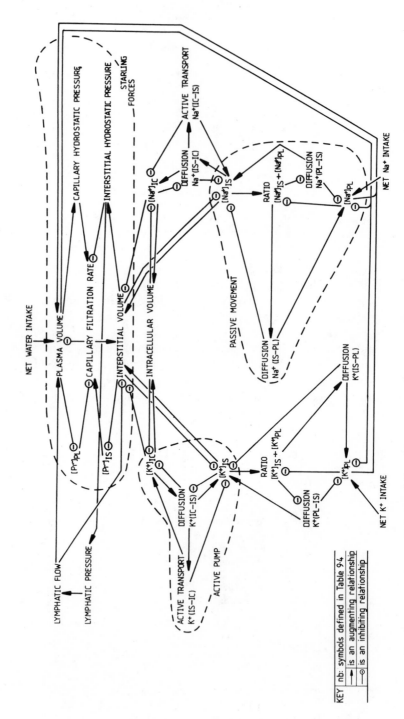

FIGURE 9.15. Signed digraph of fluid and electrolyte dynamics.

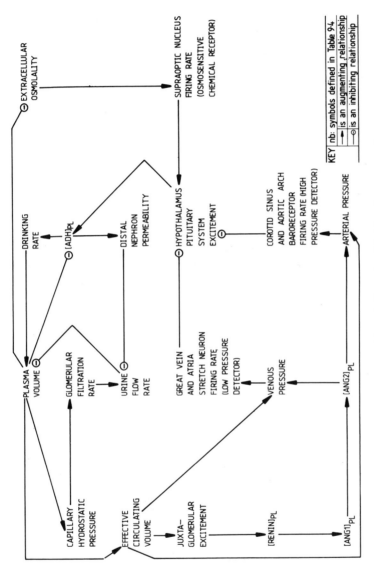

FIGURE 9.16. Signed digraph of fluid volume control.

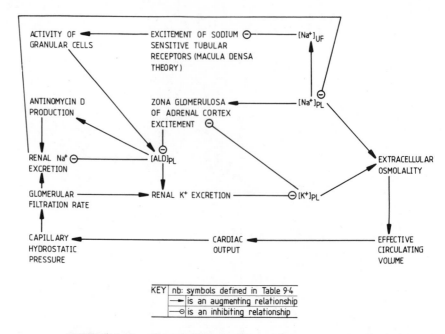

FIGURE 9.17.   Signed digraph of electrolyte content control.

models from a relational as opposed to functional viewpoint. The symbols used in the signed digraphs (Figures 9.15–9.18) are defined in Table 9.4.

If the reader wishes to consult another, more comprehensive, diagrammatic approach we recommend *Fluid and Electrolytes: A Conceptual Approach* (Smith, 1980).

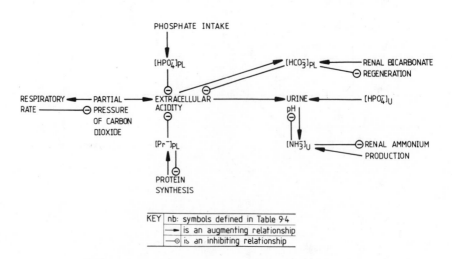

FIGURE 9.18.   Signed digraph of acid–buffer dynamics.

9.4.4. Critical Review

A critical review of extant models was carried out (Flood *et al.*, 1986a). The selection of models for review was carried out as shown in Figure 3.15 on a set of models identified during a literature search. A major finding was that almost all of them were of a large-scale, control system type. This highlighted the need to consider the potential of compact modeling and statistical approaches, and to assess their merits relative to those of the more complex approaches, with particular reference to our utilitarian objectives. It was also apparent from the research work reviewed that the data used in model development was of the ratio scale and hence the use of all statistics and mathematics was appropriate.

9.4.5. ARIMA Modeling

Introduction

A data file of critical care cases was made available. Sample size was the most important criterion used in the selection of a case for analysis, as a small sample inevitably leads to sampling error. The longest time series available was of a road traffic accident case where the patient remained in the Intensive Therapy Unit (ITU) for 27 days. Measurements were taken once every 24 hours (sample step of 1 day); urine specimens were collected using a plain bottle, and blood samples taken using the usual syringe method. A urine potassium concentration time series was selected for modeling. The following documentation is based on that of Flood *et al.* (1985).

Urine Potassium Concentration

The reference range for urine concentration is 40–120 mmol liter^{-1} (Staff of the Division of Pathology, 1979). The time series plot (see Figure 9.19) shows two outliers (highlighted by circles), which have probably arisen from error in measurement. These could be removed by changing their actual values to their expected values; however, physiologically large changes can occur

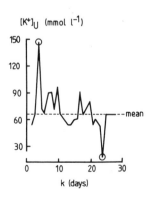

FIGURE 9.19. Time series plot of urine potassium [K$^+$] (circle highlights outliers).

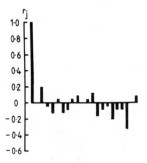

FIGURE 9.20. Correlogram of the raw data shown in Figure 9.19.

and it is difficult to determine whether the errors are due to poor measurement or physiological changes. For this reason, the values were left unchanged. In addition, there were three missing values, which were set to their expected values.

The correlogram of the raw data is shown in Figure 9.20. The autocorrelation function r_j clearly damps out slowly. This implies nonstationarity of the series (which is not clear from the plot of Figure 9.19). Consequently, the first differences of the series were taken. The autocorrelation function r_j of this is shown in the correlogram of Figure 9.21. Using Bartlett's formula, the standard error $[SE(r_j)]$ shows that only r_1 is significant. The partial-autocorrelation function of the first differences is shown in Figure 9.22 and the standard error test $[SE(\hat{\phi}_{jj})]$ shows that the first two values of the function are significant.

The interpretation of these functions is not clear-cut. An ARIMA$(2, 1, 1)$ process was tentatively chosen with ARIMA$(2, 1, 0)$ as an obvious alternative identification.

Maximum Likelihood Estimation (MLE) was the next methodological step. The ARIMA procedure on MINITAB works from initial parameter estimates of 0.1, but will allow the user to enter their own initial parameter estimates if so desired. In this first instance it was decided to compare the outcomes for both cases, thus initial parameter values had to be estimated from the autocorrelation function. This process is detailed below.

For the MA part only one parameter was estimated:

$$r_1 = \frac{-\hat{\theta}_1}{1 + \hat{\theta}_1^2} \tag{9.1}$$

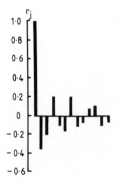

FIGURE 9.21. Correlogram of the first differences of the raw data shown in Figure 9.19.

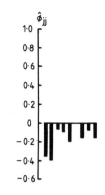

FIGURE 9.22. Estimated partial autocorrelation $\hat{\theta}_{JJ}$ on the first differences of the raw data shown in Figure 9.19.

therefore

$$\hat{\theta}_1 = \frac{1}{2r_1} \pm \left[\frac{1}{(2r_1)^2} - 1\right]^{1/2} \tag{9.2}$$

so that

$$\hat{\theta}_1 = 1.405 \pm 0.986$$

To satisfy invertibility constraints and ensure that the process is stable $|\hat{\theta}| < 1$ is a necessary condition and therefore -0.419 was chosen. For the autoregressive part, two parameters were estimated by solving the Yule–Walker equations:

$$r_1 = \hat{\phi}_1 + \hat{\phi}_2 r_1$$
$$r_2 = \hat{\phi}_1 r_1 + \hat{\phi}_2 \tag{9.3}$$

so that $\hat{\phi}_1 = -0.492$, and $\hat{\phi}_2 = -0.382$, and $\hat{\phi}_1 + \hat{\phi}_2 = -0.874$, which is within the invertible (stability) limit.

The final parameter estimates after MLE, with initial parameters all at 0.1, are shown in Table 9.5; and with initial parameters estimated from the

TABLE 9.5
Final Estimates of Parameters of ARIMA(2, 1, 1) for Urine
Potassium Concentration Data Shown in Figure 9.19
(Initial Parameters Set by MINITAB)[a]

Type	Estimate	S.D.	t-Ratio
AR(1)	0.0978	0.2369	0.41
AR(2)	−0.1805	0.2287	−0.79
MA(1)	0.8531	0.1430	5.97

[a] Differencing 1; sum of squares = 11,052.9; degrees of freedom = 23; original series = 27; after differencing = 26; S.D. is standard deviation.

TABLE 9.6

Final Estimates of Parameters of ARIMA(2, 1, 1) for Urine
Potassium Concentration Data Shown in Figure 9.19
(Estimated Initial Parameters)^a

Type	Estimate	S.D.	t-Ratio
AR(1)	−0.6965	0.2069	−3.37
AR(2)	−0.7056	0.1560	−4.52
MA(1)	−0.0633	0.2779	−0.23

^{a} Differencing 1; sum of squares = 9986.63; degrees of freedom = 23; original series = 27; after differencing = 26; S.D. is standard deviation.

autocorrelation function are shown in Table 9.6. The confidence intervals are, respectively:

$$-0.367 < \phi_1 < 0.572$$

$$-0.629 < \phi_2 < 0.268 \tag{9.4}$$

$$0.567 < \theta_1 < 1.139$$

and

$$-1.102 < \phi_1 < -0.291$$

$$-1.011 < \phi_2 < -0.400 \tag{9.5}$$

$$-0.608 < \theta_1 < 0.481$$

For the first set of confidence intervals there is less than 95% confidence that $|\hat{\theta}_1| < 1$, and $\hat{\phi}_1 + \hat{\phi}_2 = -0.996$ at the lower extremity of the interval which is near the invertible limit. For the second set of confidence intervals, at the lower extremity $\hat{\phi}_1 + \hat{\phi}_2 = -2.113$ which is nonconvergent and thus unsatisfactory. For the first case the t-ratio is significant only for $\hat{\theta}_1$; in the second case the situation is reversed as only $\hat{\phi}_1$ and $\hat{\phi}_2$ are shown to be significant. Some of these problems are undoubtedly due to the small sample size.

An alternative process has been postulated as ARIMA(2, 1, 0). This is considered below both with and without the inclusion of a constant in the process. The final parameter estimates are consolidated, respectively, in Table 9.7 and Table 9.8. The confidence intervals, respectively, are

$$-0.943 < \phi_1 < -0.352$$

$$-0.971 < \phi_2 < -0.392 \tag{9.6}$$

and

$$-0.947 < \phi_1 < -0.331$$

$$-0.984 < \phi_2 < -0.380 \tag{9.7}$$

TABLE 9.7

Final Estimates of Parameters of ARIMA(2, 1, 0) for Urine
Potassium Concentration Data Shown in Figure 9.19
(Estimated Initial Parameters)[a]

Type	Estimate	S.D.	t-Ratio
AR(1)	−0.6476	0.1506	−4.30
AR(2)	−0.6817	0.1478	−4.61

[a] Differencing 1; sum of squares = 10,035.8; degrees of freedom = 24; original series = 27; after differencing = 26; *S.D.* is standard deviation.

In both cases, there is less than 95% confidence that $|\hat{\phi}_1 + \hat{\phi}_2| < 1$. Convergence therefore has not been achieved, although in the first case the *t*-ratio shows that both AR parameters are significantly different from zero, which is also true of the second case; however, the constant is not significantly different from zero. The sums of the squares of both cases approximate to those found in Table 9.6 and are an improvement on those in Table 9.5.

Assessment of the above four tests (and further identification and parameter estimation) led to the conclusion that laboratory derived data was not attainable at a sufficiently fast rate for the requirements of ARIMA model building. The form shown in Equation (9.8) (ARIMA[2, 1, 0] using estimated parameters for MLE), for instance, gives forecasts that appear reasonable; however, the stability criteria have not been met:

$$x_t = -0.6476x_{t-1} - 0.6817x_{t-2} + U_t \tag{9.8}$$

Discussion

In the example presented above, ARIMA models were fitted to a sequence of $n = 27$ clinical data points. The small sample size caused significant problems in identification and estimation. Our findings, however, do not discount totally the use of ARIMA modeling, which may be found useful where the data rate

TABLE 9.8

Final Estimates of Parameters of ARIMA(2, 1, 0) for Urine
Potassium Concentration Data Shown in Figure 9.19
(Initial Parameters Set by MINITAB)[a]

Type	Estimate	S.D.	t-Ratio
AR(1)	−0.6390	0.1539	−4.15
AR(2)	−0.6822	0.1509	−4.52
Constant	−1.3810	4.1040	−0.34

[a] Differencing 1; sum of squares = 10,049.9; degrees of freedom = 23; original series = 27; after differencing = 26; *S.D.* is standard deviation.

is high. As the standard error of the autocorrelation estimate is approximately equal to $n^{-1/2}$, it is generally accepted that at least 50 data points are required in ARIMA modeling (Box and Jenkins, 1976). During on-line patient monitoring with frequent sampling (exception rather than the norm) this size is readily achievable; however, in data derived from laboratory results, such as that discussed above, much sparser time series are typically found.

For clinical implementation, given acceptable data rates, there remains the problem of model identification. This depends upon interpretation of the autocorrelation and partial-autocorrelation functions and has a subjective element. It has been noted that "the interpretation of correlograms is one of the hardest aspects of time series analysis and practical experience is a must" (Chatfield, 1980). This is likely to become the norm for only a small number of clinical staff. Automatic identification may be included in parameter estimation by selecting a model that minimizes the Akaike Information Criterion ($-2 \ln$ [maximized likelihood] $+ 2$), but a unique minimum cannot be guaranteed (Chatfield, 1980).

Other limitations of ARIMA modeling are its univariate nature and its adoption of linear models. In addition, long-term clinical data are likely to contain seasonal variations at different frequencies; however, seasonal ARIMA models can handle this type of data (Box and Jenkins, 1976).

9.4.6. Transfer Function Modeling

Introduction

The univariate ARIMA approach cannot take into account relations between different time series which may be of clinical importance. For instance, in one identification in Section 9.4.5, a falling urine potassium concentration would be forecast. If this was the only change in the patient it might have been important. However, if it had been counterbalanced by other changes (such as rising urine sodium) it would have been of little significance. One form of bivariate relation, where one time series corresponds to an input and another to an observable effect or output, can be investigated using discrete time transfer function (TF) models. Such models allow the dynamic response of the patient to be determined and hence better control exercised. Examples include control of fluid intake and drug infusions. An approach to TF modeling was developed by Box and Jenkins (1976) along the lines of their ARIMA methodology. Application of this approach to FAB is reported by Flood and Cramp (1987), which forms the basis of the following description.

Box and Jenkins stated that when the effect of noise is appreciable (which will usually be the case for clinical measurements), a delayed first- or second-order model of the type

$$Y_t = \delta^{-1}(B)w(B)x_{t-b} \tag{9.9}$$

would provide as elaborate a model as could be justified for that data. Therefore, where a choice arose, compact models were selected.

The following subsection provides a detailed account of a TF modeling exercise for drinking rate (input) and urine sodium concentration (output).

Urine Sodium Response to Water Intake

Figure 9.23 shows the time series data for water input (X_t) and urine sodium output (Y_t) with $n = 100$. The data illustrate the way that sodium is selectively excreted in the control of total body water.

MINITAB was used to assess the type and order of the input time series as an ARIMA process. The correlogram of the raw data (not shown) decays slowly, while the partial autocorrelation plot (not shown) spikes as lag 1 and then tails off. This seemed to suggest an ARIMA(1,0,0) process. However, taking t-ratios of the final estimates for parameters of ARIMA(2,0,0) showed that $\hat{\phi}_2$ was significantly different (but only at a low level) from zero (t-ratio of 1.02). The addition of a ϕ_3 or θ_1 term on the two previous processes proved to be insignificant on the basis of the t-ratios. The sums of the squares for ARIMA(1, 0, 0) and ARIMA(2, 0, 0) were not significantly different. An ARIMA(2, 0, 0) process was tentatively selected as being representative (although there was pressure to develop a simpler ARIMA(1, 0, 0) model).

A detailed account of a TF modeling exercise, based on an ARIMA(2, 0, 0) process for the input, is presented below. This is followed by the essential details of a similar modeling exercise, based on an ARIMA(1, 0, 0) process for the input.

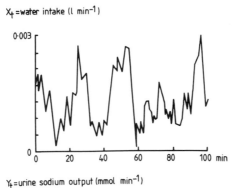

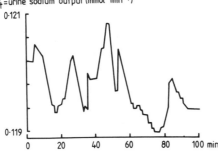

FIGURE 9.23. Time series plot of water intake and urine sodium output.

For the case of ARIMA$(2, 0, 0)$ MINITAB was used to derive the following final parameter estimates:

$$\hat{\phi}_1 = 0.8676 \quad \text{and} \quad \hat{\phi}_2 = 0.1305 \qquad \text{with } |\hat{\phi}_1 + \hat{\phi}_2| < 1$$

although these do lie close to the invertibility limit. This suggests that $n = 100$ may be too small a sample size. The 95% confidence intervals were found to be

$$0.6632 < \phi_1 < 1.0720$$

$$0.0995 < \phi_2 < 0.3335$$

$$(9.10)$$

so that the upper range of the confidence interval lies outside the invertibility limit.

Thus, an input process $x_t = \nabla^0 X_t$ has been identified that is suitably stationary and can be represented by ARIMA$(2, 0, 0)$, which is a member of the general linear class of autoregressive moving average models. Using this process, any input series x_t can be transformed to an uncorrelated white noise series α_t:

$$(1 - 0.8676B - 0.1305B^2)x_t = \alpha_t \qquad (9.11)$$

This may also be applied to $y_t(\nabla^0 Y_t)$ to obtain the uncorrelated white noise series β_t:

$$(1 - 0.8676B - 0.1305B^2)y_t = \beta_t \qquad (9.12)$$

By realizing the two series:

$$\alpha_t = x_t - 0.8676x_{t-1} - 0.1305x_{t-2}$$

$$\beta_t = y_t - 0.8676y_{t-1} - 0.1305y_{t-2}$$

$$(9.13)$$

the standard deviations $\sigma_\alpha = 3.78 \times 10^{-4}$ and $\sigma_\beta = 1.36 \times 10^{-4}$ were derived. Hence, $\sigma_\beta/\sigma_\alpha = 0.36$ and thus the estimate of the impulse response function is

$$0.36r_{\alpha\beta}(k) = \hat{v}_k \qquad (9.14)$$

From here MINITAB was used to generate the cross-correlations for $\alpha(t)$ and $\beta(t + k)$, with k representing the lag. In addition and for the sake of simplicity, the standard error was assumed to be $n^{-1/2}$ (0.1 for 100 samples). The results are shown in Table 9.9, where the impulse response function has also been calculated.

The values of $r_{\alpha\beta}(k)$ for $k = 0, \ldots, 3$ are small compared with their errors, implying that $b = 4$. The estimated impulse response function is plotted in Figure 9.24. In the figure long dashed lines are σ and 2σ confidence intervals,

TABLE 9.9
Cross-Correlations ($r_{\alpha\beta}$), Standard Error (SE), and Impulse Responses ($\hat{v}_k$) of
Urine Sodium Response to Water Intake Fitted to an ARIMA(2, 0, 0) Process

k	0	1	2	3	4	5	6	7	8	9	10
$r_{\alpha\beta}$	0.03	0.13	−0.14	0.13	0.36	0.14	0.28	0.30	0.26	0.14	−0.04
SE	0.10	0.10	0.10	0.10	0.10	0.10	0.10	0.10	0.10	0.10	0.10
$\hat{v}_k$	0.10	0.05	−0.05	0.05	0.13	0.09	0.10	0.11	0.10	0.05	−0.02

and the short dashed line is a characteristic TF(2, 1, 4) model. Comparing this
impulse response function to examples given by Box and Jenkins (1976), the
appropriate model appears to be $(r, s, b) = (2, 1, 4)$, that is

$$(1 - \delta_1 B - \delta_2 B^2)y_t = (w_0 - w_1 B)x_{t-4} \qquad \textbf{(9.15)}$$

Parameters were estimated from the following set of equations:

$$\begin{aligned} 0, & \qquad j < b \\ w_0, & \qquad j = b \\ \delta_1 w_0 - w_1, & \qquad j = b + 1 \\ \delta_1 v_{j-1} + \delta_2 v_{j-2}, & \qquad j > b + 1 \end{aligned} \qquad \textbf{(9.16)}$$

so that

$$\hat{w}_0 = v_4 = 0.13$$

and

$$\delta_1(0.13) - w_1 = v_5 = 0.09$$

$$\delta_1(0.09) + \delta_2(0.13) = v_6 = 0.10 \qquad \textbf{(9.17)}$$

$$\delta_1(0.10) + \delta_2(0.09) = v_7 = 0.11$$

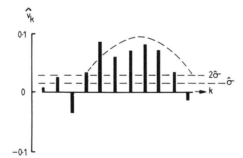

FIGURE 9.24. Estimated impulse
response function $\hat{v}_k$ assuming
ARIMA(2, 0, 0) on the input data
shown in Figure 9.23.

thus

$$\hat{\delta}_1 = 1.08, \qquad \hat{\delta}_2 = 0.02, \quad \text{and} \quad \hat{w}_1 = 0.05$$

The initial model identification was therefore

$$(1 - 1.08B - 0.02B^2)y_t = (0.13 - 0.05B)x_{t-4} \tag{9.18}$$

so that

$$y_t = \frac{(0.13 - 0.05B)}{(1 - 1.08B - 0.02B^2)} x_{t-4} \tag{9.19}$$

For this second-order model, stability will only occur if the following constraints are satisfied:

$$\delta_2 + \delta_1 < 1$$

$$\delta_2 - \delta_1 < 1 \tag{9.20}$$

$$-1 < \delta_2 < 1$$

however, the first constraint is not satisfied. For this reason, the alternative model $(r, s, b) = (2, 0, 4)$ was considered. The parameters were estimated using the following set of equations:

$$0, \qquad\qquad j < b$$

$$w_0, \qquad\qquad j = b \tag{9.21}$$

$$\delta_1 v_{j-1} + \delta_2 v_{j-2}, \qquad j > b + 1$$

so that

$$\hat{w}_0 = v_4 = 0.13$$

and

$$\delta_1(0.13) + \delta_2(0.05) = v_5 = 0.09$$

$$\tag{9.22}$$

$$\delta_1(0.09) + \delta_2(0.13) = v_6 = 0.10$$

thus $\hat{\delta}_2 = 0.395$ and $\hat{\delta}_1 = 0.54$, and hence the set of constraints, Equation 9.20, was satisfied ensuring stability. The following model was identified:

$$(1 - 0.54B - 0.395B^2)y_t = 0.13x_{t-4} \tag{9.23}$$

so that

$$y_t = \frac{0.13}{(1 - 0.54B - 0.395B^2)} x_{t-4} \qquad (9.24)$$

The nature of this second-order model can be assessed by calculating the roots of its characteristic equation. Alternatively, as $\delta_1^2 + 4\delta_2 > 0$ it is known that the roots are real and the model is "overdamped." Thus, the response of this model will be asymptotic to a new steady state following stress. Identification of the noise model was made by assuming

$$y_t = v(B)x_t + n_t \qquad (9.25)$$

where $n_t = \nabla^d N_t$, so that

$$\hat{n}_t = y_t - \hat{v}(B)x_t \qquad (9.26)$$

Noise was identified from the correlation functions for the input and output (after prewhitening) by using the following equation derived by Box and Jenkins (1976):

$$p_{\varepsilon\varepsilon}(k) = \frac{p_{\beta\beta}(k) - \sum_{j=0}^{\infty} p_{\alpha\beta}(j)p_{\alpha\beta}(j+k)}{1 - \sum_{j=0}^{\infty} p_{\alpha\beta}^2(j)} \qquad (9.27)$$

In reality, only rough estimates of $p_{\varepsilon\varepsilon}(k)$ and $r_{\varepsilon\varepsilon}(k)$ can be made using the estimated functions $r_{\alpha\beta}(k)$ and $r_{\beta\beta}(k)$. The results of applying this identification procedure are shown in Table 9.10.

From the $r_{\varepsilon\varepsilon}$ function a second-order noise model was postulated as $r_{\varepsilon\varepsilon} > 2$ is not significant. It was postulated that the process is autoregressive (no clear directions have been given by Box and Jenkins); therefore

$$(1 - 0.44B - 0.34B^2)\varepsilon_t = a_t \qquad (9.28)$$

and since

$$(1 - 0.54B - 0.395B^2)N_t = \varepsilon_t \qquad (9.29)$$

by substituting Equation 9.29 into Equation 9.28 the following expression was

TABLE 9.10
Estimation of Noise Function ($r_{\varepsilon\varepsilon}$) for ARIMA(2, 0, 0) Process
Using Correlation Functions ($r_{\alpha\beta}$, $r_{\beta\beta}$) (Small Values Set to 0)

k	0	1	2	3	4	5	6	7	8
$r_{\beta\beta}$	1.0	0.38	0.34	0	0	0	0	0	0
$r_{\alpha\beta}$	0	0	0	0	0.36	0	0.28	0.30	0.26
$r_{\varepsilon\varepsilon}$	1.0	0.44	0.34	0.02	0	0	0	0	0

obtained:

$$(1 - 0.44B - 0.34B^2)(1 - 0.54B - 0.395B^2)N_t = a_t \qquad \textbf{(9.30)}$$

so that the complete model becomes

$$y_t = \frac{(0.13)x_{t-4}}{(1 - 0.54B - 0.395B^2)} + \frac{a_t}{(1 - 0.98B - 0.497B^2 + 0.354B^3 + 0.13B^4)} \qquad \textbf{(9.31)}$$

where all $\hat{\phi}$'s and $\hat{\theta}$'s are approximate starting values.

It has previously been suggested that an ARIMA$(1, 0, 0)$ process might be appropriate for the given data:

$$(1 - \phi_1 B)X_t = \alpha_t \qquad \textbf{(9.32)}$$

where $\hat{\phi}_1 = 0.96$. Since $(1 - 0.96B) \approx (1 - B)$, the indications are that X_t was generated by a random walk process:

$$X_t = X_{t-1} + \alpha_t \qquad \textbf{(9.33)}$$

The prewhitened series α_t and transformed output series β_t were thus obtained by simple differencing:

$$\alpha_t = \nabla^1 X_t; \qquad \beta_t = \nabla^1 Y_t \qquad \textbf{(9.34); (9.35)}$$

The standard deviations were $\sigma_\alpha = 0.405 \times 10^{-3}$ and $\sigma_\beta = 0.14 \times 10^{-3}$. The estimated cross-correlation function $r_{\alpha\beta}(k)$ and an approximate estimate of its standard error (SE) are given in Table 9.11 along with the estimated impulse function $\hat{v}_k$.

The values of $r_{\alpha\beta}(k)$ for $k = 0, \ldots, 3$ are small compared with their SE, which implies $b = 4$. The estimated impulse function is plotted in Figure 9.25. In the figure long dashed lines are σ and 2σ confidence intervals, and the short dashed lines are (a) characteristic $(1, 0, 4)$, and (b) characteristic $(2, 2, 4)$ TF models. Identification of r and s using these data is not clear-cut. The

TABLE 9.11

Cross-Correlations ($r_{\alpha\beta}$), Standard Error (SE), and Impulse Responses ($\hat{v}_k$) of Urine Sodium Response to Water Intake Fitted to an ARIMA$(1, 0, 0)$ Process

k	0	1	2	3	4	5	6	7	8	9	10
$r_{\alpha\beta}$	−0.095	0.035	−0.108	−0.003	0.234	0.151	0.321	0.125	0.074	−0.094	−0.127
SE	0.1	0.1	0.1	0.1	0.1	0.1	0.1	0.1	0.1	0.1	0.1
$\hat{v}_k$	−0.033	0.012	−0.038	−0.001	0.082	0.053	0.112	0.044	0.026	−0.033	−0.045

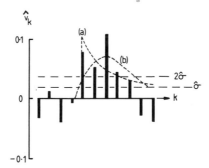

FIGURE 9.25. Estimated impulse response function $\hat{v}_k$ assuming ARIMA$(1, 0, 0)$ on the input data shown in Figure 9.23.

drop at $\hat{v}_5$ between $\hat{v}_4$ and $\hat{v}_6$ is not realizable in a physical system. This effect is probably due to the large estimation errors $\hat{\sigma}_r$ in comparison with $r_{\alpha\beta}$, despite what is considered to be a reasonable sample size.

A first-order model $(1, 0, 4)$ was postulated as an approximate description, which leads to

$$(1 - 0.75B)y_t = 0.1x_{t-4} \qquad (9.36)$$

with a steady-state gain of 0.4 in terms of its parameters. However, the characteristic impulse function of a $(2, 2, 4)$ model is an alternative possibility; see Figure 9.25.

Identification of the noise model from $r_{\alpha\beta}(k)$, $r_{\beta\beta}(k)$, and $r_{\varepsilon\varepsilon}(k)$ (see Table 9.12) suggested that a first-order noise model as $r_{\varepsilon\varepsilon} > 1$ is not significant. It was postulated that the process is autoregressive, therefore

$$(1 - 0.387B)\varepsilon_t = a_t \qquad (9.37)$$

and since

$$(1 - 0.75B)N_t = \varepsilon_t \qquad (9.38)$$

the following equation was formulated:

$$(1 - 0.387B)(1 - 0.75B)N_t = a_t \qquad (9.39)$$

TABLE 9.12
Estimation of Noise Function $(r_{\varepsilon\varepsilon})$ for ARIMA$(1, 0, 0)$ Process Using
Correlation Functions $(r_{\alpha\beta}r_{\beta\beta})$ (Small Values Set to 0)

k	0	1	2	3	4	5	6	7	8	9	10
$r_{\beta\beta}$	1.0	0.326	0	0	0	0	0	0	0	0	0
$r_{\alpha\beta}$	0	0	0	0	0.234	0	0.321	0	0	0	0
$r_{\varepsilon\varepsilon}$	1.0	0.387	0	0	0	0	0	0	0	0	0

so that the complete model becomes

$$y_t = \frac{(0.1)x_{t-4}}{(1 - 0.75B)} + \frac{a_t}{(1 - 1.137B + 0.29B^2)} \tag{9.40}$$

By algebraic manipulation of Equation 9.31, based on ARIMA(2, 0, 0) as a model of the input data, the following representation was achieved:

$$y_k = \mathbf{z}_k^T \hat{\mathbf{a}} + e_k \tag{9.41}$$

where

$$\mathbf{z} = \begin{bmatrix} y_{t-1} \\ y_{t-2} \\ y_{t-3} \\ y_{t-4} \\ y_{t-5} \\ x_{t-4} \\ x_{t-5} \end{bmatrix}; \qquad \hat{\mathbf{a}} = \begin{bmatrix} 1.520 \\ 0.362 \\ -1.000 \\ -0.135 \\ 0.210 \\ 0.130 \\ -0.127 \end{bmatrix} \tag{9.42); (9.43}$$

and similarly, manipulation of Equation 9.40, based on an ARIMA(1, 0, 0) process for the input data, gave

$$\mathbf{z} = \begin{bmatrix} y_{t-1} \\ y_{t-2} \\ y_{t-3} \\ x_{t-4} \\ x_{t-5} \end{bmatrix}; \qquad \hat{\mathbf{a}} = \begin{bmatrix} 1.887 \\ -1.151 \\ 0.224 \\ 0.100 \\ -0.114 \end{bmatrix} \tag{9.44); (9.45}$$

For Equations 9.42–9.45 the following holds:

$$e_k = y_k - \hat{y}_{k/k+1} \tag{9.46}$$

and

$$\hat{y}_{k/k+1} = \mathbf{z}_k^T \hat{\mathbf{a}}_{k-1} \tag{9.47}$$

Assuming no error, Equations 9.42/9.43 and 9.44/9.45 predict y_6 as 0.1148 and 0.1151, respectively, which appear reasonable.

Given a situation where a continuing data supply can be expected, the inclusion of a recursive estimator on **a** may well be of value. A recursive estimator updates the parameter vector **a** according to criteria based on the actual and predicted outputs of the situation and model, respectively. Young (1974) developed a recursive estimator for TF models. The updating equations (see Chapter 8 for a detailed explanation) are

$$\hat{\mathbf{a}}_k = \hat{\mathbf{a}}_{k-1} - \frac{\mathbf{P}_k^*}{\sigma^2}[\mathbf{x}_k \mathbf{x}_k^T \hat{\mathbf{a}}_{k-1} - \mathbf{x}_k y_k] \tag{9.48}$$

and

$$\mathbf{P}_k^* = \mathbf{P}_{k-1}^* - \mathbf{P}_{k-1}^* \mathbf{x}_k [\sigma^2 + \mathbf{x}_k^T \mathbf{P}_{k-1}^* \mathbf{x}_k]^{-1} \mathbf{x}_k^T \mathbf{P}_{k-1}^* \tag{9.49}$$

The initial conditions for $\hat{\mathbf{a}}_0$ may be set at those estimated above, or alternatively as $\hat{\mathbf{a}}_0 = (0)$. The initial conditions for $\mathbf{P}_0 = \mathrm{diag}(10^5, \ldots 10^5)$ which reflects the uncertainty. σ^2, the variance of the sequence of errors, should be set at

$$\sigma^2 = E(\varepsilon^2 y_1) \tag{9.50}$$

that is the noise on the raw data. In practice, however, it is acceptable to set σ^2 at 10% of $E(y)$. The tracking of four of the model parameters of the model described by Equations 9.42 and 9.43 is shown in Figure 9.26 and a comparison of the model output against the patient data is shown in Figure 9.27. In the figure the continuous line is the patient data y_k and the crosses are model forecasts $\hat{y}_k$.

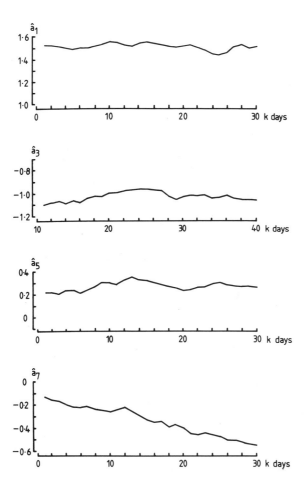

FIGURE 9.26. Recursive tracking of four parameter estimates of TF model.

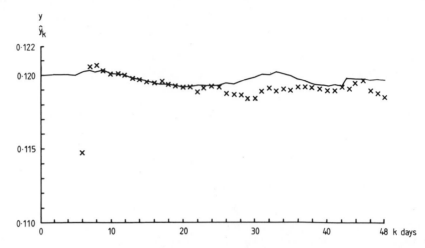

FIGURE 9.27. Recursive TF model output compared to patient data.

The parameters remain close to their true values except for $\hat{a}_7$ (and $\hat{a}_6$, not shown), whose values show a steady fall. These parameters relate to inputs rather than outputs. The depiction of model outputs against the simulated data shows an initial prediction without correction well below the data. This improves substantially on the following prediction with correction. The fit remains very good for the next 22 days, from which point on a continual underestimate begins to appear. This in fact becomes more prominent after 50 days (not shown).

The source of these problems is difficult to identify. Young (1974) stated that the recursive algorithm generates a bias that could have led to the drift on $\hat{a}_6$ and $\hat{a}_7$. Additionally, the input and output need close scrutiny. The input data, although bounded by zero, still have wide variability, whereas the output data appear to be tightly controlled within a 2% peak-to-peak amplitude. It is generally accepted that a 6%–10% measurement error is normally expected in biological situations, so that the TF model may be based mostly on noise. This raises questions concerning the ease of identification and suggests that the recursive estimator is mainly working on the noise.

These considerations are important for future work in this area. However, of most importance is the observation that in principle the technique could be used with some benefits.

Discussion

As was also found for the univariate data, a simple model may provide an adequate representation. The data requirements are high, and it appears that 100 sample pairs are not sufficient for the urine-sodium–water-intake experiment to perform identification for the particular subject. A more appropriate number of sample pairs might be 200. "Bumps" in the impulse function may be due to a sample size problem or perhaps because the underlying dynamics are nonlinear. With automatic methods of TF order determination and parameter estimation, the approach offers clinical potential where patient treatment is by physical input (for example, drugs, saline, and dextrose) and monitoring ensures a high data rate. Furthermore, the method can be generalized to the multiinput/multioutput case (Young, 1974). The value of recursive estimation of the parameters was clearly seen when comparing a first estimate (without recursive estimation) to a second one (with recursive estimation) where a significant improvement occurred.

9.4.7. Compact Compartmental Modeling

Introduction

State-space models (or control system models, Carson *et al.*, 1983) of the physiological systems and pathological processes underlying the observed variables may also be used alongside clinical time series data. If well validated, then it may be possible to use clinical observations in comparison with the model predictions in such a way as to estimate the model's parameters in a recursive fashion. De la Salle *et al.* (1984) showed that with a simple model of thyroid disease, reasonable parameter estimates and accurate predictions can be made with as few as 3 or 4 data points. Simple state-space models thus provide an alternative approach for both low- and high-data rate situations. However, a necessary precondition for the use of such models is that they are theoretically uniquely identifiable (Carson *et al.*, 1983). This is analogous to the stationarity, invertibility, and stability conditions for ARIMA and TF models.

In this case study (based on Leaning *et al.*, 1985), a compact nonlinear, stochastic compartmental model is described and the use of a recursive joint state-parameter estimator is also presented.

A Nonlinear Stochastic Model of FAB Dynamics

The model has three compartments; x_1, extracellular fluid volume (normally 15 l); x_2, extracellular sodium mass (normally 2100 mmol); x_3, normalized ADH concentration (normally 1 AU). The state equations are

$$\begin{bmatrix} \dot{x}_1 \\ \dot{x}_2 \\ \dot{x}_3 \end{bmatrix} = \begin{bmatrix} -k_{01}x_1 + p_1 x_3 \\ -k_{02}x_2 + p_2 \\ -k_{03}x_3 + p_3 \dfrac{x_2}{x_1} - p_4 x_1 \end{bmatrix} + \begin{bmatrix} u_1 \\ u_2 \\ 0 \end{bmatrix} + \begin{bmatrix} z_1 \\ z_2 \\ z_3 \end{bmatrix} \tag{9.51}$$

where u_1 and u_2 are hourly intake rates of water and sodium (0.12 l and 9.366 mmol respectively, corrected for insensible losses). z_1, z_2, and z_3 are continuous white noises representing model uncertainty and system variability. The measured "clinical outputs" at time t_k are given by

$$\mathbf{y}_k = \begin{bmatrix} y_1 \\ y_2 \\ y_3 \end{bmatrix} = \begin{bmatrix} k_{01}x_1 - p_1 x_3 \\ x_2/x_1 \\ k_{02}x_2 - p_2 \end{bmatrix} + \begin{bmatrix} n_1 \\ n_2 \\ n_3 \end{bmatrix} \tag{9.52}$$

where y_1, y_2, and y_3 are urine flow ($1\,h^{-1}$), plasma sodium concentration ($mmol\,l^{-1}$), and urine sodium flow ($mmol\,h^{-1}$). n_1, n_2, n_3 are discrete white measurement noises. The parameters of this model have been set at $k_{01} = 0.0586\,h^{-1}$, $p_1 = 0.759\,1\,h^{-1}\,AU^{-1}$, $k_{02} = 0.00446\,h^{-1}$, $p_2 = 0.0$, $k_{03} = 3.1\,h^{-1}$, $p_3 = 0.119\,AU\,1\,h^{-1}\,mmol^{-1}$, $p_4 = 0.904\,AU\,h^{-1}\,l^{-1}$.

Given a situation where there are a number of unknown parameters, or indeed where there are a number of parameters that are required to be patient-specific, then the use of an Extended Kalman Filter for recursive estimation may well be of value.

In the Extended Kalman Filter, the state vector is augmented with the unknown parameters, hence $\mathbf{x} = (x_1 x_2 x_3 k_{01} k_{02} p_2)^T$. Assuming the parameters are constant, the extended state and output equations become

$$\dot{\mathbf{x}} = \begin{bmatrix} -x_4 x_1 + p_1 x_3 \\ -x_5 x_2 + x_6 \\ -k_{03} x_3 + p_3 \dfrac{x_2}{x_1} - p_4 x_1 \\ 0 \\ 0 \\ 0 \end{bmatrix} + \begin{bmatrix} u_1 \\ u_2 \\ 0 \\ 0 \\ 0 \\ 0 \end{bmatrix} + \begin{bmatrix} z_1 \\ z_2 \\ z_3 \\ 0 \\ 0 \\ 0 \end{bmatrix} \qquad (9.53)$$

$$\mathbf{y}_k = \begin{bmatrix} x_4 x_1 - p_1 x_3 \\ x_2 / x_1 \\ x_5 x_2 - x_6 \end{bmatrix}_{x = x(t_k)} + \begin{bmatrix} n_1 \\ n_2 \\ n_3 \end{bmatrix} \qquad (9.54)$$

or

$$\dot{\mathbf{x}} = f(\mathbf{x}) + \mathbf{u} + \mathbf{z}$$
$$\mathbf{y}_k = g(\mathbf{x}(t_k)) + \mathbf{n}_k \qquad (9.55)$$

The Extended Kalman Filter updates the estimated $\hat{\mathbf{x}}_{k-1}$ and its estimated covariance $\mathbf{P}_{k-1}$ in a two-step process each time new data points y_k become available.

The model and filter algorithm were tested using data simulated from the model. x_6 was simulated as a random walk, that is, $\mathbf{z} = (z_1, z_2, z_3, 0, 0, z_6)^T$, to allow for oversimplification of the sodium dynamics, x_2. The noise matrices were $\mathbf{Q} = \mathrm{diag}(2.5 \times 10^3, 6.25 \times 10^2, 6.25 \times 10^{-4}, \quad 0, \quad 0, \quad 1)$ and $\mathbf{R} = \mathrm{diag}(3.6 \times 10^5, 1.96, 0.81)$. The recursive parameter estimates for the situation in which the model is fitted to the simulated data, and the actual model outputs and simulated data are shown in Figures 9.28 and 9.29, respectively.

The results were very encouraging. Both k_{01} and k_{02} settle relatively quickly and track close to their true values, despite the large output variability. The fit between outputs and simulated data is good.

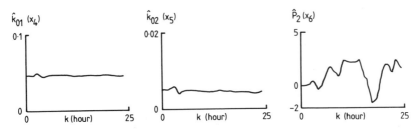

FIGURE 9.28. Recursive tracking of three parameter estimates of compact state-space model.

Discussion

Given that identifiable and well-validated models of the underlying pathophysiological processes exist, or at least are relatively easily attainable (something confirmed by the review of Flood *et al.*, 1986a), it is clear that in principle the recursive state-space approach may offer attractive possibilities. This is true not only for the technique itself, but also for the technique in relation to the types of output and the data rate encountered clinically.

The main requirement is that the model outputs relate to patient variables of particular clinical interest. The main drawbacks are that the Extended Kalman Filter is theoretically a biased estimator (Ljung, 1979) and that it requires knowledge of the noise **Q** and **R**, but does not explicitly identify the noise model as in the ARIMA and TF techniques.

9.4.8. Comparison of the Compact Approaches

The three approaches to clinical time series analysis, which have been investigated above, differ in their data requirements and knowledge of underlying physiological dynamics.

The Box–Jenkins-type methods need data sets of $n > 50$, which are large in chronic situations or laboratory terms, but small when sampling is frequent as in on-line monitoring. The recursive implementation of discrete TF models was found to be promising, and with the existence of multivariable analysis, it is possible to say that these models may have potential in on-line monitoring and control in critical care units. The omission of physiological processes is

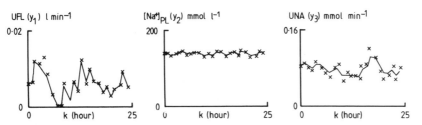

FIGURE 9.34. Decision tree for hyponatremia (adapted from Walmsley and Guerin, 1984).

disadvantageous unless the dynamics are not well understood or if they are rapidly changing, as during the course of acute disease.

Where the pathophysiological processes underlying the clinical data are codified in validated mathematical models, schemes may be devised where model estimates and predictions are made on only a few data and updated as new data arrives. The clinical implication is clear. Such an approach will be equally effective where data rates are high.

The lessons do, however, point to the need for substantial research programs focusing on this particular field. Other methodologies for time series should also be considered.

There are, however, some possibilities for complex models (Flood *et al.*, 1986a). The following case study documents substantial research efforts applied to developing a complex nonlinear model of FAB dynamics for clinical application.

9.4.9. A Complex Control System Model

In this case study a large-scale control system model is presented, adopting an integrated methodology for model formulation, identification, and validation (presented in Figures 9.1 and 9.12). This comprehensive model was developed initially to investigate complex dynamic interactions occurring at the level of physiological control. Development and testing, however, were carried out in a way that was relevant to a second level of dynamics and control, that of therapeutic attempts to restore equilibrium or maintain stability at a noncritical level.

The development of the model drew upon approaches contained in the review of Flood *et al.* (1986a). The first stage was the development of the signed-digraphs shown in Figures 9.15–9.18. This was followed by mathematical realization and parameter estimation. The main subsystems and interactions of the model are shown in Figure 9.30 with the principal variables being defined in Table 9.13. The distribution of body water and the major chemical species (electrolytes, urea, bicarbonate, protein, and so on) in the body are modeled with up to three compartments representing plasma, interstitial, and intracellular spaces. The compartmental equations are of typical mass balance form, many being nonlinear. The cardiovascular and microvascular dynamics are modeled with nonlinear algebraic equations.

Plasma protein control is effected through a set-point proportional feedback loop. Aldosterone and antidiuretic hormones, which are involved in controlling total body water and osmolality, are each modeled as a single plasma compartment with inputs linearly proportional to a weighted sum of the deviations of the controlled variables from a steady-state value. Respiratory control is exerted through the respiratory loss rate of carbon dioxide. This term is related through a nonlinear algebraic equation to the deviations of the partial pressure of carbon dioxide and plasma pH from their steady-state values.

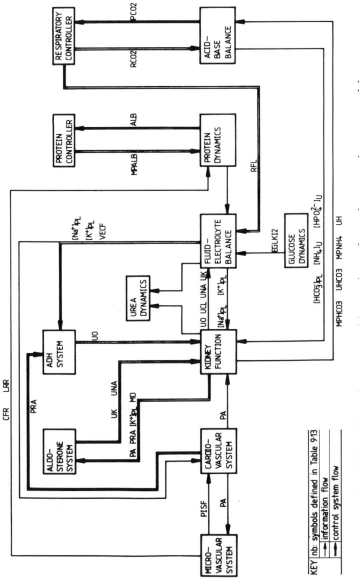

FIGURE 9.30. Main subsystems and interactions of complex control system model.

TABLE 9.13
Principal Variables of the Complex Control System
Model Illustrated in Figure 9.30

Symbol	Explanation
ALB	Plasma albumin concentration
CFR	Capillary filtration rate
EGLK12	Extracellular glucose
$[HCO_3^-]_{PL}$	Plasma bicarbonate concentration
$[HPO_4^{2-}]_U$	Urine phosphate concentration
$[K^+]_{PL}$	Plasma potassium concentration
LRR	Lymphatic return rate
MD	Macula densa theory
MPALB	Metabolic production of albumin
$MPHCO_3$	Metabolic production of bicarbonate
$MPNH_4$	Metabolic production of ammonium
$[Na^+]_{PL}$	Plasma sodium concentration
$[NH_4]_U$	Urine ammonium concentration
PA	Arterial pressure
PCO2	Partial pressure of carbon dioxide
PISF	Pressure of interstitial fluid
PRA	Right atrial pressure
RCO2	Respiration loss of carbon dioxide
RFL	Respiratory fluid loss
UCL	Urine chloride flow
UH	Urine proton flow
UHCO3	Urine bicarbonate flow
UK	Urine potassium flow
UNA	Urine sodium flow
UO	Urine output
VECF	Extracellular fluid volume

Overall, the model comprises 28 first-order differential equations and 125 algebraic equations. Full details of the realization are contained in Flood *et al.* (1987b). A microcomputer implementation using a multilanguage structure (professional PROLOG, FORTRAN 77, and BASIC) has been developed and is reported in Flood *et al.* (1986b). Implementation of the model as a teaching aid (discussed by Flood *et al.*, 1986c) is currently being undertaken by a commercial company. A number of the key assumptions made are as follows:

1. All compartments contain a single species, which undergoes complete mixing after each simulation step. Homogeneity excludes the effects of distance.
2. Lumping is a common feature of the model, for example, the systemic and pulmonary circulations, the lymphatic capillaries, compliances and resistances, and so on.
3. Body temperature is constant.
4. The concentrations of analytes are those normally found in clinics in the "Western world."

5. Stimuli acting on hormonal secretion do so as an additive weighted sum.

There are a further 35 assumptions detailed in Flood (1985).

Validation was undertaken using the adapted δ-methodology of Leaning (1980). A diagram representing this is shown in Figure 9.31. Here, V is validation, ALG is algorithmic, CON is consistency, EMP is empirical, THEOR is theoretical, HEUR is heuristic, and PRAG1 and PRAG2 are pragmatic. A comprehensive discussion of the validation program is presented in Flood *et al.* (1986d). A summary of the main empirical findings is given below.

Since the model is technically unidentifiable (unique values of the model parameters cannot be found), empirical validation proceeds by way of adaptive fitting, comparing the model response with data over a range of dynamic tests or stresses. This was carried out at five levels as shown in Figure 9.32. The

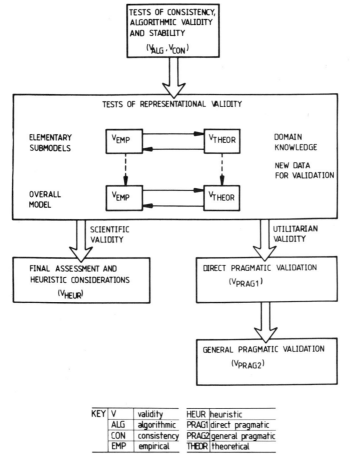

FIGURE 9.31. Adapted δ-methodology for validating complex models with utilitarian objectives (adapted from Leaning, 1980).

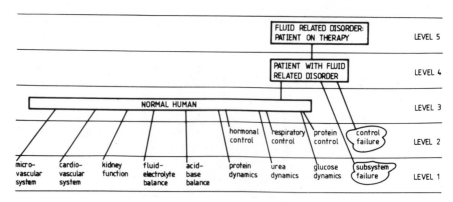

FIGURE 9.32. Hierarchy of validation at the representational stage of Figure 9.31.

data were collected variously from literature and from consultation with clinical colleagues.

We will now consider model validation at Level 3, Figure 9.32. First, the model was checked for correspondence with qualitative features of the data; see Table 9.14 for some of the expected responses (which are based on clinical and physiological reasoning). The features are classified as $\nearrow$ a fall followed by a rise; $\downarrow$ a fall; $\lrcorner$ a delayed fall; $\uparrow$ a rise; $\nearrow$ a delayed rise; $\rightarrow$ no change; $\rightsquigarrow$ oscillatory with upward trend; $\rightsquigarrow$ oscillatory with no trend.

Each matrix element has three entries: expected response, model response, and a true/false assessment. A1 is a true statement that both responses are identical. The stress descriptions (SN) are 1, intravenous 5% dextrose feed; 2, venous fluid loss; 3, ADH antagonist; 4, aldosterone antagonist; 5, Na$^+$ input rise; 6, Na$^+$ starvation; 7, increased CO_2 production rate; 8, hypertonic saline infusion; 9, K$^+$ starvation. $\sum r$ and $\sum c$ indicate the summation of true assessments in each row and column, respectively. From these and other tests reported by Leaning *et al.* (1985), there was good matching of qualitative response features. Qualitative feature matching is an important test of structural validity in nonlinear models.

Quantitative feature testing of the model, the next stage of model validation, was restricted to stresses and variables for which real data were available, namely, aldosterone loading, hypertonic loading, and water loading. The results of water loading are shown in Table 9.15 with the quantitative measures of validity explained in Figure 9.33. These results increase confidence in model parameter values within the overall structure.

9.4.10. Consideration of the Complex Approach

The computer simulation of the model produces realistic responses. Differences between normal subjects are represented by changes in initial conditions, and not by parameter changes. For clinical application, it is highly desirable that a larger set of parameters (free parameters) be estimated with

TABLE 9.14

Qualitative Feature Analysis of the Complex Control System Model[a]

SN	Plasma concentration						Intracellular concentration	Whole body	Fluid volume			Σ_r
	Na^+	K^+	ADH	ALD	HCO_3^-	H^+	K^+	PCO_2	ICF	ISF	PV	
1	→↓1	→↓1	→↓1	→↓1	↑↑1	↑↑1	↑↑1	↑↑1	↺↑1	←↑1	←↑1	11
2	↑↑1	↑↑1	←↑1	↑↑1	↑↑1	↑↑1	↑↑1	↑↑1	↑↑1	↑↑1	→↓1	11
3	↺↑0	↺↑1	→↓1	←↑1	↑↑1	↑↑1	↑↑1	↑↑1	↺↓1	→↓1	→↓1	10
4	↺↓1	↺↓1	←↑1	→↓1	↑↑1	↑↑1	↺↓1	↑↑1	↺↓1	→↓1	→↓1	11
5	←↑1	↑↑1	→↓1	↓↑1	↑↑1	↑↑1	↑↑1	↑↑1	←↑1	←↑1	←↑1	11
6	→↓1	↑↑1	↺↺1	←↑1	↑↑1	↑↑1	↑↑1	↑↑1	↺↓1	→↓1	→↓1	11
7	←↑1	←↑1	←↑1	→↓1	←↑1	→↓1	↑↑1	←↑1	↺↓1	→↓1	→↓1	11
8	←↑1	→↑1	→↓1	→↓1	↑↑1	↑↑1	↑↑1	↑↑1	↺↓1	←↑1	←↑1	11
9	→↝0	→↓1	→↝0	↓↓1	↑↑1	↑↑1	↺↓1	→↑1	↺↓1	→↓1	→↓1	9
Σ_c	7	9	8	9	9	9	9	9	9	9	9	

[a] Explanation of symbols: ADH, antidiuretic hormone; ALD, aldosterone; H^+, proton; HCO_3^-, bicarbonate; ICF, intracellular fluid; ISF, interstitial fluid; K^+, potassium; Na^+, sodium; PCO_2, partial pressure of carbon dioxide; c, column; r, row; SN, stress number (defined in text); Σ, sum of.

TABLE 9.15
Quantitative Feature Analysis of the Complex Control System Model

Water loading 20 ml kg⁻¹ infused over 30 min		Empirical data	Model prediction
Plasma osmolality	Peak time (min)	50–100	65
	Peak value ($mosm\,l^{-1}$)	279	280.5
	Settling time (day)	30–50	55
Plasma volume	Peak time (min)	50–100	65
	Peak value (l)	3.5	3.33
	Settling time (min)	60	65
Plasma ADH concentration	Fall time (min)	0	0
	Peak time (min)	50–65	65
	Peak value (AU)	0.25	0.25
	Settling time (min)	100–210	150
Urine osmolality	Fall time (min)	20	15
	Peak time (min)	70	60
	Peak value ($mosm\,l^{-1}$)	80	110
	Settling time (min)	210	240

an automatic estimation algorithm which functions during simulation. Techniques such as those described in the earlier case studies may be used to estimate these parameters. This has the added advantage of providing continual validation of the model through goodness-of-fit, parameter error matrices, and other measures. Let us discuss this further.

By its nature, the large-scale model described above is capable of representing the range of behavior of individual subjects within the modeled class.

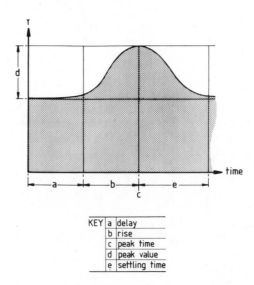

KEY

	a	delay
	b	rise
	c	peak time
	d	peak value
	e	settling time

FIGURE 9.33. Explanation of quantitative measures of validity detailed in Table 9.15.

However, one problem is the uncertainty as to whether the model parameter values are a true reflection of the subject's condition. Unfortunately, with the data available, it is not possible to estimate all the parameters in these models; they are theoretically unidentifiable. In the former case studies, however, we considered some small-scale models whose patient-specific parameters were estimated from clinical data. This is ideal for compact models, but for complex models is unfortunately problematic. The desire to have a relatively complex model, providing many useful outputs of clinical relevance, conflicts with the constraints on the number of parameters which may be estimated from available data. The more complex the model the less strictly will it be able to represent any one individual patient. Additionally, in pathological cases an expert component may be necessary to identify the key parameters, which are changing during a disease process, so that these may be updated.

9.4.11. Logical Modeling

An example of the use of a decision tree as a logical model is presented in Figure 9.34. Again the focus is fluid balance, concentrating on the diagnosis

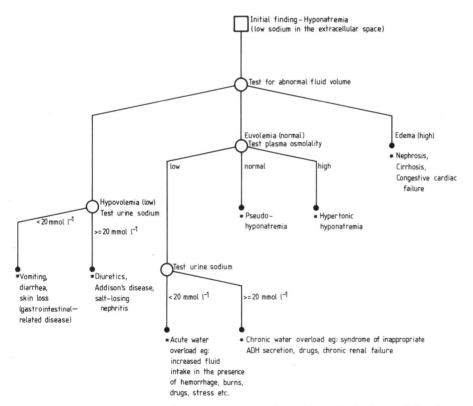

FIGURE 9.34. Decision tree for hyponatremia (adapted from Walmsley and Guerin, 1984).

of diseases, one of the symptoms of which is a low concentration of extracellular sodium (hyponatremia). Sodium salts comprise most of the solutes in the extracellular space. Hyponatremia could be due either to a fall in the total body mass of sodium or to a rise in the fluid volume or to a combination of these processes.

The mechanisms giving rise to the finding of hyponatremia are complex and it is therefore helpful as an aid to understanding to make use of a logical model such as depicted in Figure 9.34. This highlights the sequence of tests that can be carried out (measuring extracellular volume, plasma osmolality, and urine sodium concentration as appropriate), where in effect the various test outcomes (high, normal, or low values of the particular variable) constitute decision points. Each possible underlying disease process (an end point of the decision tree marked by an asterisk) giving rise to the initial finding of hyponatremia is thus defined in terms of a set of test outcomes.

It should be noted, however, that whereas Figure 9.34 depicts the logic of the decision-making process in a complete and consistent manner, clinical practice usually proceeds in a somewhat different fashion. The doctor normally begins by testing for the more common underlying causes before proceeding to look for more unusual disease processes. His approach to the decision-making process might typically be summarized by 1–5 below:

1. Suspect the disturbance (hyponatremia) from the clinical signs and symptoms presented by the patient.
2. Has the patient pseudohyponatremia, that is, normal plasma osmolality associated with a severe hyperlipidemia (elevated concentration of lipids in the bloodstream), or hyperproteinoemia (elevated concentration of proteins)?
3. Is the patient's extracellular fluid hypertonic—for example, high plasma levels of glucose or mannitol?
4. If the answer to (2) and (3) is "no" then what is the patient's extracellular volume status—hypovolemia (dehydration), euvolemia (normal or near normal extracellular volume and total body sodium), or hypervolemia (edema)?
5. Take a urine sample and estimate (a) urine/plasma osmolality ratio and (b) urinary sodium concentration.

An example of a logical conceptual model is shown in Figure 9.35. In the graph, concept nodes (square blocks) represent entities, attributes, or states. The relational nodes (circles) show how the concepts are interconnected. This type of graph can be applied to logic and computation (Sowa, 1984).

The particular example focuses upon a particular feature of the complex interaction processes whereby fluid–electrolyte, acid–base balance is maintained. Other illustrations taken from this physiological/medical system appear elsewhere in this chapter exemplifying other types of model. In essence the physiological basis of the model is that the osmolality of the extracellular sodium space controls the effective circulatory blood volume. In turn, one of the hormones that controls the osmolality of the extracellular sodium space is aldosterone.

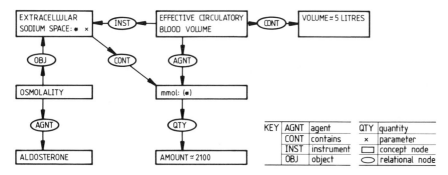

Figure 9.35. Part of conceptual graph of effective circulatory blood volume.

The schema for the extracellular sodium space shown in Figure 9.35 can thus be interpreted as follows. Extracellular sodium space contains approximately 2100 mmol of sodium, which is the instrument of effecting circulatory blood volume at, say, approximately 5 liters. The generic set {*} represents an unspecified set of sodium molecules that conform to type mmol and the subrange ≈2100. This limits the possible referents for the corresponding concepts.

The information contained in Figure 9.35 can also be incorporated within a program written in one of the logic programming languages such as microPROLOG. Such programs are used to encapsulate expert knowledge, to assist, for example, the doctor in the processes of diagnosis and medical decision making, for instance by expressing a chain of causal reasoning in the form of a set of logical decision rules.

As a necessary precursor to developing the microPROLOG code, the information contained in Figure 9.35 should be assembled as a set of statements:

1. Aldosterone is one of the hormones (agent) that controls the osmolality of the extracellular sodium (Na) space.
2. Extracellular sodium osmolality controls effective circulatory blood volume (ECV).
3. The normal value for sodium in the extracellular space is 2100 mmol.
4. The normal value of effective circulatory blood is approximately 5 liters.

A possible microPROLOG implementation of 1–4 is

```
((normal ECV 5 liters))
((normal Xcellular-Na 2100mmol))
((dependent/related ECV Osmolality-Xcellular-Space))
((dependent/related Osmolality-Xcellular-Space Aldosterone))
```

9.4.12. Qualitative, Quantitative, and Logical Modeling Approaches

This subsection deals with the differences and complementarity between qualitative, quantitative, and logical modeling approaches.

As we have seen, one traditional approach to computer-based decision support, before the wider availability of techniques of artificial intelligence (AI), is to design, develop, and validate dynamic mathematical models of the underlying process of interest. These models enable investigators to simulate physicochemical mechanisms and/or pathophysiological processes of disease in the human subject, while allowing experimental intervention of a medical nature (see, for example, Deland, 1975, and Ikeda *et al.*, 1979). A further sophistication is the addition of algorithms that tune model parameters to the structure of the patient (see, for example, Flood *et al.*, 1985).

A number of researchers, however, have maintained an essentially qualitative approach, for example, arguing that in many instances the system control properties might not be self evident from the solution of parametrized equations, although sensitivity analysis would quantitate the control features (Kohn and Chiang, 1982; Kohn and Letzkus, 1983).

The application of graph theory to represent fluid volume maintenance has been assessed by Flood (1985), although a more sophisticated methodology for loop analysis can be found in Puccia and Levins (1985) and applied by Flood and Carson (1987). Nicolosi (1986) reviewed the qualitative simulation of differential equations as described by Kuipers (1984) and noted that the aim was to achieve a knowledge representation scheme able to describe human commonsense reasoning and explanation about physical causality.

Recently, efforts have switched to AI, where mechanisms and representations are investigated by use of symbols, language, and knowledge.

Commonalities and Differences

The approaches considered here are dynamic mathematical, dynamic graphical, and logical conceptual models. The former two approaches are models of control systems; they are cybernetic representations. The third approach is a symbolic knowledge-based or AI representation.

Much of cybernetics is concerned with the microstructure of dynamic systems, such as feedback loops (positive and negative) and levels of control (reflexive and strategic) using quantitative (mathematical and graphical-block diagrams) or qualitative (graphical) differential equations. AI looks for mechanisms and representation by use of symbols, language, and knowledge. This can also be presented as a graph (conceptual).

The elements of the various graphs belong to different levels of mental processing; the simpler control representations respond to efferent information signals producing afferent control signals, whereas the more complex conceptual processes are relational, involving a great complexity of interacting neurons. The notion of these levels helps us to find an appropriate way of mixing approaches, as discussed below.

In cybernetics, control is in part explained by the concept metalanguage (discussed in Chapters 1 and 5). A controlled process possesses an object language, whereas a controller possesses a metalanguage capable of explaining the behavior of the controlled process. An object language has a relatively limited vocabulary and lack of syntax and structure. A controller, possessing a metalanguage over the controlled process, sits "above" the object language. A conceptual graph can be thought of as a metalanguage over the object language of a control system model. In AI it is also necessary to have a metalanguage to help describe the object language of a conceptual graph. This hierarchical structure identifies a means of integrating the dynamic and logical approaches.

A qualitative approach may offer a better model than a mathematical one for the purpose of prototype systems. A number of factors described by Puccia and Levins (1985) highlight this point:

1. Nature cannot be controlled in the sense of creating uniformity.
2. There are real variables that are either nonquantifiable or change in value with any attempt to measure them.
3. In a complex system of only a modest number of variables and interconnections, any attempt to describe the system completely and measure the magnitude of all the links would be the work of many people over a lifetime (also see Brewer, 1973).
4. In biological (hence physiological) problems the search for quantification of links or establishment of accurately measured base lines ignores the fact that often the biological (physiological) reality resides in the rules of construction of the system and not in the absolute values.

Thus, the qualitative approach allows the inclusion of variables that are difficult or even impossible to measure. A model of diabetes, such as Cramp and Carson (1981), which includes glucose, insulin, and other chemicals, could also include anxiety. The important criterion is that the direction and effect of one variable on another is known.

Mixing Dynamic Mathematical and Logical Models

When reviewing the combination of mathematical and logical approaches, Nicolosi (1986) commented that in almost all the papers reviewed, classical mathematical methods were subsumed in AI techniques. It was noted that, in contrast, Uschold *et al.* (1984) used AI as a means of enhancing development of mathematical models (as a user-friendly front end). Of equal importance was the observation that in most of the papers reviewed the goal was achieving a diagnosis or interpretation for which AI proved very important in using and merging quantitative data and qualitative facts in the knowledge base.

Nicolosi also suggested a spectrum of approaches for interfacing Intelligent Knowledge Based Systems (IKBS). The two extremes are as follows:

1. An IKBS *linked* to an external dynamic mathematical model. Interaction between the two requires multilanguage interfacing. An advantage is that the IKBS disregards the mathematical representation of the model's differential equations.
2. A dynamic mathematical model *incorporated* within an IKBS. An advantage is the increase in the knowledge base of IKBS with physiological knowledge.

Many intermediate possibilities must also exist; however, the hierarchical structure identified above does seem to suggest that extreme (2) is appropriate for the purpose of tools for clinical decision support.

The notion that there is a continuum of modeling approaches has been suggested by Flood and Carson (1986), and the case of qualitative cybernetic models is presented in Flood and Carson (1987). These contributions are important because they highlight the broader idea of mixing modeling approaches that has not been considered in this section.

9.4.13. Summary

In this section we have considered a variety of quantitative and logical modeling approaches in the context of patient fluid balance management. The topic area is common to all case studies, thus facilitating a concentration of the reader's efforts on the modeling types. Reflecting on fluid dynamics, however, may be of value at this stage, particularly by considering the successes and failures of the modeling approaches adopted to represent this structured situation.

The data-driven approaches suffered somewhat from limited sequences of measurements. Laboratory tests on clinical specimens provide the low data rate used in the ARIMA models. This produced models with poor confidence limits. A high data rate is necessary for better representations; however, this requires on-line patient measurement. The reality of such measurements for fluid-electrolyte variables is some way off general availability. Additionally, there is the problem of model identification, experience of which is unlikely to become the norm for practicing clinicians. Computer implementation for automatic identification is problematic as the interpretation of correlation and autocorrelation functions has a subjective element. Nevertheless the techniques and methodologies have shown some real possibilities in this area.

Compartmental modeling approaches showed more immediate prospects of application. This is certainly due to the generally accepted understanding of FAB structure. The need to develop well-validated models of the underlying pathophysiological processes is paramount, and offers attractive possibilities when included in a recursive state-space approach. One issue here is how complex can a model be without losing the potential for a recursive approach.

Logical approaches are relatively new. It is not clear at this time whether the new computer modeling languages, alongside appropriate methodological approaches, will provide an effective medium by which expert knowledge may be represented and manipulated in the area of medicine. A most promising prospect is some form of integration with dynamic models.

This set of studies offers the reader a sample of available approaches and types, and provides some insight as to their relative merits and limitations in application.

9.5. CONCLUSION

The aim of this chapter has been to consider the modeling process for structured situations by investigating modeling philosophy, methodology, and techniques. This has been achieved by considering statistical, mathematical, and logical approaches, looking at a sample of types from each approach.

This chapter will have presented a major challenge for a number of readers. All, however, will have been able to gain at least a conceptual understanding of quantified structured modeling approaches. This has been made possible by omitting all equations and the like until the final section. Here, a series of case studies presented the processes of quantification and symbolic description. The uses of such methods of representation are wide-ranging.

This and the previous chapter contain the quantitative material of the book which complements the earlier chapters. The whole text up to this point has presented an account of the theory and application of systems science, the main thesis of the book. The final chapter considers systems science at a philosophical level in a search for some additional understanding that will tie together some of the more controversial issues that have emerged in this and the preceding chapters.

PROBLEMS

9.1. What are the three general types of purpose associated with modeling?

9.2. What are the relative successes of mathematical, statistical, conceptual, and logical modeling approaches in achieving each of the three purposes in your answer to Question 9.1?

9.3. Write a detailed explanation of the modeling process as shown diagrammatically in Figure 9.3.

9.4. Review the types of modeling approach discussed under the headings
1. Mathematical
2. Statistical
3. Logical

9.5. By referring to Figure 9.3, briefly describe the following modeling methodologies:
1. Mathematical
2. Statistical ARIMA
3. Statistical TF
4. Markov chains

9.6. Describe the comprehensive modeling methodology for structured situations as shown in Figure 9.13.

SYSTEMS SCIENCE

Making Sense of the Philosophical Issues

10.1. INTRODUCTION

The content of the preceding chapters is designed to present an overview of systems science. This has been achieved by looking at the concepts that make up the systems framework, and by considering the breadth of application achievable with such a framework. We have seen that, emerging from the presentation, there is universal agreement among the systems movement that systems thinking is at least "a good idea" worth exploring and developing in order to ascertain whether a coherent body of knowledge can be developed under the overall umbrella of systems science. If this ultimately is achievable, then proponents of the systems movement will have succeeded in justifying the existence of systems science. One of the roles of this book is to bring together fundamental systems thinking and theory and to show the application of systems ideas. This constitutes one small step in the search for a coherent body of knowledge.

Also emerging from the presentations of the previous chapters, and despite the universal harmony in the systems movement that systems thinking is at least "a good idea," is the disagreement on the way these ideas should be extended and developed beyond the natural sciences. For instance, Chapter 4 made a thorough appraisal of the ideas and concepts of measurement developed over a number of preceding centuries, only to find that the development of such ideas in the social sciences (questionnaires as the main example) was wholly unacceptable to some researchers who propose learning (and labeling—the nominal scale) by carrying out action research. In Chapter 5 we saw a distinction between the ideas and approaches of the dominant functionalist paradigm and the interpretive paradigm. In Chapter 6 we again saw differences in approach. In this case, the issue was how we might best deal with what have traditionally been called social problems, which, the non-traditionalists say, are better termed problematical situations.

The differences are unfortunately not trivial, nor are they bridgeable. They relate to what we think or can say about what the world is, to how we can represent or express this knowledge; to the nature of man himself, and, consequently, to how we can properly investigate the world. These differences are philosophical. They relate to opposing sets of beliefs on the causes and nature of things, and of the principles governing existence, perception, human behavior, and the material universe.

There is of course much debate between the protagonists of different sets of beliefs. But as long as this is set within a shared paradigm, there is a real possibility that viewpoints can shift and evolve via this process, and the theory of the paradigm may consequently mature. Transparadigm discussion, however, is of a different nature. It can lead to three possible outcomes: First, that the opposing camps literally ignore each other and carry on maturing their own paradigm by "in-house" debate. Second, that transparadigm discussion leads to further entrenchment in a battle between paradigms. Third, and last, that an individual may change camps, adopting in its entirety the new set of philosophical beliefs and rejecting wholly the set of beliefs previously subscribed to. There are no gray areas, and the experience of switching paradigms has been likened to the "realization" or "discovery" of a set of religious beliefs.

The task set for this concluding chapter is thus to try and make some sense of the philosophical issues. To achieve this we will initially present an overview of these issues and then use this to cast some light on the differences in approach apparent in a number of the previous chapters.

10.2. THE PHILOSOPHICAL ISSUES

10.2.1. Introduction

In this section we will present some understanding of the philosophical issues themselves, by reviewing four main areas of dispute: ontology, epistemology, methodology, and the nature of man. This has been presented in more detail elsewhere, for example, Burrell and Morgan (1979). The brief insight we offer is in part based on their presentation.

10.2.2. Four Main Areas of Dispute

Ontology is theory associated with what the world is or contains. The ontological debate concerns the nature of reality. The two opposing extremes of thought are as follows:

1. Realism: reality is external to the individual imposing itself on individual consciousness; it is a given "out there," and is of an objective nature.
2. Nominalism: reality is a product of individual consciousness, a product of one's own mind or of individual cognition.

An extension of this is the epistemological debate. Epistemology deals with the two assumptions about the grounds of knowledge, about how one might begin to understand the world and communicate this as knowledge to fellow human beings, and ideas about what forms of knowledge can be obtained. The two opposing extremes in this debate are the following:

1. Positivism: knowledge is hard, real, and capable of being transmitted in a tangible form.
2. Antipositivism: knowledge is soft, more subjective, spiritual, or even transcendental—based on experience, insight, and essentially of a personal nature.

Related to these ideas is how we view the nature of man. The two opposing extremes of this debate are as follows:

1. Determinism: man is mechanistic, determined by situations in the external world; human beings and their experiences are products of their environment; they are conditioned by external circumstances.
2. Voluntarism: man has a creative role, has free will; man is the creator of his environment; he is voluntaristic.

Ontology, epistemology, and our view of man directly influence the methodological approach that we adopt. Methodology is concerned with our attempts to investigate and obtain knowledge about the world in which we find ourselves. If we have a hard objective view of an external world, then the following ideas would be appropriate:

(1) Nomothetic: it is appropriate to analyze relationships and regularities between the elements of which the world is composed; the concern is the identification and definition of the elements and the way relationships can be expressed. The methodological issues are concepts themselves, their measurement, and identification of underlying themes. In essence, there is a search for universal laws that govern the reality that is being observed. Methodologies are based on systematic process and technique.

If, however, we adhere to a subjective, experiential view of a subjective world then the following alternative ideas would be appropriate:

(2) Ideographic: the principal concern is with an understanding of the way an individual creates, modifies, and interprets the world. The experiences are seen as unique and particular to the individual rather than general and universal. An external reality is questioned. An emphasis is placed on the

relativistic nature of the world to such an extent that it may be perceived as not amenable to study using the ground rules of the natural sciences. Understanding can be obtained only by acquiring first-hand knowledge of the subject under investigation.

10.2.3. Summary

The philosophical issues that underly many of the differences in approach that have been encountered in this book have been discussed under the headings of ontology, epistemology, methodology, and the nature of man. Our concern, now, is to make some sense of the philosophical issues and cast some light on those encountered in the preceding chapters.

10.3. MAKING SENSE

10.3.1. Introduction

The philosophical issues extend from the historical development of Western society and the dominant scientific approach that has been so successful in advancing our knowledge in the natural sciences. The issues arise from the adoption of such an approach for societal investigations. The fundamental controversy is whether the adoption of such an approach is at all appropriate for dealing with complex issues arising in society.

10.3.2. The Scientific Approach

The scientific approach has four main characteristics:

1. Hypothesis testing: making propositions or suppositions for reasoning, investigation, or experimentation
2. Reductionism: the reduction of complexity under experimental conditions
3. Repeatability: the validation of experimental results by repetition; this may be viewed in two ways:
   (a) Verification—hypotheses can be verified by an appropriate experimental research program
   (b) Falsification—hypotheses can be subject only to attempts at falsification and never demonstrated as finally true
4. Refutation: knowledge building by the refutation of hypotheses.

Adopting a scientific approach initially requires the reduction of a portion of the situation of interest and design of an artificial situation where a small number of variables are investigated while the remainder are held constant.

Experimental design is important here, with the experiment purposely devised in order to test the hypothesis with the aim of refutation.

The scientific approach is clearly functionalist, that is, it is associated with a realist ontology, positivist epistemology, and nomothetic methodology. It has had huge successes in the natural sciences. If applied to the study of man it would, however, imply a high degree of determinism.

10.3.3. Science and Matters of Society

Kuhn (1975) noted that much of the agreement shared in Western society is via science itself, rather than being freely achieved. In fact, it is the result of the scientist's mode of education. Agreement arises, not because it is inherent in the structure of physical reality itself, but because the scientist has been trained to look for agreement and seek an "objective" account of nature. Education consists of solving textbook problems for which there exists common agreement upon formulation and a single answer. Agreement is indeed a cultural phenomenon.

Models of patterned regularity are thus used in description and to pursue prediction and explanation. Instruments of measurement are designed and constructed in order to gather data at as high a level of measurement as is attainable. This approach has been adopted by social system theorists in, for instance, the design and use of questionnaires. Churchman (1971) has, however, strongly attacked this approach to social events when he noted that pure empirical inquiring systems cannot seriously consider the task of, for example, predicting future events. He has additionally stated (Churchman, 1968) that it is

> silly and empty [to] claim that an observation is objective if it resides in the brain of an unbiased observer [instead,] one should say an observation is objective if it is the creation of many different points of view.

The implication of this viewpoint is to question the use of scientific measurement and to tend toward action research as an effective alternative for the social sciences (see Chapter 4).

In the context of methodology (the subject of Chapter 6) Checkland (1981) noted that all hard system methodologies (HSM) have an inherent positivist ontology that assumes that worldly investigations will lead to the identification of systems, that is, HSM and traditional management science assume that systems exist in the real world. Checkland states that a soft systems methodology (SSM) is fundamentally different as it "embodies a paradigm of learning and orchestrates a process of never ending learning." He found many parallels between SSM and the philosophical, sociological tradition of interpretive social science (discussed in Chapter 5), which he consolidated in five main points. These are summarized as follows:

1. SSM declines to accept the idea of a problem, rather, it works within the notion that there are situations in which varying actors may perceive various aspects to be problematical. Emphasis is not placed on external reality but on

people's perception of reality, on their mental processes rather than on the objects of these processes.

2. Any human activity system may be described in many different ways with many different *Weltanschauungen*. Any of these may be expressed in a root definition.

3. Each model of a relevant human activity system embodies a single one-sided concept of such a system, a purer view than the complex perspectives we manage to live with in our everyday life.

4. Stage 5 of the SSM offers a way of describing "the universal structures of subjective orientation in the world" rather than "general features of the objective world."

5. An action research approach is preferred for SSM as it is consistent with the idea that one can start virtually in any place in the SSM cycle. This is necessary for iterative learning. In positivist natural science, there are starting and end points.

Taking this viewpoint it seems that the interpretive paradigm holds a nominalist ontology, is antipositivist in epistemology, adopts ideographic methodologies, and sees man as voluntaristic. However, it is not meaningful for interpretivists to make realistic ontological statements, and epistemological ones appear only to come about from methodological studies since there is no confidence in what the real world actually is. Jackson (1982) has shown in some detail how "soft systems" methodologies of Ackoff, Checkland, and Churchman all adhere to the assumptions of the interpretive paradigm. He also demonstrates that these methodologies both gain (in relation to hard systems approaches) and suffer (in relation to their ability to bring about radical change) from adopting this theoretical position.

A challenge has thus been set within systems science which broaches many areas of social systems theory. Measurement, management, and methodology are three of these areas we have identified and discussed, although the challenge extends to a broad sweep of all societal matters.

10.3.4. Summary

In this section we have drawn out the major philosophical issues that are apparent in the current writings in systems science. We have stated that the scientific approach has been successful in the natural sciences where structure is not a major issue of debate, although not always easy to identify. In societal matters, however, structure is replaced by messiness, that is, sets of beliefs, values (and so on) that may or may not overlap. Thus, there are different viewpoints on situations relevant to particular sets of beliefs, values (and so on). Interestingly, Churchman's (1968) statement (see earlier) implies that sets of beliefs, values (and so on) may share some commonalities that lead us toward agreement, away from total anarchy, and toward a reduction in messiness. This is one of the considerations of the next section.

10.4. TYING IT ALL TOGETHER

10.4.1. Introduction

As a final contribution we will present an impressionistic view of the current state of the philosophical debate. This view develops ideas from Chapter 2 on complexity and draws on ideas from Chapter 4 on measurement. This provides a sort of framework within which the content of the whole book may be considered.

10.4.2. An Impressionistic View

The impressionistic view that we offer here is illustrated in Figure 10.1. (developed from Flood, 1987b). We will initially describe the way that this figure was constructed.

The first idea we drew upon comes from Chapter 2. Essentially, the argument was that complexity can be disassembled into ideas on systems and people. This idea was further developed by drawing upon Weaver's (1948) idea that complexity may be "sliced" into organized simplicity, organized complexity, and disorganized complexity. The systems–people idea was used to develop the thesis that complexity can usefully be considered in two

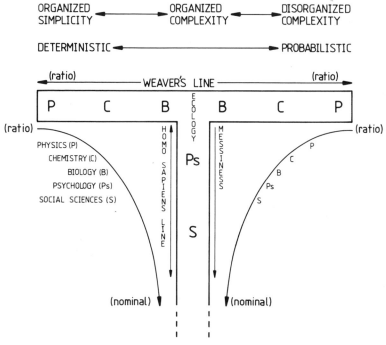

FIGURE 10.1. Impressionistic view of the philosophical debate in systems science (adapted from Flood, 1987b).

dimensions; these we labeled "Weaver's line" and the "*Homo sapiens* line." The former is characterized by situations with structure that can be identified; the latter is characterized by messiness, which occurs as a result of different values, beliefs (and so on). These two dimensions form the basis of our impressions and are drawn purposely as being orthogonal to each other.

The horizontal line refers to the three ranges of "structured" complexity, whereas the vertical lines in contrast relate to ideas of messiness. Weaver's line may also be considered as a deterministic–probabilistic spectrum (not at all appropriate to the *Homo sapiens* line), where simple deterministic analytical mathematics typifies organized simplicity, and complex probabilistic statistics typifies disorganized complexity.

The classification of experimental sciences can then be superimposed on this idea. This has been achieved by drawing a concave curve from the extreme left- and right-hand ends of the T down toward its base. This stretches out the classification, which can then be mapped onto the T. The ecology component (a subset of biology) provides the connection between the two dimensions, where human populations can be considered as structured in ecological terms.

The next addition to this impression comes from the ideas of the scales of measurement. Along Weaver's line we can say that the highest level of measurement that can be used is the ratio scale. Along the *Homo sapiens* line, as the messiness increases, the highest level of measurement that can be used is the nominal scale. Theorists of the interpretive paradigm would, with their nominal ontology, attach only nominal measurements to the *Homo sapiens* line, labeling being achievable through the development and sharing of mental constructs. Functionalists, however, would allow the higher levels of measurement to stretch down into the *Homo sapiens* line. Conversely, social systems theorists' statements from either paradigm do not interfere with reasoning associated with Weaver's line.

If we take the viewpoint that it is not meaningful to look for social generality, then we may wish to uncover notional social systems, and compare our labeling and understanding of them. These "social systems" would thus be the products of our perceptions, and nominal measurement only is achievable, in that we perceive that we share the same idea on the purpose of a notional system, which is associated with our similar experiences. Social "anarchy" arises when we can find no similar experiences. Social "order" arises when we are able to attach shared labels to notional social systems and attach similar purposes to those shared experiences. As we move away from messiness, toward ecological science, we tend to find a higher degree of agreement among people over the purposes of the social situations, and, at some point, degrees of structure may be agreed upon. At this point, which varies according to an individual's philosophical stance, we feel comfortable in dropping the word "notional" and tend to talk in terms of systems in a realist fashion. The position of this transitional point varies according to each individual's philosophical stance—a transitional point that does not exist at all for those who follow nominalism to its extreme (into the natural sciences) and those who follow realism to its extreme (into the social sciences).

10.4.3. Summary

This section has presented an impressionistic view of the philosophical issues in systems science as a final offering in our attempt to make some sense of this difficult area. To achieve this we have additionally drawn upon ideas about complexity and measurement.

10.5. CONCLUSION

There is agreement in the systems movement that systems science is at least "a good idea." There is, however, disagreement at a philosophical level concerning the way in which we can use systems thinking to deal with complex situations. The disagreements are fundamental and unbridgable, relating to differences in ontology, epistemology, methodology, and views on the nature of man. Making some sense of the philosophical issues has been achieved by painting an impressionistic view, drawing upon ideas of complexity and measurement.

PROBLEMS

10.1. Contrast the philosophical extremes of

1. Ontology
2. Epistemology
3. Methodology
4. The nature of man

10.2. Describe the scientific approach.

10.3. Use Figure 10.1 to discuss your view of the appropriateness of adopting a traditional scientific approach and an interpretivistic approach to investigating and representing social situations.

REFERENCES

Ackoff, R. L. (1974). The systems revolution. *Long Range Planning*, 7, pp. 2-20.

Ackoff, R. L. (1981). *Creating the Corporate Future*. New York: John Wiley & Sons.

Ampère, A. M. (1884). Essay on the philosophy of the sciences. (Trans). Essai sur la philosophie des sciences, ou exposition analytique d'une classification naturelle de toutes les connaissances. Paris (1834).

Ashby, R. W. (1956). *An Introduction to Cybernetics*. London: Chapman & Hall.

Ashby, R. W. (1973). Some peculiarities of complex systems. *Cybernetic Medicine*, 9, pp. 1-7.

Atkinson, C. J. (1986). Towards a plurality of soft systems methodology. *Journal of Applied Systems Analysis*, 13, pp. 19-31.

Atthill, C. (1975). *Decisions: West Oil Distribution*. London: B.P. Educational Service.

Attinger, E. O. (1985). Parsimonious systems description. A necessary first step in the development of predictive indicators. In Carson, E. R., and Cramp, D. G. (eds.), *Computers and Control in Clinical Medicine* (pp. 175-211). New York: Plenum Press.

Banks, M. (1969). Systems analysis and the study of regions. *International Studies Quarterly*, 13(4), pp. 408-429.

Barnard, C. (1938). *Functions of the Executive*. Cambridge, Mass.: Harvard University Press.

Beer, S. (1979). *The Heart of the Enterprise*. Chichester: John Wiley & Sons.

Beer, S. (1981). *Brain of the Firm* (2nd ed.). Chichester: John Wiley & Sons.

Beer, S. (1985). *Diagnosing the System for Organizations*. Chichester: John Wiley & Sons.

Beishon, J. (1980). *Systems Organization: The Management of Complexity*. Milton Keynes: Open University Press.

Berlinski, D. (1976). *On Systems Analysis*. Cambridge, Mass.: MIT Press.

Besant, J. (1982). *Microprocessors in Production Processes*. London: Policy Studies Institute.

Binder, L. (1958). The Middle East as a subordinate international system. *World Politics*, 10(3), pp. 408-429.

Birkhoff, G. D. (1933). *Aesthetic Measures*. Cambridge, Mass.: Harvard University Press.

Bittner, E. (1965). The concept of organisation. In Turner, R. (ed.), *Ethnomethodology*. Harmonsworth: Penguin.

Boulding, K. E. (1956). General systems theory—The skeleton of science. *Management Science*, 2, pp. 197–208.

Bowman, L. W. (1968). The subordinate state system of Southern Africa. *International Studies Quarterly*, 12(3), pp. 231–261.

Box, G. E. P., and Jenkins, G. M. (1976). *Time-Series Analysis, Forecasting and Control* (2nd ed.). San Fransisco, Cal.: Holden Day.

Brecher, M. (1963). International relations and Asian studies. *World Politics*, 15(2), pp. 213–235.

Brewer, G. D. (1973). Analysis of complex systems: An experiment and its implications for policy making (Report no. P-4951). Santa Monica, Cal.: RAND Corporation.

Brown, T. A., Roberts, F. S., and Spencer, J. (1972). Pulse processes on signed digraphs: A tool for analysing energy demand (Report no. R-926-NSF). Santa Monica, Cal.: RAND Corporation.

Bunge, M. (1977). Levels and reduction. *American Journal of Physiology*, 233(3), R75–R82.

Burrell, G., and Morgan, G. (1979). *Sociological Paradigms and Organisational Analysis*. London: Heinemann.

Burton, J. (1965). *International Relations—A General Theory*. London: Cambridge University Press.

Burton, J. (1968). *Systems, States, Diplomacy and Rules*. London: Cambridge University Press.

Carson, E. R., Cobelli, C., and Finkelstein, L. (1983). *Mathematical Modeling of Metabolic and Endocrine Systems: Model Formulation, Identification and Validation*. New York: John Wiley & Sons.

Chatfield, C. (1980). *The Analysis of Time-Series* (2nd ed.). London: Chapman & Hall.

Checkland, P. B. (1971). A systems map of the universe. *Journal of Systems Engineering*, 2(2), pp. 107–114.

Checkland, P. B. (1972). Towards a systems-based methodology for real world problem solving. *Journal of Systems Engineering*. 3(2), pp. 87–116.

Checkland, P. B. (1975). The development of systems thinking by systems practice—A methodology from an action research program. In Trappl, R., and Harika, F. de P. (eds.), *Progress in Cybernetics and Systems Research* (Vol. V). Washington, D.C.: Hemisphere Publications.

Checkland, P. B. (1978). The origins and nature of "hard" systems thinking. *Journal of Applied Systems Analysis*, 5, pp. 99–110.

Checkland, P. B. (1979). Techniques in "Soft" systems practice: Part I. Systems diagrams—Some tentative guidelines. *Journal of Applied Systems Analysis*, 6, pp. 33–40.

Checkland, P. B. (1980). Are organisations machines? *Futures*, 12, pp. 421–424.

Checkland, P. B. (1981). *Systems Thinking, Systems Practice*. Chichester: John Wiley & Sons.

Checkland, P. B. (1986, July). Soft systems methodology. Handouts from a tutorial event organised by the Operations Research Society, Manchester.

Churchman, C. W. (1968). *Challenge to Reason*. New York: Basic Books.

Churchman, C. W. (1971). *The Design of Inquiring Systems*. New York: Basic Books.

Churchman, C. W. (1979). *The Systems Approach*. New York: Dell.

Clemson, B. (1984). *Cybernetics: A New Management Tool* (Cybernetics and Systems Series). Tunbridge Wells: Abacus Press.

Coplin, W. D. (1966). International simulation and contemporary theories of international relations. *American Political Science Review*, 40(3), pp. 562–578.

Coyle, R. G. (1977). *Management Systems Dynamics*. Chichester: John Wiley & Sons.

Cramp, D. G., and Carson, E. R. (1981). The dynamics of short-term blood glucose regulation. In Cobelli, C., and Bergman, R. N. (eds.), *Carbohydrate Metabolism* (pp. 349–367). Chichester: John Wiley & Sons.

Cyert, R. M., and March, J. G. (1963). *A Behavioral Theory of the Firm*. Englewood Cliffs, N.J.: Prentice-Hall.

Daellenbach, H. G., George, J. A., and McNickle, D. C. (1983). *Introduction to Operations Research Techniques* (2nd ed.). Boston, Mass.: Allyn & Bacon.

Davis, L. E., and Cherns, A. B. (1975) (eds.). *The Quality of Working Life* (Vols. 1 & 2). New York: Free Press.

De la Salle, S., Leaning, M. S., Carson, E. R., Edwards, P. R. and Finkelstein, L. (1984). Control system modeling of hormonal dynamics in the management of thyroid disease. In Gertler, J., and Keviczky, L. (eds.), *Proceedings of the Ninth IFAC World Congress: A bridge between control science and technology* (Vol. 6). Oxford: Pergamon Press.

Deland, E. C. (1975). Classic electrolyte distribution and transport—Mathematical principles. *Advances in Pathology*, 1, pp. 21–28.

Delbecq, A. L., Van de Ven, A. H., and Gustafson, D. H. (1975). *Group Techniques for Program Planning: A Guide to Nominal Group and Delphi Processes.* Glenview, Ill.: Scott, Foresman and Company.

Deutsch, K. W. (1963). *The Nerves of Government.* New York: Free Press.

Dichter, E. (1960). *The Strategy of Desire.* London: Boardman.

Drucker, P. F. (1979). *Management.* London: Pan Books.

Eden, C., Jones, S., and Sims, D. (1983). *Messing About in Problems.* London: Macmillan.

Ellison, A. J. L., and Flood, R. L. (1986). An introduction to international relations, the systems view of international relations, and the use of systems science in social theory building (Research memorandum DSS/AJLE-RLF/245). London: City University.

Espejo, R. (1987). Cybernetic method to study organizations. In *Problems of Constancy and Change* (Proceedings of the thirty-first Conference of the International Society for General Systems Research, Budapest). 1, pp. 323–336.

Eykhoff, P. (1974). *Systems Identification and State Estimation.* Chichester: John Wiley & Sons.

Fayol, H. (1949). *General and Industrial Management.* London: Pitman.

Festinger, L. (1962, October). Cognitive dissonance. *Scientific American*, pp. 93–100.

Fielder, F. E. (1967). *A Theory of Leadership Effectiveness.* New York: McGraw-Hill.

Finkelstein, L. (1973). Foundations of measurement, *Quest* (Journal of the City University, London), 23, pp. 30–33.

Finkelstein, L. (1974). Fundamental concepts of measurement: Definition and scales. *Measurement and Control*, 8, pp. 105–110.

Finkelstein, L., and Carson, E. R. (1985). *Mathematical Modeling of Dynamic Biological Systems.* Letchworth: Research Studies Press.

Flagle, C. D., Huggins, W. H., and Roy, R. H. (1960) (eds.). *Operations Research and Systems Engineering.* Baltimore, Maryland: Johns Hopkins Press.

Flood, R. L. (1985). Quantitative Modeling of the Fluid-Electrolyte, Acid–Base Balance for Clinical Application. Ph.D. thesis, City University, London.

Flood, R. L. (1987a). Some theoretical considerations of mathematical modeling. In *Problems of Constancy and Change* (Proceedings of the thirty-first Conference of the International Society for General Systems Research, Budapest), 1, pp. 354–360.

Flood, R. L. (1987b). Complexity: A definition by construction of a conceptual framework. *Systems Research*, 4(3), pp. 177–185.

Flood, R. L., and Carson, E. R. (1987). A continuum of modeling approaches: The case of qualitative cybernetic modeling in physiology. In *Proceedings of Ninth Annual IEEE Conference on Engineering in Medicine and Biology Society*, New York: IEEE.

Flood, R. L., and Carson, E. R. (1988). Mathematical models in medicine: Do they still have a future? *First IFAC Symposium on Modeling and Control in Biomedical Systems* (Venice). Oxford: Pergamon Press.

Flood, R. L., and Cramp, D. G. (1987). Transfer function (TF) simulation and recursive estimation of pathophysiological processes. In Hogan, P. (ed.), *Modeling and Simulation on Microcomputers* (pp. 141–145). San Diego, Cal.: SCS.

Flood, R. L., and Jackson, M. C. (1988). Cybernetics of organization theory: A critical review. *Cybernetics and Systems* (in press).

Flood, R. L., Leaning, M. S., Cramp, D. G., and Carson, E. R. (1985). Clinical time series. Analysis, modeling, and recursive estimation. In Barker, H. A., and Young, P. (eds.), *Proceedings of the Seventh IFAC Symposium on Identification and Systems Parameter Estimation* (pp. 1613–1618). Oxford: Pergamon Press.

Flood, R. L., Carson, E. R., and Cramp, D. G. (1986a). The control of body fluid volume in man: Mathematical models of the regulatory process. In Carson, E. R., and Cramp, D. G. (eds.), *Measurement in Medicine I: The Circulatory System.* Beckenham: Croom Helm.

Flood, R. L., Nicolosi, E., Carson, E. R., Leaning, M. S., and Cramp, D. G., (1986b). Micro-computer implementation and clinical application of a user-friendly decision support system for fluid volume maintenance. In Barnett, C. C. (ed.), *Modeling and Simulation on Micro-computers* (pp. 76-81). San Diego, Cal.: SCS.

Flood, R. L., Carson, E. R., and Cramp, D. G. (1986c). Medical research models as educational tools. In Kondraske, G. V., and Robinson, C. J. (eds.), *Proceedings of the Eighth Annual Conference of the IEEE Engineering in Medicine and Biology Society* (pp. 859-862). Fort Worth, Texas. New York: IEEE.

Flood, R. L., Carson, E. R., and Cramp, D. G. (1986d, July). *Validation of a large-scale simulation model of fluid-electrolyte, acid-base balance*. Paper presented at the Summer Computer Simulation Conference. Reno, Nevada: SCS.

Flood, R. L., Stupples, D., and Charlwood, F. J. (1987a). Decomposition of representations of finite complex biomedical systems using NCDMT. *Biomedical Measurement Informatics and Control* (in press).

Flood, R. L., Leaning, M. S., Cramp, D. G., and Carson, E. R. (1987b). A mathematical model of the fluid-electrolyte, acid-base balance: Formulation and validation (Research memoran-dum MIM/RLF-MSL-DGC-ERC/6). London: City University.

Gowers, E. (1954). *The Complete Plain Words*. HMSO, Crown copyright reserved.

Godfrey, K. (1983). *Compartmental Models and Their Application*. London: Academic Press.

Habermas, J. (1971). *Towards a Rational Society*. London: Heineman.

Hamwee, J. (1986). Personal communication to R. L. Flood.

Handleman, J. R., Vasquez, J. A. O'Leary, M. K., and Copling W. D. (1973). *Color it Morganthau: A Database Assessment of Quantitative International Relations Research*. New York: Syracuse University.

Holsti, O. R. (1965). The 1914 case. *American Political Science Review*, 2(59), pp. 365-378.

Hoos, I. (1972). *Systems Analysis in Public Policy: A Critique*. Berkeley, Cal.: University of California Press.

Hussey, M. (1971). *Using Letters Instead of Numbers*. Milton Keynes: Open University Press.

Ikeda, N., Marumo, F., Shiritaka, M., and Sato, T. (1979). A model of overall regulation of body fluids. *Annals of Biomedical Engineering*, 7, pp. 135-166.

Jackson, M. C. (1982). The nature of "soft" systems thinking: The work of Churchman, Ackoff, and Checkland. *Journal of Applied Systems Analysis*, 9, pp. 17-29.

Jackson, M. C. (1985). Social systems theory and practice: The need for a critical approach. *International Journal of General Systems*, 10, pp. 135-151.

Jackson, M. C. (1986). The cybernetic model of the organization: An assessment. In Trappl, R. (ed.), *Cybernetics and Systems 1986*. Dordrecht, The Netherlands: Reidel.

Jackson, M. C. (1987). New directions in management science. In Jackson, M. C., and Keys, P. (eds.), *New Directions in Management Science*. Aldershot: Gower.

Jackson, M. C., and Keys, P. (1984). Towards a system of systems methodologies, *Journal of the Operations Research Society*, 35(6), pp. 473-486.

Jenkins, G. M. (1969). The systems approach. In Beishon, J., and Peters, G. (eds.), *Systems Behavior* (2nd ed.). London: Harper & Row.

Jones, L. (1982). Defining systems boundaries in practice: Some proposals and guidelines. *Journal of Applied Systems Analysis*, 9, pp. 41-55.

Jordan, N. (1981). Some thinking about "systems." In Emery, F. (ed?), *Systems Thinking* (Vol. 2). Harmondsworth: Penguin.

Kaplan, M. A. (1957). *Systems and Process in International Politics*. New York: John Wiley & Sons.

Katz, D., and Kahn, R. L. (1966). *The Social Psychology of Organizations*. New York: John Wiley & Sons.

Keeney, R. L., and Raiffa, H. (1976). *Decisions with Multiple Objectives: Preferences and Value Tradeoffs*. New York: John Wiley & Sons.

Keohane, R. O., and Nye, J. S. (1977). *Power and Interdependence*. Boston, Mass.: Little Brown.

Klir, G. (1985a). *Architecture of Systems Problem Solving*. New York: Plenum Press.

Klir, G. (1985b). Complexity: Some general observations. *Systems Research*, 2(2), pp. 131-140.

Kohn, M. C., and Chiang, E. (1982). Metabolic network sensitivity analysis. *Journal of Theoretical Biology*, 98, pp. 109-126.

Kohn, M. C., and Letzkus, W. (1983). A graph-theoretical analysis of metabolic regulation. *Journal of Theoretical Biology*, 100, pp. 293–304.

Koontz, H., O'Donnell, C., and Werhrich, H. (1984). *Management* (8th ed.). New York: McGraw-Hill.

Kuhn, T. S. (1975). *The Structure of Scientific Revolutions* (2nd ed.). Chicago, Ill.: University of Chicago Press.

Kuipers, B. (1984). Common sense reasoning about causality: Deriving behavior from structure. *Artificial Intelligence*, 24, pp. 169–203.

Lawrence, P. R., and Lorsch, J. W. (1967). *Organizations and Environment*. Cambridge, Mass.: Harvard Graduate School of Business.

Leaning, M. S. (1980). The Validity and Validation of Mathematical Models, Ph.D. thesis, City University, London.

Leaning, M. S., Flood, R. L., Cramp, D. G., and Carson, E. R. (1985). A system of models for fluid-electrolyte dynamics. *IEEE Transactions on Biomedical Engineering*, BME-32, pp. 856–864.

Lilienfeld, R. (1978). *The Rise of Systems Theory*. New York: John Wiley & Sons.

Ljung, L. (1979). Asymptomatic behavior of the extended Kalman filter as a parameter estimator for linear systems. *IEEE Transactions on Automation and Control*, AC-24, pp. 36–50.

Mason, R. O., and Mitroff, I. I. (1981). *Challenging Strategic Planning Assumptions*. New York: John Wiley & Sons.

Maxwell, J. C. (1864). *Proceedings of the Royal Society*, 13, London.

McClelland, C. A., (1966). *Theory and the International System*. New York: Macmillan.

McGregor, D. (1960). *The Human Side of the Enterprise*. New York: McGraw-Hill.

Mill, J. S. (1859). *Essay on Liberty*. London: Parker.

Miller, J. (1978). *Living Systems Model*. New York: McGraw-Hill.

Miller, G. (1967). The magical number seven, plus or minus two: Some limits on our capacity for processing information. In Miller, G., *The Psychology of Communication: Seven Essays*. New York: Basic Books.

Mitchell, C. R. (1978). Systems theory in international relations. In Groom, A. J. R., and Mitchell, C. R. (eds.), *International Relations Theory, A Bibliography* (pp. 78–103). London: Frances Pinter.

Mitroff, I. I., and Emshoff, J. R. (1979). On strategic assumption making: A dialectical approach to policy and planning. *Academic Management Review*, 4, pp. 1–12.

Modelski, G. (1961). International relations and area studies. The case of South-East Asia. *International Relations*, 2, p. 148.

Morganthau, H. J. (1967). *Politics Among Nations: The Struggle for Power and Peace* (4th ed.). New York: Knopf.

M'Pherson, P. K. (1974). A perspective on systems science and systems philosophy. *Futures*, 6(3), pp. 219–239.

M'Pherson, P. K. (1980). Systems engineering: An approach to whole system design. *Radio and Electronic Engineer*, 50(11/12), pp. 545–558.

M'Pherson, P. K. (1981). A framework for systems engineering design. *Radio and Electronic Engineer*, 51(2), pp. 59–93.

Nachmias, C., and Nachmias, D. (1981). *Research Methods in the Social Sciences*. New York: St. Martin's Press.

Naughton, J. (1977). *The Checkland Methodology: A Readers Guide* (2nd ed.). Milton Keynes: Open University Press.

Naughton, J. (1979). Review of Lilienfeld (1978). In *Futures*, 11(2), pp. 165–166.

Naughton, J. (1981). Theory and practice in systems research. *Journal of Applied Systems Analysis*, 8, pp. 61–70.

Nelson, C. R. (1973). *Applied Time-Series Analysis for Managerial Forecasting*. San Francisco, Cal.: Holden Day.

Nicolosi, E. (1986, March). Interfacing dynamic mathematical models of physiological systems and IKBS for clinical systems. In *Proceedings of the Inst MC Symposium on Expert Systems in Medicine*, 3, Royal Free Hospital, London.

Petrie, H. G. (1968). The strategy sense of methodology. *Philosophy of Science*, pp. 248–257.

Pippenger, N. (1978, June). Complexity theory. *Scientific American*, pp. 114–125.

Puccia, C. J., and Levins, R. (1985). *Qualitative Modeling of Complex Systems.* Cambridge, Mass.: Harvard University Press.

Pugh, D. S., and Payne, R. L. (eds.). (1977). *Organizational Behavior in Its Context: The Aston Program III.* Farnborough: Saxon House; and Lexington, Mass.: Lexington Books.

Rapoport, A. (1986). *General Systems Theory* (Cybernetics and Systems Series). Tunbridge Wells, Kent, and Cambridge, Mass.: Abacus Press.

Reynolds, P. A. (1980). *An Introduction to International Relations.* New York: Longman.

Rhodes, D. J. (1985). Root definitions and reality in manufacturing systems. *Journal of Applied System Analysis,* 12, pp. 93–100.

Rice, A. K. (1958). *Productivity and Social Organization: The Ahmedebad Experiments.* London: Tavistock Publications.

Robb, F. F. (1985). Cybernetics in management thinking. *Systems Research,* 1(1), pp. 5–23.

Roberts, E. B. (ed.). (1978). *Managerial Applications of System Dynamics.* Cambridge, Mass.: MIT Press.

Roberts, N., Andersen, D., Deal, R., Garet, M., and Shaffer, W. (1983). *Introduction to Computer Simulation: A System Dynamics Modeling Approach.* Reading, Mass.: Addison-Wesley.

Roethlisberger, F. J., and Dickson, W. J. (1939). *Management and the Workers.* Cambridge, Mass.: Harvard University Press.

Rosencrance, R. (1963). *Action and Reaction in World Politics.* Boston, Mass.: Little Brown.

Rowntree, S. (1921). *The Human Factor in Business.* London: Longmans.

Schein, E. (1980). *Organizational Psychology* (2nd ed.). Englewood Cliffs, N.J.: Prentice-Hall.

Selznick, P. (1948). Foundations of the theory of organizations. *American Sociological Review,* 13(1), pp. 25–35.

Silverman, D. (1970). *The Theory of Organization.* London: Heinemann.

Silverman, D., and Jones, J. (1976). *Organizational Work: The Language of Grading/The Grading of Language.* London: Collier-Macmillan.

Simon, H. A. (1957). *Administrative Behavior: A Study of Decision Making Processes in Administrative Organizations* (2nd ed.). New York: Collier-Macmillan.

Simon, H. A. (1965). The architecture of complexity. *General Systems Yearbook,* 10, pp. 63–64.

Singer, J. D., and Small, M. (1966). The composition and status ordering of the international system. *World Politics,* 1(17), pp. 236–282.

Smith, K. (1980). *Fluid and Electrolytes: A Conceptual Approach.* Edinburgh: Churchill Livingston.

Sowa, J. F. (1984). *Conceptual Structures: Information Processing in Mind and Machine.* Reading, Mass.: Addison Wesley.

Staff of the Division of Pathology. (1979). *Practical Notes on Hospital Pathology* (5th ed.). London: Royal Free Hospital Group.

Stephens, J. (1972). An appraisal of some system approaches to international relations. *International Studies Quarterly,* 16(3), pp. 321–349.

Strank, R. H. D. (1982). *Management Principles and Practice: A Cybernetic Approach.* London: Gordon & Breach.

Taylor, F. W. (1911). *The Principles of Scientific Management.* London: Harper & Row.

Taylor, F. W. (1947). *Scientific Management.* London: Harper.

Trist, E. L., and Bamforth, K. W. (1951). Some social and psychological consequences of the longwall method of coal getting. *Human Relations,* 4(1), pp. 3–38.

Uhr, L., Vossier, C., and Weman, J. (1962). Pattern recognition over distortions by human subjects and a computer model of human form perception. *Journal of Experimental Psychology,* 63, pp. 227–234.

Uschold, M., Harding, M., Muetzelfeldt, R., and Bundy, A. (1984). An intelligent front end for ecological modeling (DAI Research Paper) Edinburgh.

Vemuri, V. (1978). *Modeling of Complex Systems.* New York: Academic Press.

Vickers, G. (1970). *Freedom in a Rocking Boat.* London: Allen Lane.

Walmsley, R. N., and Guerin, M. D. (1984). *Disorders of Fluid and Electrolyte Balance.* Bristol: John Wright & Sons.

Warfield, J. N. (1976). *Societal Systems: Planning Policy and Complexity.* New York: John Wiley & Sons.

Weaver, W. (1948). Science and complexity. *American Science,* 36, pp. 536–544.

Weber, M. (1947). *The Theory of Social and Economic Organization* (Trans.). Glencoe: Free Press.

Weltman, J. J. (1973). *Systems Theory in International Relations.* Lexington, Mass.: D. C. Heath & Co.

Wiener, N. (1948). *Cybernetics.* Cambridge, Mass.: MIT Press.

Willetts, P. (1982). *Pressure Groups in the Global System.* London: Frances Pinter.

Wilson, B. (1984). *Systems: Concepts, Methodologies, and Applications.* Chichester: John Wiley & Sons.

Wilson, R. J. (1979). *Introduction to Graph Theory* (2nd ed.). London: Longman Group.

Wolstenholme, E. F. (1983a). System dynamics in perspective. *European Journal of Operations Research Society,* 33, pp. 547–556.

Wolstenholme, E. F. (1983b). The relevance of system dynamics to engineering systems design. *European Journal of Operations Research Society,* 14, pp. 116–126.

Woodburn, I. (1985). Some developments in the building of conceptual models. *Journal of Applied Systems Analysis,* 12, pp. 101–106.

Woodward, J. (1965). *Industrial Organization, Theory and Practice.* Milton Keynes: Open University Press.

Yates, F. E. (1978). Complexity and the limits to knowledge. *American Journal of Physiology,* 4, R201–R204.

Young, P. (1974). Recursive approaches to time series analysis. *Bulletin of the Institute of Mathematics and Its Applications,* 10, pp. 209–224.

Zartman, W. I. (1967). Africa as a subordinate state system in international relations. *International Organization,* 21(3), pp. 545–564.

Zimmerman, D. H., and Wieder, D. L. (1970). The everyday world as a phenomenon. In Douglas, J. D. (ed.). (1970), *Understanding Everyday Life.* Chicago, Ill.: Aldine Publishing.

INDEX